BEING GODLESS

Studies in Social Analysis
General Editor: Martin Holbraad
University College London

Focusing on analysis as a meeting ground of the empirical and the conceptual, this series provides a platform for exploring anthropological approaches to social analysis while seeking to open new avenues of communication between anthropology and the humanities, as well as other social sciences.

BEING GODLESS
Ethnographies of Atheism and Non-Religion

Edited by

Ruy Llera Blanes and Galina Oustinova-Stjepanovic

berghahn
NEW YORK · OXFORD
www.berghahnbooks.com

First published in 2017 by

Berghahn Books

www.berghahnbooks.com

© 2017 Berghahn Books

Originally published as a special issue of *Social Analysis*, volume 59, issue 2.

Library of Congress Cataloging-in-Publication Data

Names: Blanes, Ruy Llera, 1976- editor. | Oustinova-Stjepanovic, Galina, editor.
Title: Being godless : ethnographies of atheism and non-religion / edited by Ruy Llera Blanes and Galina Oustinova-Stjepanovic.
Description: New York : Berghahn Books, [2017] | Series: Studies in social analysis ; 1 | Includes bibliographical references and index. |
Identifiers: LCCN 2017000378 (print) | LCCN 2017014832 (ebook) | ISBN 9781785335747 (ebook) | ISBN 9781785336287 (hardback : alk. paper) | ISBN 9781785335730 (pbk. : alk. paper)
Subjects: LCSH: Irreligion. | Atheism. | Secularism.
Classification: LCC BL2747 (ebook) | LCC BL2747 .B45 2017 (print) | DDC 306.6–dc23
LC record available at https://lccn.loc.gov/2017000378

British Library Cataloguing in Publication Data

A catalogue record for this book is available from the British Library.

ISBN 978-1-78533-628-7 (hardback)
ISBN 978-1-78533-573-0 (paperback)
ISBN 978-1-78533-574-7 (ebook)

CONTENTS

INTRODUCTION
Godless People, Doubt, and Atheism

Ruy Llera Blanes and Galina Oustinova-Stjepanovic

Being Godless

In the current climate of false prophecies of secularism and numerous theories of the resurgence of religions, it is rather unusual to study a way of disengaging from religion. A bulk of recent ethnographies tell stories about technologies of self and the adept cultivation of religious dispositions (Mahmood 2005), learning to discern God (Luhrmann 2007), and enacting divine presences in physical rituals, speech acts, dream visions, or materials (Engelke 2007). Rituals of presencing the transcendent, the divine, or the immaterial (e.g., Orsi 2005) and well-rehearsed arguments about the resilience of religious spiritualities in politics (Bubandt and van Beek 2012) seem to be the order of the day. Building on the growing interest in researching how people demarcate the boundaries of religion and what falls outside (Engelke 2012b, 2014), this volume suggests that 'being godless' is an important empirical reality that encompasses processes, aspirations, and practices that purposefully or inadvertently lead to the attenuation of one's religious life. Through ethnographies of 'godless people', we propose to explore modalities of disengagement from religion, such as aspirations to move away from one's religious tradition and attempts to maintain one's atheist sensibilities and dispositions in encounters with religious phenomena

References for this section begin on page 16.

and people. The contributors to this volume illuminate several moments and movements within such processes: the materiality and bodily consequences of atheist configurations (Copeman and Quack), questions of certainty and doubt (Tremlett and Shih), problems of defining a non-religious identity (Lee), and political narratives and ontologies (Blanes and Paxe). We also interrogate the non-religious construction of scientific scholarship (Luehrmann) and the atheism of anthropology and anthropologists (Oustinova-Stjepanovic). These contributions exemplify possible questions and itineraries in the empirical study of atheism and non-religion and raise anthropological questions beyond a specific sub-disciplinary scope. As Matthew Engelke brilliantly exposes in the afterword to this book, this exercise is conceptually uncomfortable but can be productive for both a hypothetical anthropology of non-religion *and* an anthropology of religion. In this introduction, we set an agenda for the study of non-religion and atheism and critically review the work of our intellectual predecessors.

Achieving holistic religious devotion and terminating all religious connections are equally impossible tasks. Being godless connotes discourses and practices that aim to place limits on religion in one's daily life. In her study of Soviet-style secularism, Sonja Luehrmann (2011: 155) suggests that icons placed in the corners of Russian and Soviet houses would "simultaneously create a perceptible divine presence and help restrict that presence to a particular location and to ritually sanctioned occasions for interaction." Marilyn Strathern (1996) is also critical of the proliferation of idioms of hybrids, flows, and networks in ethnographic descriptions that cannot account for how networks and relations can stop. In other words, people appear to be anxious not only about maintaining relations with gods, spirits, and human-managed religious institutions, but also about terminating religious connections and cutting religious networks. Godless people, as introduced by our interlocutors in this book, seem to be motivated by disaggregating and abridging religious traditions, keeping them at bay.

Consider this ethnographic vignette. At the first sound of the call to prayer, a young Muslim in Skopje, a mystical leader (*shaykh*) by birth and the head of all Sufi orders in Macedonia, could be seen running away from mosques and his own religious lodge. As he sprinted across the yard and out the gate, the *shaykh* was watched by a handful of bitter followers, whom he was supposed to lead in prayer. During the clearly defined time of five daily prayers, the *shaykh* would feign stomach cramps or simply ignore the divine appeal to worship God, muffled by the blaring of a television set. Yet this *shaykh* did not renounce religion. On the contrary, he claimed that he was a "staunch believer" in God, angels, and demons as described in the Muslim Holy Book, the Qur'an. The young leader was eager to advertise and sell his services as a spiritual healer to Muslim and Christian clientele, but he was reluctant to reinvest his income into the leaning walls of the lodge and sweep the dirty carpets around the tombs of ancient saints. This *shaykh* turned a deaf ear to God's urgent demands to be worshiped and served. He also ignored the pleas of his religious followers (*dervish*) to join the religion-building social efforts within their lodge. Bound by an oath of loyalty to the dead saints buried in the lodge, these followers continued to gather for rushed, disappointing rituals and took part in bitter debates over what their religious tradition was about and why their lodge was experiencing a rapid decline. At the same time, each *dervish* restricted his involvement in the religious and administrative life of the lodge to the practices he enjoyed most: reading books or praying in solitude or communal feasting at the end of Ramadan, the month of fasting. Under the roof of one *dervish* lodge in Skopje, these Muslims showed selective disinterestedness in different aspects of their religious tradition, be it prayer, ritual, administration, financial obligations, and so on. It seemed as if religion in its totalizing complexity had become a burden that these people actively sought to avoid.

These Macedonian Sufis did not identify as atheists in the sense of somebody who rejects the validity and efficacy of religion per se. Going beyond a study of articulate atheists alone, whose efforts are guided by their intellectual commitment to the elimination of religion from their own and other people's personal and social lives, we suggest that being godless can take multiple forms of partial indifference, unease, ambivalence, reluctance to be drawn in, and attempts at withdrawal from religious traditions—modalities that are sometimes fraught with tension between subjective and public loyalties. The tension arises because not every context creates enabling conditions for an unequivocal break away from one's religious tradition. This impossibility of open defiance is apparent in Louis Frankenthaler's (pers. comm.) incisive account of how ultra-Orthodox Jewish men gradually negotiate their way out of obligations and regulations imposed on them by their Haredi learning and sociality. For them, the disruption of habitual religious bonds entails the clandestine reading of books on politics and psychology that are banned as 'secular' subjects in the strictly religious Haredi education. Similarly, Daniel Dennett and Linda LaScola (2010) have encountered atheist Christian priests, who hesitate to abandon religion completely. Some are not prepared to sever their social and professional relations for practical reasons. Others continue to see God as a significant symbol in their life but cannot agree with God's conventional representations in Christian discourses. Their lives are a struggle to hide or to articulate their opinions from the pulpit.

We suggest that anthropology has not paid enough attention to experiences of being godless, although there has recently been a modest upsurge of research on non-religious formations across disciplines (Bullivant and Lee 2012). Some studies explore correlations between gender, education, wealth, and non-religion, but the general demographic findings are too crude to understand the actual empirical complexities of withdrawal, indifference, or militant rejection of religious traditions (ibid.: 23). Currently, we still lack nuanced ethnographic and historical studies of varieties of meanings, claims, and practices of being disengaged from religion. The exception to the ethnographic silence around godless experiences is a somewhat better-documented history of Soviet and allied socialisms. It is not accidental that we have borrowed the term 'godless' from the early Soviet era when, during the first experimental decade after the

1917 October Revolution, the Communist Party created an organization called the League of the Militant Godless (Soiuz voinstvuiushchikh bezbozhnikov) to promote and teach atheism (Peris 1998). The League agitated against religious observance, published atheist leaflets, and convened numerous meetings, but it failed to create an unequivocally atheist population. Rather, the League's activities succeeded in inserting a degree of uncertainty about religious commitments among Soviet citizens. Pointing out how pre-socialist reforms were instrumental to the marginalization of religious institutions within the social and political administration of Uzbekistan, Kehl-Bodrogi (2008: 11) argues that theological ignorance, lax observance, and ritual neglect cannot be blamed on Soviet or other socialist religious policies without a careful analysis of previous and current forms of affective religiosity, both local and global. Awkward relations, embarrassment, and ironic reflexivity about being religious endure in post-Soviet spaces (Louw 2012). In post–Cold War Mongolia, some people are also apprehensive of renewing unknown and threatening contracts with shamanic forces exiled by socialist modernization (Højer 2009; Pedersen 2011). These relations are resisted because they suggest the darker possibilities of madness and spirit possession. This volume brings together ethnographies that can further illuminate the historical and contemporary experiential complexities of thinning out religion.

'Being godless' is a descriptive ethnographic category rather than an analytical one because we are interested in the experiential quality of being godless. The adjective 'godless' is treated here as an attribute of different practices rather than a reified phenomenon and object of analysis. To illustrate our ethnographic orientation, it is easy to find fault with Marxist theories of religion as an ideology that conceals real life inequalities by promising salvation. However, it is a different matter to identify and ethnographically engage with people who live Marxist theories of religion in practice. Julie McBrien and Mathijs Pelkmans (2008: 89) describe how Marxist values and their unanticipated effects continue to play an important role among atheist Muslims of Kyrgyzstan who clash with Muslim and Christian missionaries eager to undo their socialist education. Atheist Muslims participate in life-cycle rituals that they interpret as non-religious—that is, these rituals are part of people's cultural ethno-national heritage rather than an expression of 'fanatical' or proselytizing motives of new Muslim and Christian missionaries. Muslims of Kyrgyzstan are atheist not because they do not believe in God but because they resist missionary proselytism. Although socialist secularisms have created conditions for openly professing atheism and unbelief, deterministic causal frameworks, such as socialist education in atheism or Western-style secularism, offer an inadequate explanation of the everyday meanings of being godless.

There are, of course, several concrete historical legacies that have been conducive to the appearance of godless people. These include Soviet secularism, post-colonial Angolan pragmatism, and British or Indian humanist movements. This book does not suggest that disenchantment, religious indifference, and godless dispositions are inevitable teleological outcomes of modernization or secularization campaigns. Rather, these are complex, troubled realities, not only in the geographical West or post-Soviet spaces, but in other parts of the world as well. In the shadow of the publicized Islamic revival in today's Cairo, one can encounter Egyptians who question the basic premise of their faith, which others pronounce and practice conventionally, idiosyncratically, or impiously (Schielke 2012: 302). Falling short of Islamic ideals is common-place, while accusations of infidelity to the Qur'an, hypocrisy, and apostasy are instrumental admonitions to Muslims to adhere to their faith. But the socially isolated and occasionally electronically connected lives of Muslim atheists—with their rhetoric of freedom from religious intolerance and cruelty, their critique of the presumed irrationality and inconsistencies of Islamic history, their trust in education, and their moral qualms about social injustice com-mitted within religious frameworks—are becoming known only now (ibid.). To press the point, in this volume, being godless is an attribute of cultural and subjective figurations rather than an entified state, system, or abstract concept of 'godlessness'. That is why we grapple with the problem of living a godless life comparatively and ethnographically, although through a lens of theories relevant to our ethnographic material.

We are reluctant to coin a new term—'godlessness'—and to provide a general, monothetic definition of it because what we learn from the above examples is that a single definition of atheism or godlessness would be mis-leading at the moment when these phenomenological realities in different parts of the world have been poorly explored. One particularly illustrative example of this has been Engelke's (2012b, 2014) recent work on how the British Humanist Association (BHA) engages in a complex definitional debate concerning its non-religious identity, revealing the multiplicity of the stakes involved in such definitional exercises. In his afterword, Engelke rightly intro-duces these complexities into the anthropological debate, questioning the pertinence of the negative term ' non-religion'. Therefore, we do not want to add 'areligion', 'irreligion', and 'non-religion' to the terminological confusion. Areligion and irreligion describe autonomous practices carried out without explicit reference to religion, although this raises the question about demar-cating the boundaries between things religious or areligious. Currently, the term 'non-religion' has gained epistemological ground. As a rule of thumb, non-religion is defined in relation to religious phenomena. Non-religion can be understood narrowly in opposition to religion, or as a more inclusive term that encompasses the articulation of functional alternatives, such as human-ism, scientific naturalism, and secular morality (Quack 2014). Nevertheless, we are not sure that this concept can act as an umbrella term for the diverse forms of cutting religious networks under discussion in this collection. Rather, we feel that all these concepts—irreligion, non-religion, unbelief, and so on—describe specific empirical phenomena that might not be easily subsumed under one category.

Looking for a flexible analytical framework for this volume, we initially con-sidered the concepts of secularism and secularity but found them restrictive. In our reading, the notions of secularism, secularity, and secularization refer to aspects of a political project that variously aims to define relations between religious and political institutions with repercussions for mundane experiences of those arrangements. Needless to say, the empirical forms that these relations take are neither self-evident nor singular, and the growing body of literature on cultures of secularism addresses the internal contradictions, political implications, and experiential feel of plural secularisms (see, e.g., Bubandt and van Beek 2012; Jakobsen and Pellegrini 2008). This volume is not isolated from the debates on secularity, but we seek to break out of the binary logic of religion versus politics. One way to do so is by showing that this binary logic does not hold water under ethnographic scrutiny. Alternatively, and this is our take on the issue, we can search for original frameworks of analysis. That is why we position this publication in the recent studies of doubt and atheism rather than secularism. We find doubt and atheism to be particularly relevant concepts because they help us explore a situated relation between a self and religion instead of that between politics and religion. This is not to say that doubt and atheism cannot become a foundation for a political program, but we are interested in how people distance themselves from religion rather than how, for example, 'the state' engages with religion.

To pre-empt a charge of reification and ethnocentrism, we are aware that 'religion' is not an appropriate term in every context, and that not all religious traditions consist of worshipping 'gods'. For instance, our comparative agenda unavoidably raises concerns about the applicability and translation of the attribute 'godless' into non-monotheistic contexts or even its consistency across monotheistic denominations. From our definition above, it follows that being godless implies religious scarcity, having less contact with God and God's religious networks on earth. Yet God means very different things in theistic, deistic, pantheistic, or animistic religious traditions (Martin 2007b: 2). Such a loose definition suggests that our interlocutors might assume very different positions toward God or gods, depending on their definition (ibid.). God might figure as an engaged, aloof, or ubiquitous deity. This is not to forget that learned and everyday debates and speculations about the form and agency of monotheistic God fragment the notion even within a single, nominally uniform religious tradition. Non-monotheistic traditions pose additional challenges. For example, Johannes Quack and Jacob Copeman's ethnography (this volume) is set in India, where the spiritual pantheon consists not only of gods but also half-gods, ghosts, demons, human godmen, and even abstract principles such as truth, liberation, and pure consciousness. Some Hindu paths to liberation, such as Sāṃkhya, are necessarily 'a-theistic' as they are independent of relations with gods (Quack 2012a, 2013). To sidestep this thorny issue, we understand being godless broadly as the reluctance of humans to engage with any divinized beings or notions of transcendental agency, regardless of theories about a god's position in any given religious cosmology. The idea of God has a lot of mileage in anthropology, but in this book it will, unfortunately, remain woefully under-researched. Instead, we focus on ways that humans disengage from the web of religious traditions, making them less immediate. Still, it would be productive to find out what kind of god people have in mind when they cut and attenuate their religious networks.

Religious Mentalities

So why do anthropologists tend to reiterate arguments for the abiding presence of religion instead of simply acknowledging that there are contexts in which religion plays an important role and other contexts, not necessarily geographical, in which religion is an unwelcome tradition? If we hark back to Malinowski's (1948: 9) critique of the 'primitive mentality' debate (see Lévy-Bruhl [1926] 1985), anthropological discomfort at demarcating partly autonomous spheres of non-religious routines and religious traditions can be traced to residual notions of the mystical holism of religious lives that do not differentiate between the admittedly Durkheimian dyad of the sacred and the profane. This concept of mystical holism is applied equally to non-Western indigenous traditions and to the European past. For instance, medieval Europe is painted as black as the Dark Ages, when 'superstitious' or 'ignorant' people inhabited a cosmic order alongside angels, demons, and other celestial and earthly bodies. Supposedly, this sense of immediacy (Taylor 1992: 3; 2007: 10–11) endured until scientific progress, secularization, and political modernization ripped this texture apart (Bennett 2001: 60–62). However, this mystical holism hypothesis obscures the extent to which the modernity that we live is an outcome of internal debates and tension within Christianity (ibid.: 67). Thus, an attempt to historicize modernity depends on the contrast between the Age of Faith and relentless secularization, which inconsistently refers to deinstitutionalization, the decline of personal piety and belief, and the separation of religion and politics (Stark 1999). Some might argue that in medieval Europe church attendance was nearly 100 percent, but this would be a poor indication of the scope of personal piety and the intensity of religious experiences (Casanova 1994: 16). Instead, it seems plausible that medieval knowledge of formal religious creed and observance might have been low and ambivalent for centuries before industrial and digital modernity (Stark 1999: 42ff.). People simply would not know their prayers or would misbehave or would not go to church at all, while understaffed parishes were managed in the most haphazard manner. In fact, our notions of an all-encompassing medieval Christianity are derived from anachronistic nineteenth-century images of medieval religion.

This mystical bias is especially apparent when it comes to non-Western contexts. For example, much African ethnography points out that witchcraft is a serious concern of people caught in webs of sorcery and anti-witchcraft rituals. An otherwise wonderful monograph by Harry West (2005) explores in detail the means of sorcery in Mozambique, its language and effects. We learn mostly about witches and witch doctors, but who were the people behind the ideologies and practices of the socialist ruling party FRELIMO, which famously condemned sorcery beliefs and counter-sorcery practices as false consciousness but simultaneously 'tolerated tradition' in order to enact neo-liberal reforms? What happened to them? Focusing on the intersections between ideological regimes, discourse, political agency, and social praxis, the chapter by Ruy Blanes and Abel Paxe (this volume) explores the historical moment when a top-down anti-religious stance was imposed in post-colonial Angola. The authors examine the motivations behind such impositions, including the utopian association between independency and modernity, which produced a redefinition of the objects and subjects of belief and the legacies created by them with regard to the establishment of social values.

Doubt

Since Tylor's ([1871] 2008: 23) notorious definition of religion as "the belief in Spiritual Beings," only the idea of belief itself has been an anthropological staple. The concept has been surrounded by controversies over its universal applicability and Christian genealogy, with its ethnocentric connotations of propositional meanings (Ruel 1982) and impenetrable qualities of cognitive dispositions (Needham 1972). There have also been arguments over the manifestation of beliefs in relational practices (Street 2010), material cultures (Keane 2008), and power relations (Asad 1993). However, in the heat of the debates for and against belief (see Lindquist and Coleman 2008), anthropologists are more likely to describe what people assert as propositional content within their theologies and cosmologies than what they reject, question, caricature, and avoid. Where uncertainty and doubt are incorporated into analysis, intrinsic instabilities of belief and the malleability of intellectual and ritual commitments to one's religious traditions are often seen as problematic only in the contexts of conversion and denominational switch (Kirsch 2004) and iconoclastic rejection of ancestral and popular practices in favor of authoritative global traditions such as Christianity and Islam. In sum, anthropologists have been far more interested in belief, whether as a socially significant phenomenon in its own right or a problematized field of relations within secular contexts (Agrama 2012; Cannell 2010; Starrett 2010).

Recently, several publications have engaged with the questions of doubt and atheism that constitute our inter-textual space for the study of godless people (Hecht 2003). We maintain that doubt is an intrinsic quality of most, maybe all, religious traditions, while atheism has historically acquired a reputation for rather extreme certainty about its anti-religious premises. Let us say that doubt is commonplace, while atheism is radical. With doubt and atheism as two reference points, it is important to bear in mind that in addition to routine questioning and outright rejection of some or all religious premises and practices, respectively, there are other experiential forms of being godless. These include finding no room for God in one's everyday life; being indifferent to the point of not even making a passing comment about divinities and institutions that mediate human-divine relations; and even mocking religions through spoof religious discourses and liturgies, such as the Church of the SubGenius, the Maradonian Church, and the Church of the Flying Spaghetti Monster (Cusack 2010).

Doubt is not an exclusively religious process (Kelly 2011); however, this book looks only at its religious manifestations. Doubt is located in relations between people, among people and spirits, and within people themselves in specific socio-historical contexts. It is a thought process, a performative technique, and a social mechanism. It has been suggested that doubt has a material quality, but it remains to be seen how doubt is lodged in objects and how embodied activities, such as touching icons, kneeling, lighting candles, hearing church bells, and reading books, might be relevant (Naumescu 2013: 86). Although doubt is understood as a multifaceted phenomenon, it is usually located in the mind and given a social function. Thus, it has been argued that doubt implies a capacity for 'religious reflexivity', or casting a critical glance at one's conventionally accepted beliefs and practices (Lewis 2002: 11). It is an agentive process of considering alternative values or actions that is distinct from uncertainty and skepticism, which do not entail a search for resolution (Pelkmans 2013b: 4). Doubt also indicates a choice between alternatives and trying to arrive at a decision (ibid.). As a process of thinking and judgment, doubt is implicated in belief. Jean Pouillon (1982) points out the inherent ambiguity of the French verb *croire* (to believe), which simultaneously expresses bonds of trust and uncertainty. Pouillon argues that if the existence of gods (and spirits) becomes an object of belief, doubt becomes a distinct possibility (ibid.: 2). Another early attempt to conceptualize doubt was made by Benson Saler (1968: 32), who sought to revive William James's terminological distinction between belief, unbelief, and disbelief and differentiated firm rejection of theological propositions, or disbelief, from uncertainty, the gray zone of unbelief that is comparable to agnosticism. Even if the notion of unbelief has raised concerns about the negative analytical polarity between the presence and absence of something as vague as propositional beliefs (Quack 2010), the argument has a valid point that 'a kernel of doubt' (Goody 1996) is intrinsic to all human experiences.

Doubt features prominently in European history. For example, it is well-known that Hellenic 'humanists', like the sophists or Protagoras, claimed that 'a man is the measure of all things' and that gods played no role in human affairs (Goody 1996: 669). Although many classical Greek and Roman philosophers and Islamic and Indian scholars did not have the strength of conviction to believe or disbelieve in gods beyond doubt, some of them questioned liturgical, imaginative, and philosophical forms of being religious. The figure of the Devil in scriptural religions—a trickster who leads people astray and sows doubts—might be an incarnation of "a structural necessity" (ibid.: 674) to relate conviction and uncertainty. Furthermore, doubt is not a European monopoly. In the early twentieth century, Paul Radin (1927) raised a question of philosophical proclivities and skepticism among 'primitive people'. Arguing against Lévy-Bruhl's theory that 'primitive' societies are not capable of abstract, scientific thought, Radin insisted that every political, linguistic, and social formation has stakes in speculative philosophy and religious critique, even if indigenous philosophies do not necessarily take coherent, integrated forms along the lines of Greek philosophical traditions. Radin reviewed early ethnographic records of interaction with Winnebago of North America and Ewe of West Africa that had revealed cases of doubt about the potency and existence of their divinities and exposed people's vented frustration with the gods' failure to deliver the promised prosperity and justice (ibid.: 375–384).

Because expressions of doubt are invariably linked with larger social contexts, such as historical change, socio-political crisis (Pelkmans 2013b: 8), and conversion to global religions, and with mundane relations, including kinship and cultural politics of modernization, cosmopolitanism, progress, and local traditions versus global development (Pigg 1996), one can sweepingly argue that pervasive doubt about ritual efficacy, and even about the existence of gods in Western Africa, is caused by colonial and cultural encounters that transmit 'Western modernities'. Building on the contemporary example of renegotiation and rejection of ancestral customs among Manjaco in Guinea-Bissau, Eric Gable (1995: 249) suggests that people's interactions with spirits point to the existence of the "indigenous landscape" within which skepticism makes sense. During ritual interactions, people cajole spirits into action while questioning their ability to hear and respond to people's pleas. Manjaco display a profoundly pragmatic attitude toward their spirits, who are expected to work hard in return for a ritual sacrifice. Spirits' failure to do so inevitably casts a shadow of doubt over the utility of the human-spirit contract. Seeing no signs of successful intervention on behalf of humans suffering from droughts and hunger, some Manjaco speak of losing faith in spirits, even though the loss of faith in ancestral spirits could be coupled with belief in the Christian God.

Attitudes toward witchcraft and shamanic healing have always elicited complex responses. Public assertions of their efficacy co-exist with critical discussions about the validity of rituals, private doubts, and evidence of failure. Doubt is not strictly a cognitive mechanism, because it also has a social dimension. People often distrust inept and corrupt religious practitioners rather than turn their back on spirits and gods as such. During healing rituals, Iban shamans in Borneo work in the invisible realm and plead with their audiences to accept their actions as genuine and efficacious. But audience members can be divided in their opinion as to whether a shaman is a charlatan (Wadley et al. 2006: 44–46). For example, people can be selectively skeptical of practitioners and their ability to deceive spirits and restore health to an afflicted person. They might consult several religious experts and then dismiss their verdicts as invalid. In some contexts, the performative incompetence of a shaman can give rise to suspicions that a shaman plays tricks on the audience rather than on spirits. The circulation of popular comic tales about shamans who succeed in their rituals by luck and deception rather than extraordinary powers reinforces people's incredulity (ibid.: 45). A skeptical public can attempt to expose fraudulent shamans or parody their peregrinations. In essence, audiences need to be convinced by a sorcerer that his magic works.

Here, doubt is not simply a correlate of belief but a communicative technique of ritual professionals (Good et al. 2014). Although we have suggested that doubt is an intrinsic aspect of any religious tradition, it cannot be naturalized because it can be actively managed. Doubt can be generated and/or dispelled in the process of judgment, persuasion, decision making, and arbitration in religious and judicial settings. Doubt opens these processes to contestation and negotiation because it is imbricated in questions about legitimacy and the authority of predictions and verdicts.

Doubt, however, is not only situated intersubjectively in relations between people and among people and spirits; it is also an internal conversation with the self. For example, ritual experts seem to sustain their commitment to the efficacy of their actions even when they are fully aware of the staged, simulated qualities of their ritual practices (Houseman 2002). Feigning to kill novices during initiation rites or drugging a goat whose silent 'death' is a guaranteed sign of divine intervention is not a secret to initiated operators and participants in such rituals. Awareness of the 'theatrical' character of ritual routines and of their technological aspects is not detrimental to creating and recreating the relational contexts that we call religious traditions.

However, a sorcerer might question whether his or her own actions are genuine and efficacious. If a shaman or a sorcerer hides a stone in his mouth before spitting it out as tangible evidence of successful healing, "how does he justify this procedure in his own eyes?" (Lévi-Strauss 1963: 168–169). How does self-persuasion take effect? Lévi-Strauss tells us a story about Quesalid, a sorcerer "driven by curiosity about [shamans'] tricks and by the desire to expose them" (ibid.: 172). Quesalid uses a shamanic technique on a patient who then is cured, despite the sorcerer's skepticism. How can we account for doubts, misgivings, and confusion that cannot be easily overcome? Engelke (2005: 783) discusses Michael Lambek's view that moments of self-questioning and self-denying among religious enthusiasts are not well-known. Engelke reminds us that these moments illuminate processes of coming under conviction or of developing an inwardly oriented language of persuasion that accompanies a religious transformation such as conversion. His work with the BHA highlights precisely the continuous process of producing conviction despite inward and outward questioning (see Engelke 2014).

Atheism

Anthropologists have highlighted that doubt about religious cosmologies and practices is intrinsic to all cultures, whether more or less saturated with religion. What is more, we know that religiously motivated people are often playful with their religious premises and practices. Members of the Vineyard Christian Fellowship, a neo-charismatic evangelical denomination, explained to Tanya Luhrmann (2012) that God is not imaginary, but his presence entails an act of imagination. For instance, by pretending to have God to dinner, people "behaved both as if God was foundationally real and as if their particular experiences of God were deeply satisfying daydreams that they had no difficulty recognizing as daydreams" (ibid.: 380). In other words, Vineyard Christians were wary of the possibility of disbelief in the reality of their religious world. It is an important ethnographic insight because the potential for doubt within religion is a premise that some atheists would deny. Among some well-known atheists, the notion that doubt is constitutive of religious subjectivities runs counter to the representation of religiously motivated people as deluded and 'blinded' by their faith. In order to engage with this problem productively and to avoid essentializing and flattening out atheism, we need to address the question of who atheists are and what their ideas, practices, and everyday realities are like, ethnographically and historically rather than ideologically.

Unsurprisingly, there is no simple answer. Conceptually, atheism is often defined as the explicit denial of God's existence or simply the lack of belief in a god (Bullivant 2008: 363). Negatively, it is a conscious, articulated credo against God's existence. A positive value of self-described atheists is their conviction (or rhetoric, at least) regarding the supremacy of a scientific worldview over 'irrational' traditional beliefs. This has been the main stance underpinning the political project of the New Atheists, a movement of authors and prominent figures who have, through several controversial books and publicity campaigns, criticized the 'nonsense' of religion and its negative repercussions for society. Some New Atheists use the logic of natural science as an argumentative standpoint against the 'wrongness' of theistic belief in order to prove the 'failed hypothesis' of God's existence (see, e.g., Dawkins 2006; Dennett 2006; Harris 2004, 2006; Hitchens 2007; Stenger 2007). Disregarding the problematic aspects of their arguments, which in any case are not new per se but instead reflect a long tradition of 'scientific enlightenment', the impact provoked by their initiatives has shown how specific conceptions of non-religion can become powerful and politically influential, without any discomfort concerning the self-ascribed trope of atheism.

In any case, as the chapters in this volume also prove, 'being an atheist' differs across cultural and historical contexts. This places the New Atheism critique as but one chapter in a long history. Forms of atheism have existed for centuries, but the popularization of public denial of God's existence is the marker of the twentieth century (Hyman 2007: 32). Classical and later Hellenic Greece had a fair share of philosophers and playwrights who addressed the problem of atheism (Bremmer 2007). Yet long lists of philosophical atheists compiled in the second century BC did not mention any "practicing atheists" (ibid.: 20). Instead, the charge of atheism was wielded as a political labeling weapon. For some time, atheism was a convenient way of accusing somebody of disloyalty, as happened in the Roman Empire in the first to second century AD when atheism was imputed to early Christians by pagans and vice versa. Up until the sixteenth century, the writings of Christian fathers suggest that atheism denoted heresy. But by the seventeenth century, the meaning of atheism had changed: it emerged as a recognized phenomenon linked to Enlightenment reasoning and its notion of modernity, which was understood as rational and tied to the scientific mastery of reality (Hyman 2007: 28–29). In Britain and France in particular, several thinkers, including Hume, Diderot, Descartes, Locke, and Hobbes, began to question the religious premises of their cosmos and argued for a rational or empirical quest for truth—one that discredited or expelled God, metaphysics, and revelation as a "hypostatization of rational concepts or empirical realities" (ibid.: 35).

By the end of the nineteenth century, the historical conditions were ripe for atheism to acquire institutional legs, and several secular organizations in Britain and France made a case for explicit intellectual and moral commitment to atheism (Budd 1977). In 1876, prominent figures of the Society of Anthropology of Paris created what became known as the Society of Mutual

Autopsy (Dias 1991; Hecht 1997, 2003). This research group was firmly committed to the advancement of science, in particular by proving that the soul does not exist—thus embodying a particular form of evangelical atheism. Each of the society's members would pledge to donate his or her brain to the society after death and agree to postmortem autopsy in order to investigate the relation between the human brain and an individual's personal and intellectual qualities. The group did not outlive the world wars of the twentieth century. The case of the Society of Mutual Autopsy is particularly interesting, not only because it is a nod to our discipline's historical self-conception as a secular, positivist science, but also because it highlights the thin line that separates belief from knowledge—a separation that is bridged precisely by the notion of certainty, in opposition to that of credulity.

Practices like this have never been confined to the geographical and cultural West and have contemporary purchase. A number of atheist, rationalist, and humanist associations in India emerged in the nineteenth century in interaction with similar British organizations (Quack 2012b: 70; see also Joshi 2012: 170). Frequently, atheists in India are activists who seek to promote literacy, science, ecological consciousness, social equality, sex and health education, and liberation from religious 'superstition', as well as an individual's responsibility for his or her own life (Quack 2012b: 71–74). Many Indian atheists aim to expose miracles as tricks and miracle workers as charlatans as a means to effect a reform of their social milieu, but they must also transform their personal lives and offer alternatives to traditional rites and concepts in order to confirm their 'genuine' atheist convictions. Jacob Copeman and Johannes Quack (this volume) suggest that, for Indian atheists, body donation is a practice that stands in metonymic relation to atheism because it annuls the transcendental premises of Indian religions and foregrounds materialism as a moral and experiential quality of being an atheist. Here, atheism is less a matter of intellectual debates than of material practices, including the treatment of objects and dead bodies. For an Indian atheist, cadaver donation plays a dual role—ridiculing religious mortuary practices as wasteful and making an affirmation of constructive 'godless morality', even in the face of imminent death.

Thus, atheists might present themselves as well-educated rational thinkers who disapprove of the presumed 'prejudice' of believers (see Engelke 2014, this volume). Indeed, the juxtaposition of uncritical 'blind' faith with scientific doubt informs the binary logic of New Atheists' discourses in Britain, although New Atheists themselves are in pursuit of certainty; some of them proclaim, with confidence, that there is no God and promise 'definitive evidence' to prove it (see Engelke 2012a). In their contribution to this volume, Paul-François Tremlett and Fang-Long Shih explore how discourse and texts of New Atheists, represented by Dawkins, Dennett, Harris, and others, misconstrue religions as intellectual hypotheses about divinities that govern this empirical world. Because New Atheists interpret religions in terms of private cognitive beliefs that are allegedly immune to new scientific evidence, they remain insensitive to the imperatives of many religious traditions that prioritize experiential efficacy of their practices over cognitive convictions. Much of New Atheist reasoning leads to a peculiar self-aggrandizing that casts New Atheists as critical and open-minded explorers in sharp contrast to stubborn, dogmatic 'believers'. This aggressive intellectual position of 'rational freethinkers', Tremlett and Shih emphasize, caricatures religiously motivated people as scriptural literalists and their practices as atavisms of modernity while failing to recognize the combination of continuity and innovation that goes into any religious tradition. Conversely, their religiously motivated opponents can caricature atheists as immoral deviants and puppets of authoritarian regimes, drawing a pernicious isomorphism between atheism and communist politics. Thus, atheists themselves might be subjected to stereotyping and moralizing discourses. In US opinion polls, atheists are associated with illegality, immorality, materialist values, and the lack of social obligations (Bainbridge 2005; Edgell et al. 2006). Even when tolerance of religious diversity is extended to numerous denominations, atheists test the limits of social acceptance. In American society, where religious belonging is conceptualized as a foundation of national unity (Edgell et al. 2006: 213), atheists are a category that is excluded from symbolic membership.

The antagonism between religiously and atheistically motivated people might give rise to mutual stereotyping, but the reality is even more complex. Apprehensive of the belligerent language of New Atheists, some godless people hesitate to subscribe to the name 'atheist' (see Engelke 2012b). Lois Lee (this volume) argues that, in Britain, institutional and overt forms of atheism are not the only modes of non-religion. Some people prefer to self-identify with a survey and census category of 'non-religious', thus differentiating their position from religious belonging and atheist cultures alike, yet making claims to legitimacy in their own right. What matters to these non-religious residents in north London boroughs is that their disengagement from religion does not signal that they endorse the more aggressive or militant atheist discourses and techniques of New Atheists. The fact that non-religious Londoners are ambivalent about representing themselves as atheists points to their problematic perception of New Atheists as intolerant castigators of religions. Moreover, this ambivalence is key to understanding how the refusal to be cast as an atheist generates and/or undermines the power to interpret or misinterpret non-religious personhood.

The presumed divide between believers and atheists goes so far as to impute to the latter the inability to 'know' religion. The religious and atheist positions are seen as incommensurable and untranslatable. This issue becomes critical with regard to the social sciences and anthropologists. Taking into consideration that atheists are often charged with ideological blindness and the failure to engage productively with religion, does the work of atheist Soviet scholars carry any epistemological value? Can non-religious anthropologists productively conduct ethnographic research in an intensely religious culture? Sonja Luehrmann (this volume) challenges the idea that Soviet scholarship on religion was a case of blatant propagandism. For several decades, the bureaucratic condition of mandatory scientific atheism constrained the interpretive possibilities of Soviet social scientists, but their bafflement with religious resilience led them to refine their methodological and theoretical tools. Never challenging the official critique of religious belonging, Soviet scholars had to pursue increasingly sophisticated empirical research to explain the reasons why Soviet people continued to baptize their children and perform other life-cycle rituals. Their findings contradicted the Communist Party's assertions that only ignorant people held religious convictions. Their studies also pointed to polarization between younger and older generations, the city and the countryside, and different ethnic groups, as well as the role that religions might play in creating divisions. Soviet social scientists remained oblivious of their biases; for instance, they saw ritual and religious objects as mechanisms of religious propaganda. But their anti-religious stance allowed for many interesting insights into the complexities of religious traditions.

Luehrmann persuasively argues that antagonism and empathy are productive yet problematic ways of engaging with religious 'others'. By analogy with Soviet social scientists, she touches upon the methodological pressure to achieve ethnographic empathy in anthropological research that has sprung from an assumption that religious traditions might be alien to secularized scholars. While Luehrmann's work is historical in its scope, Galina Oustinova-Stjepanovic's chapter (this volume) is motivated by the problem of being an atheist anthropologist among seriously religious people. In addition to reviewing the debates on methodological atheism in anthropology as a secularized—and potentially biased—discipline, Oustinova-Stjepanovic shows that reflexivity, intellectual sensitivity to our interlocutors' religious ideas and practices, and professional commitment to ethnographic empathy might crumble when an anthropologist is suddenly drawn into the physically and affectively demanding world of a religious ritual. It becomes apparent that the suspension of disbelief might be obstructed by the inability to participate bodily in a ritual. This line of inquiry complements and expands the analysis of atheism and New Atheism, which see religion in terms of beliefs (Tremlett and Shih, this volume), by disclosing visceral aspects of atheism as a disposition.

Conclusion

With this volume, we hope to contribute to a critical understanding of the different ways of being godless and the manifestation of their problematics somewhere between mundane doubt and ideological atheism. Despite our reluctance to define (and essentialize) godlessness, we contend that the line of the ethnographic inquiry that we pursue here allows us to capture the experiential quality of being godless and perspectives of godless people on the role of religion in their personal and public lives. These chapters recognize the historical, social, cultural, and political complexities that underpin the daily realities of godless people. All of us are familiar with the idea that being religious is difficult: one has to commit to theistic and social obligations, invest time and money, learn and polish ritual techniques, and much more. But being godless implies an equally unsettling endeavor: one must remove oneself from ancestral traditions, find rationalizations and ethical justifications for one's position, struggle against familial and institutional responsibilities, and look for ways to insulate oneself from the potential encroachment of religious mysteries and compelling qualities of religious liturgies. Most people dwell somewhere in between total immersion and the unequivocal rejection of religion. By focusing on godless people, we hope to understand what some people do to disengage from religion and the challenges and paradoxes that they face.

Acknowledgments

Galina and Ruy would like to thank their colleagues in the Department of Social Anthropology at the University of Edinburgh, the Department of Anthropology at University College London, the Institute of Social Sciences at the University of Lisbon, and the Department of Social Anthropology at the University of Bergen. Shawn Kendrick has provided invaluable editorial comments on this volume.

Ruy Llera Blanes, who received his PhD from the University of Lisbon in 2007, is a Ramon y Cajal fellow at the Spanish National Research Council (CSIC). His current research site is Angola, where he is working on the topics of religion, mobility (diasporas, transnationalism, the Atlantic), politics (leadership, charisma, repression, resistance), temporalities (historicity, memory, heritage, expectations), and knowledge. He is also co-editor of the journal *Religion and Society: Advances in Research.*

Galina Oustinova-Stjepanovic has been working as a Teaching Fellow in the Department of Anthropology at University College London since 2012. She is also a resarcher in the Department of Anthropology at the University of Edinburgh. Her research interests include anthropology of religion, especially Islam, and political anthropology.

References

Agrama, Hussein Ali. 2012. "Reflections on Secularism, Democracy, and Politics in Egypt." *American Ethnologists* 39, no. 1: 26–31.

Asad, Talal. 1993. *Genealogies of Religion: Discipline and Reasons of Power in Christianity and Islam.* Baltimore, MD: Johns Hopkins University Press.

Bainbridge, William. 2005. "Atheism." *Interdisciplinary Journal of Research on Religion* 1, no. 2: 1–26.

Bennett, Jane. 2001. *The Enchantment of Modern Life: Attachments, Crossings, and Ethics.* Princeton, NJ: Princeton University Press.

Bremmer, Jan N. 2007. "Atheism in Antiquity." Pp. 11–27 in Martin 2007a.

Bubandt, Nils, and Martijn van Beek, eds. 2012. *Varieties of Secularism in Asia: Anthropological Explorations of Religion, Politics and the Spiritual.* London: Routledge.

Budd, Susan. 1977. *Varieties of Unbelief: Atheists and Agnostics in English Society, 1850–1960*. London: Heinemann.

Bullivant, Stephen. 2008. "Research Note: Sociology and the Study of Atheism." *Journal of Contemporary Religion* 23, no. 3: 363–368.

Bullivant, Stephen, and Lois Lee. 2012. "Interdisciplinary Studies of Non-religion and Secularity: The State of the Union." *Journal of Contemporary Religion* 27, no. 1: 19–27.

Cannell, Fenella. 2010. "The Anthropology of Secularism." *Annual Review of Anthropology* 39: 85–100.

Casanova, José. 1994. *Public Religions in the Modern World*. Chicago: University of Chicago Press.

Cusack, Carole M. 2010. *Invented Religions: Imagination, Fiction and Faith*. Surrey: Ashgate.

Dawkins, Richard. 2006. *The God Delusion*. New York: Bantam Books.

Dennett, Daniel. 2006. *Breaking the Spell: Religion as a Natural Phenomenon*. New York: Viking Press.

Dennett, Daniel, and Linda LaScola. 2010. "Preachers Who Are Not Believers." *Evolutionary Psychology* 8, no. 1: 122–150.

Dias, Nélia S. 1991. "La Société d'Autopsie mutuelle ou le don du corps à la science." *Gradhiva* 10: 26–36.

Edgell, Penny, Joseph Gerteis, and Douglas Hartmann. 2006. "Atheists as 'Other': Moral Boundaries and Cultural Membership in American Society." *American Sociological Review* 71, no. 2: 211–234.

Engelke, Matthew. 2005. "The Early Days of Johane Masowe: Self-Doubt, Uncertainty, and Religious Transformation." *Comparative Studies in Society and History* 47, no. 4: 781–808.

Engelke, Matthew. 2007. *A Problem of Presence: Beyond Scripture in an African Church*. Berkeley: University of California Press.

Engelke, Matthew. 2012a. "Angels in Swindon: Public Religion and Ambient Faith in England." *American Ethnologist* 39, no. 1: 155–170.

Engelke, Matthew. 2012b. "In Spite of Christianity: Humanism and Its Others in Contemporary Britain." Paper presented at the NSRN Annual Lecture, London, 28 November.

Engelke, Matthew. 2014. "Christianity and the Anthropology of Secular Humanism." *Current Anthropology* 55, no. S10: S292–S301.

Gable, Eric. 1995. "The Decolonization of Consciousness: Local Skeptics and the 'Will to Be Modern' in a West African Village." *American Ethnologist* 22, no. 2: 242–257.

Good, Anthony, Daniela Berti, and Gilles Tarabout. 2014. "Introduction: Technologies of Doubt in Law and Ritual." Pp. 1–18 in *Of Doubt and Proof: Ritual and Legal Practices of Judgment*, ed. Daniela Berti, Anthony Good, and Gilles Tarabout. Farnham: Ashgate Publishing.

Goody, Jack. 1996. "A Kernel of Doubt." *Journal of the Royal Anthropological Institute* 2, no. 4: 667–681.

Harris, Sam. 2004. *The End of Faith: Religion, Terror, and the Future of Reason*. New York: W.W. Norton.

Harris, Sam. 2006. *Letter to a Christian Nation*. New York: Knopf.

Hecht, Jennifer. 1997. "Scientific Materialism and the Liturgy of Death: The Invention of a Secular Version of Catholic Last Rites (1876–1914)." *French Historical Studies* 20, no. 4: 703–735.

Hecht, Jennifer. 2003. *The End of the Soul: Scientific Modernity, Atheism, and Anthropology in France*. New York: Columbia University Press.

Hitchens, Christopher. 2007. *God Is Not Great: How Religion Poisons Everything*. New York: Twelve Books.

Højer, Lars. 2009. "Absent Powers: Magic and Loss in Post-Socialist Mongolia." *Journal of the Royal Anthropological Institute* 15, no. 3: 575–591.

Houseman, Michael. 2002. "Dissimulation and Simulation as Forms of Religious Reflexivity." *Social Anthropology* 10, no. 1: 77–89.

Hyman, Gavin. 2007. "Atheism in Modern History." Pp. 27–46 in Martin 2007a.

Jakobsen, Janet R., and Ann Pellegrini, eds. 2008. *Secularisms*. Durham, NC: Duke University Press.

Joshi, Vibha. 2012. *A Matter of Belief: Christian Conversion and Healing in North-East India*. New York: Berghahn Books.

Keane, Webb. 2008. "The Evidence of the Senses and the Materiality of Religion." *Journal of the Royal Anthropological Institute* 14: S110–S127.

Kehl-Bodrogi, Krisztina. 2008. *"Religion Is Not So Strong Here": Muslim Religious Life in Khorezm after Socialism*. Berlin: Lit Verlag.

Kelly, Tobias. 2011. "The Cause of Human Rights: Doubts about Torture, Law, and Ethics at the United Nations." *Journal of the Royal Anthropological Institute* 17, no. 4: 728–744.

Kirsch, Thomas G. 2004. "Restaging the Will to Believe: Religious Pluralism, Anti-Syncretism, and the Problem of Belief." *American Anthropologist* 106, no. 4: 699–709.

Lévi-Strauss, Claude. 1963. *Structural Anthropology*. Trans. Claire Jacobson and Brooke Grundfest Schoepf. New York: Basic Books.

Lévy-Bruhl, Lucien. [1926] 1985. *How Natives Think*. Trans. Lilian A. Clare. London: George Allen and Unwin.

Lewis, Gilbert. 2002. "Between Public Assertion and Private Doubts. A Sepik Ritual of Healing and Reflexivity." *Social Anthropology* 10, no. 1: 11–21.

Lindquist, Galina, and Simon Coleman. 2008. "Introduction: Against Belief?" *Social Analysis* 52, no. 1: 1–18.

Louw, Maria. 2012. "Being Muslim the Ironic Way: Secularism, Religion and Irony in Post-Soviet Kyrgyzstan" Pp. 143–162 in Bubandt and van Beek 2012.

Luehrmann, Sonja. 2011. *Secularism Soviet Style: Teaching Atheism and Religion in a Volga Republic*. Bloomington: Indiana University Press.

Luhrmann, Tanya. 2007 "How Do You Learn to Know That It Is God Who Speaks?" Pp. 83–102 in *Learning Religion: Anthropological Approaches,* ed. David Berliner and Ramon Sarró. New York: Berghahn Books.

Luhrmann, Tanya. 2012. "A Hyperreal God and Modern Belief: Toward an Anthropological Theory of Mind." *Current Anthropology* 53, no. 4: 371–395.

Mahmood, Saba. 2005. *Politics of Piety: The Islamic Revival and the Feminist Subject*. Princeton, NJ: Princeton University Press.

Malinowski, Bronislaw. 1948. *Magic, Science and Religion, and Other Essays*. Boston: Beacon Press.

Martin, Michael, ed. 2007a. *The Cambridge Companion to Atheism*. New York: Cambridge University Press.

Martin, Michael. 2007b. "General Introduction." Pp. 1–7 in Martin 2007a.

McBrien, Julie, and Mathijs Pelkmans. 2008. "Turning Marx on His Head: Missionaries, 'Extremists' and Archaic Secularists in Post-Soviet Kyrgyzstan." *Critique of Anthropology* 28, no. 1: 87–103.

Naumescu, Vlad. 2013. "Old Believers' Passion Play: the Meaning of Doubt in an Orthodox Ritualist Movement." Pp. 85–118 in Pelkmans 2013a.

Needham, Rodney. 1972. *Belief, Language, and Experience*. Oxford: Basil Blackwell.

Orsi, Robert. 2005. *Between Heaven and Earth: The Religious Worlds People Make and the Scholars Who Study Them*. Princeton, NJ: Princeton University Press.

Pedersen, Morten Axel. 2011. *Not Quite Shamans: Spirit Worlds and Political Lives in Northern Mongolia*. Ithaca, NY: Cornell University Press.

Pelkmans, Mathijs, ed. 2013a. *Ethnographies of Doubt: Faith and Uncertainty in Contemporary Societies*. London: I.B. Tauris.

Pelkmans, Mathijs. 2013b. "Outline for an Ethnography of Doubt." Pp. 1–42 in Pelkmans 2013a.

Peris, Daniel. 1998. *Storming the Heavens: The Soviet League of the Militant Godless*. Ithaca, NY: Cornell University Press.

Pigg, Stacy Leigh. 1996. "The Credible and the Credulous: The Question of Villagers' Beliefs in Nepal." *Cultural Anthropology* 11, no. 2: 160–201.

Pouillon, Jean. 1982. "Remarks on the Verb 'To Believe.'" Pp. 1–8 in *Between Belief and Transgression: Structuralist Essays in Religion, History, and Myth*, ed. Michel Izard and Pierre Smith; trans. John Leavitt. Chicago: University of Chicago Press.

Quack, Johannes. 2010. *Disenchanting India: Organized Rationalism and Criticism of Religion in India*. New York: Oxford University Press.

Quack, Johannes. 2012a. "Hinduism, Atheism, and Rationalism." Pp. 626–632 in *Brill's Encyclopedia of Hinduism*, vol. 4, ed. Knut A. Jacobsen, Helene Basu, Angelika Malinar, and Vasudha Narayanan. Leiden: Brill.

Quack, Johannes. 2012b. "Organized Atheism in India: An Overview." *Journal of Contemporary Religion* 27, no. 1: 67–85.

Quack, Johannes. 2013. "India." Pp. 651–663 in *The Oxford Handbook of Atheism*, ed. Stephen Bullivant and Michael Ruse. Oxford: Oxford University Press.

Quack, Johannes. 2014. "Outline of a Relational Approach to 'Nonreligion.'" *Method & Theory in the Study of Religion* 26, no. 4–5: 439–469.

Radin, Paul. 1927. *Primitive Man as Philosopher*. New York: Dover Publications.

Ruel, Malcolm. 1982. "Christians as Believers." Pp. 9–33 in *Religious Organization and Religious Experience*, ed. John Davis. London: Academic Press.

Saler, Benson. 1968. "Beliefs, Disbeliefs, and Unbeliefs." *Anthropological Quarterly* 41, no. 1: 29–33.

Schielke, Samuli. 2012. "Being a Nonbeliever in a Time of Islamic Revival: Trajectories of Doubt and Certainty in Contemporary Egypt." *International Journal of Middle East Studies* 44, no. 2: 301–320.

Stark, Rodney. 1999. "Atheism, Faith, and the Social Scientific Study of Religion." *Journal of Contemporary Religion* 14, no. 1: 41–62.

Starrett, Gregory. 2010. "The Varieties of Secular Experience." *Comparative Studies in Society and History* 52, no. 3: 626–651.

Stenger, Victor J. 2007. *God: The Failed Hypothesis. How Science Shows That God Does Not Exist*. Amherst NY: Prometheus Books.

Strathern, Marilyn. 1996. "Cutting the Network." *Journal of the Royal Anthropological Institute* 2, no. 3: 517–535.

Street, Alice. 2010. "Belief as Relational Action: Christianity and Cultural Change in Papua New Guinea." *Journal of the Royal Anthropological Institute* 16, no. 2: 260–278.

Taylor, Charles 1992. *The Malaise of Modernity*. Concord, Ont.: Anansi.

Taylor, Charles. 2007. *A Secular Age*. Cambridge, MA: Belknap Press of Harvard University Press.

Tylor, Edward B. [1871] 2008. "Religion in Primitive Culture." Pp. 23–33 in *A Reader in Anthropology of Religion*, 2nd ed., ed. Michael Lambek. Oxford: Blackwell.

Wadley, Reed, Angela Pashia, and Craig Palmer. 2006. "Religious Scepticism and Its Social Context: An Analysis of Iban Shamanism." *Anthropological Forum* 16, no. 1: 41–54.

West, Harry G. 2005. *Kupilikula: Governance and the Invisible Realm in Mozambique*. Chicago: University of Chicago Press.

Chapter 1

AMBIVALENT ATHEIST IDENTITIES
Power and Non-religious Culture in Contemporary Britain

Lois Lee

First and second waves of research into secularism, non-religious atheism, and other non-religious[1] cultures have been biased in their interest toward the organized expressions of these cultures. There are two sensible reasons for this. Firstly, organized non-religion (e.g., humanist associations, identifiable cultural movements like New Atheism, or anti-theist governmental policy) is empirically and theoretically significant, increasingly so in some regards (see Engelke 2015). Secondly, part of this significance relates to the high visibility of these forms. This prominence shapes their impact in society and also makes them readily identifiable as subjects for social research. In all likelihood, however, these organized forms present the 'tip of the iceberg' when it comes to social and cultural expressions of non-religion in contemporary societies. There are, for example, several indications that the number of people involved with overt,

Notes for this chapter begin on page 36.

representational modes of atheism is vastly overshadowed by the number associated with implicit, non-representational modes (Lee, forthcoming).

In this chapter, I consider the scope for ethnographies of non-religion and non-religious atheism beyond the most centralized or codified expressions of these phenomena. Drawing on exploratory fieldwork conducted in South East England, I focus on issues of representation and identity, concentrating on the more ambivalent non-religious identities that are easily lost from view. Like other forms of self-representation, these identifications reveal, enable, and determine subjective experiences. Representation makes something of the self available to multiple audiences, subjecting it to the interpretation and interests of others. The diffuseness of these representations, however, prevents them from being recognized and therefore restricts their direct influence in public discussion and space. At the same time, it prevents others from understanding and interpreting these subjectivities—and from misunderstanding and misinterpreting them. Thus, ambivalent identities are themselves deeply ambivalent, with complicated and contradictory effects for the actors involved. This chapter argues that asymmetries in the ways that religious and non-religious positions are identified are, ultimately, problematic and draws attention to the particular role ethnographers can play by shedding light on cultural forms that are at once naturalized and difficult to comprehend.

Beyond Organized Atheism

Contemporary Western discourses have focused on 'atheism' as the dominant form of non-religious identity and have typically imagined these atheist identities to be coherent, clearly understood by those adopting them, and confident in attitude. While social researchers have been more open-minded about how assertively religious identities need to be in order to be meaningful, they have required those who identify themselves as atheist to be more definite in their self-understanding and self-representation. Concerns have been raised about the 'convinced atheist' category that appears in a major international survey alongside denominational responses that are not qualified (e.g., 'Christian' rather than 'convinced Christian') (Bruce 2002: 193). Similarly, both academic and popular writing is littered with ideas of 'aggressive atheism' and 'militant atheism'. Although some space is made for uncertainty and complexity, this is often achieved not by studying the specific relationship between ambivalence and atheism but by displacing the idea of atheism and reidentifying the phenomenon in terms of (weak) agnosticism, which is seen to occupy a middle ground between theism and atheism. There is, however, evidence that atheist and other non-religious cultures can be decentered in a range of ways, not all of which imply that the individual is uncertain in his or her atheist or non-religious cultural or intellectual positions but rather that these decentered cultures are concrete in their own right. Organized atheist and other non-religious cultures have been and continue to be a significant feature in societies and present an important subject for research. In this section, I aim to highlight the significance of atheist and non-religious cultures beyond these centers. I argue that although they are often less tangible or explicit, these more diffuse forms of symbolic representation also shape social life and require scholarly attention.

In the first place, many atheists do not adopt representations that are associated with organized non-religion, such as atheist, humanist, rationalist, or Bright,[2] yet they appear to be clear in their non-theist perspectives. To take an example from the British case that this chapter focuses on, in 2000 only 5 percent of Britons described themselves as "convinced atheists" (European Values Survey, cited in Bullivant 2010: 114), compared to 28 percent who expressed an atheist view on the existence of God.[3] Alternatively put, only one-fifth of those who professed atheistic beliefs understood or represented themselves in a way that reflected this. This might appear to be evidence that the majority of Britons are not significantly or substantively atheist—that they consider their beliefs to be atheist only if pressed to do so. However, the number of people who state that being non-religious is meaningful is much closer to the number of 'actual' atheists than to the smaller number of people who identify themselves as atheist. In the 2008 British Social Attitudes survey, 26 percent of Britons said that they are "very or extremely non-religious," and a further 11 percent described themselves as "somewhat non-religious."[4] The 26 percent echoes, almost exactly, the number of people expressing atheist beliefs in that year. This is an indication that bare atheistic principles are not an insignificant appendage to the real business of everyday life, but rather are part of broader and meaningful non-religious complexes. In this light, the disinclination to express atheism in public and personal self-representations is paradoxical and an interesting problem for empirical researchers. Certainly, it is a reason to investigate further.

Additional evidence of diffuse but culturally significant expressions of nontheism, or 'positive atheism' (Bullivant 2013), comes precisely from the array of media representations of atheism, non-theism, and non-religion that do not focus on dedicated, organized atheist and non-religious communities. The concept of atheism itself has a notable but decentered presence in mainstream public discourses in the UK, as in other places around the world (see the various contributions to this volume). This is partly due to wide interest in the cultural movement known as New Atheism and, in particular, the work of Richard Dawkins,[5] but it extends far beyond that, with 'atheism' central to many discursive spaces dedicated to religion. For example, on its blog Comment Is Free: Belief, the *Guardian* newspaper organizes its postings according to major religious traditions (Anglicanism, Catholicism, evangelicalism, Judaism, Islam) and includes atheism as representative of the non-religious. In recent years, the British Humanist Association (BHA) has sought to shape British culture by means of high-profile advertising campaigns in public spaces in which representations of atheism and non-religious secularism have been central. These include the Atheist Bus Campaign ("There Probably Is No God. Now Stop Worrying and Enjoy Your Life") (see Sherine 2008), as well as the Census Campaign ("If You're Not Religious, for God's Sake Say So") (BHA 2011). These examples illustrate how representations emanating from nonreligious organizations are diffused more widely in socio-cultural space.

Kim Knott et al. (2013) report that, between 1980 and 2000, the presence of secularism and/or *atheism* has increased in British media outlets in general, with the coverage of religion also having grown. Meanwhile, works such as Teemu Taira and Ruth Illman's (2012) recent special issue of *Approaching Religion* on the visibility of atheism in Europe recognize this emphasis on atheism in popular cultures. Indeed, this volume and many of its contributions (including my own) focus on atheism, emerging from and attempting to speak to a discursive tradition centered on non-religious atheism rather than other types or aspects of non-religion. In short, atheist discursive threads are woven through the fabric of many societies and should extend the empirical reach of any anthropology of atheism (and of non-religion in general) far beyond the study of individuals and institutions that understand or represent themselves as atheist.

This is not to mention the implicit and indirect aspects of non-religious identities—their manifestation in related symbols, social formations, and embodied practice (Lee 2012b). As well as identifying as 'atheist' or 'humanist'—terms associated with developed and institutionalized non-religious identities in British and several other contexts—non-religious people might represent themselves as 'not religious', 'non-religious', or 'secularist'. They might choose to participate in humanist life-cycle rituals and ceremonies without identifying as humanist or express an atheist identity by taking part in civil ceremonies. Alternatively, they might reject life-cycle ceremonies entirely due to their association with religious cultures. Unbelief might play a role in the 'talking about' religion that Courtney Bender (2012) has recently described as a central concern to researchers of religion and the secular,[6] or in talking about or having existential experiences—in negotiating the precariousness of life and death and the sources of meaning and ideas of individual agency and human purpose that people experience in relation to these negotiations (Lee, forthcoming).

This open, relational approach to understanding atheist subjectivity and identity (Lee 2012c; Quack 2014) looks beyond the rejections of theism and religion that have also governed engagements with the non-religious. In some ways, this approach is broader than the already pliant framework provided for this volume. The notion of non-religion used in this chapter is contingent and elastic and therefore consistent with Ruy Blanes and Galina Oustinova-Stjepanovic's suggestion in the introduction that, standing as we do at the cusp of a relatively new field of inquiry, the use of firm or closed definitions is ill-advised. Blanes and Oustinova-Stjepanovic are particularly interested in the concept of 'being godless', understanding it broadly "as the *reluctance* of humans to engage with any divinized beings or notions of transcendental agency, regardless of theories about a god's position in any given religious cosmology" (this volume; emphasis added), echoing Colin Campbell ([1971] 2013) and many others' focus on the *rejection* of religion or 'irreligion'. By contrast, the idea of non-religion as any form of difference, not merely rejection, and as distance from any aspect of religion, not just theism, draws attention to processes and representations that involve not only moving away from god or religion but also moving closer to non-religious godlessness or non-religious cultures and experiences that may be positive and concrete.

Methodologically, the common incidence of non-religious activity and expression that is not represented in highly codified symbolic forms or in highly centralized social ones calls especially for ethnographic research. With its focus on situated methods and detailed interpretative analysis, ethnographic research is especially suited to shedding light on and giving color to some of the mysteries that remain despite research focused on self-description and self-reporting. The empirical focus of this chapter—the discrepancy between the number of atheists and the number of people who clearly self-identify as atheist—is one such mystery.

Fieldwork and New Opportunities for Ethnography

This chapter draws on data collected as part of a doctoral research project piloted in 2006 and conducted between 2007 and 2011 (Lee 2012a). A sociological investigation of the nature and variety of secularity, my research initially followed a limited qualitative sociological methodology, relying on semi-structured interviews. I identified a group of people commonly understood to be 'secular'—namely, those who disaffiliate from religion in large-scale surveys. In practice, participants were included in the research if they preferred the label 'not religious' (or 'non-religious') to 'religious' to describe themselves. The broad sampling population was narrowed to a frame that focused on South East England, an area that includes particularly high numbers of non-affiliates (Voas 2009; Voas and McAndrew 2012), but within this I aimed to work with people who potentially had diverse non-religious positions in order to explore the extent of this variety and the parameters of any non-religious field. Formal interviews were conducted with 42 people. The research then investigated how this population related and stood in relation to various aspects of 'conventional religion' (Robert Towler, cited in Knott 2005: 59). In view of the fact that so little could be said about secularity *a priori*, given the lack previous of empirical work, the methodology was exploratory and the analysis inductive. This meant that the research could adapt to new possibilities for data collection, many of which were not anticipated at the outset.[7] Although the project cannot claim to be a full-fledged ethnographic endeavor, it was able to indicate sites for ethnographic work that were not previously in view and used ethnographic methods to understand the nature of those non-religious representations that are substantial but hard to identify.

It became clear through this work that even diffuse forms of atheist and non-religious identities are often tacitly known by people and are difficult to put into words. Interviews opened with a discussion of self-classification—of how the participants would identify their 'religious' or 'non-religious' position if asked to do so for a survey—followed by a wider discussion of this classification and whether it and other available classifications succeeded in expressing what participants wanted. These explicit discussions of classifications were analyzed in light of other aspects of interview conversations and contextualized by other ethnographic data gathered (discussed below). They were also triangulated with data collected from a second interview method developed in the field, which was conducted at the end of the interview session described above. This involved a qualitative social network exercise, conducted as part of formal interview meetings, in which the participants were asked to list 10 people to whom they are close (their 'personal network') and then to identify, if they could, the religious or non-religious positions of those people. This method proved particularly fertile in terms of exploring intersubjective aspects of (non-) religious language and the ways in which non-religious positioning relates to social relationships, including how people recollect social interactions concerning or mediated by religion or non-religion in some way. These discussions showed that both played a role in social life and identity formation, even when people were not aware of or had not narrativized this process. Most people could say something about the religious, spiritual, or non-religious positions of those around them and, in reflecting on this, could identify moments of conversation or ongoing practice that had led to this knowledge. This method revealed more subtle or embedded forms of atheist identification than could emerge from directly asking individuals to identify themselves in relation to religion—the affiliation questions that have been popular in quantitative research.

I also became increasingly aware of the role of the material and the aesthetic in non-religious experience and the possibilities of more rounded ethnographic work to investigate this subject (Lee 2012b; see also the chapters by Blanes, Copeman and Quack, and Oustinova-Stjepanovic, this volume). Having begun the project with an interview methodology, I increasingly used a mixed methods approach to situate these discussions in a wider cultural context. Ethnographic data were gathered in private settings—the homes of research participants and small, organized secularist and atheist meetings—as well as public settings, including representations in the national media and at larger-scale commercial events. Ethnography of place was also a factor: fieldwork was conducted in the London boroughs of Islington and Camden, areas that have a 'top ten' concentration of people who do not affiliate with a religion (Voas 2009; Voas and McAndrew 2012), which is where I lived for the duration of this research. Additional data were obtained through informal interviews with people involved in organized non-religious activity or simply in the locale more generally (see Lee 2012b). Local ethnography enabled an exploration of the trajectories that might give rise to 'non-religious encounters'—that is, encounters with religion experienced by those with some sense of 'otherness' from it—and demonstrated the possibility of using spatial methods to investigate 'lived non-religion'.

Because they are not always aware of them, both research participants and researchers are likely to overattribute secularity (i.e., the marginalization of the religious and, necessarily, the non-religious) to situations in which religious and non-religious cultures are in fact meaningful. By contrast, instances in which non-religion and religion appear to be insignificant or irrelevant are frequently sites of engagements that are part of, and constituted in, wider constellations of symbols and meanings. Ambivalent atheist and non-religious identities, so long taken at face value, are an important example of this.

Ambivalent Non-religious Identities

Previous scholars have focused on atheism and (less often) humanism, perceived to be the most significant non-religious cultural representations. As identities, however, these are usually adopted by small minorities, and, as they are outside of the mainstream to that extent, it may in fact be right to suppose that their use implies a degree of conviction. In Britain, for example, atheists may be more likely to be 'convinced' in their view than Christians. By contrast, non-religious identities that are more generic appear to be more ambivalent. Indeed, scholars have assumed that identifying as 'not religious' rather than 'atheist' is to adopt this as a default option or to merely fall into a residual category (see, e.g., Campbell [1971] 2013; Lee 2012a: 154; 2014; Pasquale 2007). As Frank Pasquale (2007: 762) points out: "The most prevalent survey category relevant to the irreligious is known as 'nones,' a term that indicates that this is a function of survey method rather than a self-description."

Certainly, 'not religious' and related categories, such as 'non-religious', 'no religion', and 'none', have been offered as residual categories on social scientific surveys and population censuses. There is also evidence, however, that these categories are not merely imposed upon people but are appropriated and mobilized by them to specific ends. As well as sometimes being used in these scenarios as a proxy for a form of self-understanding that is not included as a survey option (e.g., specific identities such as 'atheist' or 'humanist', or in lieu of a 'spiritual' or 'spiritual but not religious' option), people also use generic non-religious categories to reject category labels or to identify as 'indifferent to religion' (Lee 2014).

This section draws out the last two of these as exemplary ambivalent non-religious identities and discusses the extent to which these identities are concrete and meaningful. These cases are particularly interesting as situations in which people identify as non-identifying subjects. This intrinsic paradox is even greater when those who reject classification or identify as being indifferent to religion also display a range of engagements with religion and non-religion—something that I encountered several times in my research and has led me to make a distinction between indifference and 'engaged indifferentism' (see Lee 2014).

To illustrate with an example—of indifferentism in this case—Victoria,[8] a 28-year-old editor whom I interviewed in her flat in Islington, said that she preferred to call herself 'non-religious' rather than 'atheist', although she was an atheist in terms of her (un)belief in God. As she put it: "If I was to say I was 'atheist', it sort of suggests I actively pursue [atheism] in a kind of formal way ... whereas, I don't really give it a huge amount of thought very often." Other research participants told me more explicitly that religion, and sometimes non-religion as well, did not matter to them. This often happened in the process of distancing themselves from the 'God wars'—the battle between New Atheists and 'old theists' of traditional and conservative perspectives—that has achieved such prominence in the British media over the past decade. People often expressed confusion or exasperation with the strong feelings associated with both sides of the debate. In these cases, 'non-religion' was a useful category for communicating disengagement.

However, Victoria was typical of many people self-identifying as 'indifferent' while also, over the course of the interview, discussing a number of ways in which she engages with religion, including clear philosophical and moral statements on issues relating to religion, non-religion, theism, and atheism. For example, later on in the interview, she said: "I'm not probably keen on marriage, but were I to want to get married, there's no way I would have a church wedding, and if someone was to [ask why], I would say, 'because I'm an atheist', I suppose." While it might not be useful to her as a 'main' identity, then, Victoria's atheism nevertheless emerges as an aspect of her self-understanding that is expressed in certain situations (Lee 2012a). Similarly, the embeddedness of non-religious identities is evidenced by the fluency with which people, like Victoria, select the default category 'non-religious' (or 'not religious') and are able to provide a reasoning for the decision. Struggling to express disengagement would be a powerful illustration of such disengagement, but instead people are able to take up 'non-religious' categories to represent themselves in particular ways. Thus, such representations of the self as ambivalent stand in contrast with more authentically incoherent self-understandings and modes of self-expression.

In what follows, I want to explore this 'inauthentic ambivalence' as an example of the significance of more diffuse non-religious cultures in general and as an interesting empirical case in its own right. Ambivalence emerges as something that needs to be understood in its specificity and historicity,[9] even when it is manifest not in easily identifiable forms but is woven through cultural life. Although the very nature of the diffuse and the ambivalent makes them intrinsically hard to locate, it is important that this effort be made because these types of identity are, I argue, socially significant and culturally formed.

Inauthentic Ambivalence

Inauthentic ambivalence is, then, core to some non-religious representations. This is not because people are disinclined to determine their position, nor is it a reflection of their disengagement with religion and non-religion. Rather, it is because ambivalence itself has meaning and can be expressed—non-ambivalently—as part of an individual's identity.

Representing oneself as ambivalent may communicate several positions. In this research context, ambivalent atheist and non-religious identities were used to express non-partisanship, independence from a community or culture, disinterestedness or neutrality, non-piousness, or tolerance and openness. Ambivalent identities also expressed antipathy toward closed, institutionalized cultures and a preference for more liberal orientations. These attitudes might have been combined or given different weight so that distinctive forms of ambivalence emerged that were mutually incompatible and could not be integrated within one framework (see also Lee 2011). The following three examples are instructive and illustrate the dangers of oversimplification.

First, some people identify as ambivalent or indifferent to non-religious cultures because they see themselves as occupying a 'rational'—and therefore ahistorical or non-cultural—position (see also Fitzgerald 2000). In the rationalist framework, cultural and emotional investments are seen to cloud one's judgment and undermine the claims to knowledge that are being made.[10] During my fieldwork, non-religious rationalism was visible in the resistance I often encountered to the very idea of the sociological and/or social anthropological study of religion and, especially, non-religion—to the idea, that is, that religious and non-religious perspectives could be understood sociologically or as a type of cultural commitment. Tellingly, such resistance was manifest in emotionally charged as well as intellectual opposition to this kind of research. On occasion, I have proposed to non-religious activists that recognizing their positions as cultural and emotional investments might lead to sympathetic audiences and political gains, and this has sometimes been met with similar antipathy.

Second, while some people prefer self-representations that emphasize a 'non-cultural' status and seek legitimacy via claims to unconstrained, clear thinking, other people prefer ambivalent identities precisely because they do not want to be categorized or do not believe in categorizing people in general—a group I have referred to as 'non-nominal' (Lee 2014). In this case, generic category labels such as 'not religious' or 'non-religious' are preferred because they seem to be the sparest form of categorization available. For people of this persuasion, however, identifying as 'not religious' may still be the bottom line—the point at which not being categorized becomes unacceptable. Although some people in the study emphasized the permeability of the boundary between religion and non-religion, or argued that there is no divide at all, for others an opposition to cultural classification operated alongside a firm sense of being located outside of the religious 'field'. The corollary of this is that these people were placing themselves inside a non-religious one (Quack 2014), whether they recognized this or not. In this way, many people who eschewed category labels and cultural affiliations did not want to go so far as to communicate ambivalence about whether they were located in or out of the religious field. Instead, they had a coherent sense of their otherness to religion, and their ambivalence extended only to that point.

Third, ambivalent identities and the residual 'not religious' category can be used by people to position themselves as 'other' to both religious and non-religious practice—that is, to position themselves as fundamentally secular. This is the indifferentism, mentioned above, in which self-understanding as indifferent is bound up with some kind of performance as indifferent, in addition to other forms of engagement (Lee 2014).[11] As seen with Victoria, understanding oneself to be indifferent or dispassionate may be combined with one or several committed positions that emerge in relation to specific scenarios, encounters, and practices. The idea that claims of indifference may not be all that they seem is supported by recent theoretical work that calls into question the idea of secular neutrality. Indifferentism can be seen as an aspect of the types of secular normativity discussed by scholars such as Timothy Fitzgerald (2000), among others. On the other hand, unproblematized notions of indifference continue to be commonplace in much work. Indifference plays a central role in discussions of irreligion, for example, where it is presented as one of two irreligious modes. In his seminal work, *Toward a Sociology of Irreligion*, Campbell ([1971] 2013) advocates the dictionary definition of irreligion as 'hostility' or 'indifference' toward religion, and this understanding has shaped the field without being subject to scrutiny.Yet indifference is a difficult concept for anyone adopting a relational epistemology, which is becoming increasingly common in the social sciences and has been a significant influence on my work. In relation to this, I have argued that it may be helpful to distinguish between secularity—as a situation in which religion or non-religion counts as a secondary point of reference or authority (where indifference might be relevant)—and non-religion when describing phenomena in which an engagement with religion (as other) is paramount (Lee 2012a, 2012c, forthcoming).

In these different ways, ambivalence—expressed as uncertainty, fluidity, and lack of commitment—can be seen as socially constructed. As such, it becomes interesting in terms of the different ways it is manifested in empirical scenarios and as an object for ethnographic research. The next section explores these representations in more detail, focusing on issues of power. Establishing the power relations that shape these representations is not only a matter of social significance but also another method of considering the depth and weight of meaning associated with un- or disorganized and decentralized forms of atheist and non-religious culture. I discuss the political significance of inauthentic and authentic ambivalent identities in turn.

The Politics of Inauthentic Ambivalence and Indifferentism

Following Bourdieu, 'fields of play' are necessarily fields of power—spaces of struggle for limited resources.[12] Hence, the notion of a field of non-religious studies should be accompanied by an analysis of the power relations that it involves (Quack 2014). In the scenarios discussed above, it is clear that 'not religious' identities can involve making plays for power when authenticating knowledge claims or claiming disinterestedness or neutrality. What I want to explore in this section is the extent to which these attempts express already powerful positions or vulnerable ones from which individuals seek to advance. Scholars who focus on secularist ideologies tend to discuss the ways in which non-religious secularists wield power. However, these critiques have not normally been based on empirical work (Turner 2010). Such studies reveal, unsurprisingly perhaps, that empirical realities are far more complicated and, importantly, that non-religious subjectivities are subject to external forces as well as exerting force on others. Even non-religious normativity emerges not only as something that the non-religious impose on the religious but as something that they also experience and perform without conscious reflection, which constrains their own subjectivities and action.

Many of the people I worked with in South East England understood themselves as occupying positions of power. Indeed, this sense of strength was another reason why ambivalent self-representations might be preferred to more unequivocal ones. For example, the category 'non-religion' was used as an alternative to 'atheism', not only because identifying as an atheist might, as Victoria says, suggest too high a level of engagement, but also in order to avoid the aggressive connotations of identifying as such. Victoria raised this possibility herself: "I suppose it depends who you're talking to. 'Cause if I was talking to someone who was really religious, it might somehow seem a bit, um, *aggressive* to say I was an 'atheist' or something, so I'd probably say I'm not religious." Even those who said that they normally self-classify as 'atheist' described a similar concern about how the term might be perceived. Hermione, a 36-year-old writer living in London, said: "Yeah, I am [happy to call myself an 'atheist']. The only, my only concern with it is it often comes across as being quite aggressive. Calling yourself an atheist in *company* can occasionally seem like holding up a big sign saying, 'If any of you are anything other than atheists, I think you're all fucking morons.' Um, which ... [pause] is disrespectful in the extreme. Obviously."

Comparison with similar data from the US suggests that the perceived forcefulness of identifying as an atheist might be related to the strength of non-religious positions in at least some UK contexts. The idea that identifying as 'atheist' might be aggressive differs markedly from its implications in the US setting. Jesse Smith (2010, 2013) describes atheism as a stigmatized position and discusses how collective identification—and 'coming out' as an atheist—is an empowering resource that counters experiences of exclusion. Several other authors have described cases in which people identifying as atheist are denigrated in American culture or discriminated against (Cragun and Hammer 2011; Cragun et al. 2012; Edgell et al. 2006). By contrast, in the British settings explored here, being an atheist is seen to be so established and strong a position that using 'atheism' as a collective identification appears to be gratuitous and therefore bullying in nature.

Aggression and atheism have also become associated with one another through New Atheist culture. This movement has made God a central motif in its discussion, and its categorization as 'New Atheism' has affirmed its association with theism in particular, rather than with, say, radical secularism. As a result, its forceful, often controversial anti-religious expressions have, in this context, become linked with the concept of atheism. Elsewhere in our conversation, Hermione said that some people (excluding herself) do not like to call themselves 'atheist' because it is associated with "other people's hate figures." She did not say who these were, but in the British context it is likely that she had New Atheist writers and broadcasters such as Dawkins in mind. Certainly, contemporary British public discourse has involved many strongly critical views about Dawkins's and others' particular brand of non-religion, and this is likely to have played some role in the forming and reforming of recent understandings of the term 'atheism'.

In addition to the provocative tone in which Dawkins's and other New Atheists' arguments have been made, there may be sociological factors to consider as well. Stephen Bullivant's (2010: 119) formative sociological discussion of

New Atheism raises this point, drawing attention to an important feature of this public atheist culture, namely, that the leading New Atheist commentators are all establishment figures who have been trained or work in elite institutions and, moreover, are male, white, and generally of high socio-economic standing. This may work against the idea of atheism as countercultural in the US case (where New Atheism is also popular), and it reinforces the sense that British non-religious people often speak from a position of power. Indeed, participants who were aware of the value of ambivalent identities often occupied privileged socio-economic positions in my study. The two women quoted above are examples of this: both Hermione and Victoria identified themselves as white, and both were comfortably well-off, working in professional occupations with high cultural capital. Both women were recruited via the same occupational network—an e-mail list used by people working in the literary industry. Both interviews took place in pleasant, book-lined living rooms in homes that the participants owned. Neither woman mentioned suffering any form of social exclusion in relation to her non-religious identity.

There are other indications that, in the British context, non-religious people can speak from positions of power. In the UK (as in several other European countries) two-thirds of those with a decided stance toward the existence of God are atheists or strong agnostics (Voas and Ling 2010: 68). Non-theism is therefore a dominant category in demographic terms, with non-believers occupying a position of power in the 'strength in numbers' sense alone (Lee 2013). This makes non-theism comparable to other dominant socio-cultural positions—maleness, for example, or whiteness—that are similarly undeveloped as collective identities precisely because of the power already wielded by people who occupy these socio-cultural positions.

The situation is all the more acute if, as Bullivant (2010) suggests, the sources of strength associated with non-religious positions are not only those particular to it (large numbers, status in public discourse) but also those that intersect with other sources of power (white skin, maleness, affluence, cultural capital). Returning to the field of study explored in this ethnographic project, one passage from a 'highbrow' publication describing the locale of this research is instructive. It is comes from a piece of commentary published in the British literary magazine, the *London Review of Books*, and written in response to the London riots (or England riots) of 2011, which took place toward the end of my fieldwork. In it, the author, James Meek (2011), takes the opportunity of these riots to consider social divisions in the borough of Hackney, where the author lives and which borders on the borough of Islington, in which my research was largely situated. Meek (ibid.) writes:

On the face of it my area's mixed, ethnically and socially. They've just built a new Hindu temple on Rhondda Grove. The students at the girls' school across the road are almost entirely Muslim. The church along the way which would, I assume, be derelict otherwise, has been taken over by a black congregation. *Middle-class white atheists like me sail around on our bikes to buy our coffee beans in Broadway Market or Victoria Park Village*; there are Georgian houses round the corner that a million pounds wouldn't buy you, and there's the eastern stretch of Roman Road, with pound stores and pawn shops and elderly geezers who never made it out to Essex and a market that makes Albert Square look posh. But this isn't mixing. It's the ingredients for something—nobody knows what—laid out side by side and not being mixed, not touching. (Emphasis added)

For my purposes, what is striking here is the association made between atheism and middle-class status, expressed in practices as well as a codified identity: the leisurely trip for coffee beans, the confident 'sailing' about on bicycles (Lee, forthcoming).[13] The implied connection between these people and million-pound dwellings may suggest that the atheist group is rather wealthier than the 'middle' stratum, but this only emphasizes the economic power associated with it. The casual, taken-for-granted link between atheism and embodied socio-economic status also appears to assume that audiences will be familiar with it. At the same time, the commentary reproduces these associations while hiding other non-religious socio-economic positions from view.

This text reflects the British discursive context outlined at the beginning of this chapter, in which atheism is a particularly prominent way of identifying the non-religious. But it is also significant that the term 'atheist' is presented, ambivalently, in the lower case, while the words 'Hindu' and 'Muslim' are capitalized. Hinduism and Islam are recognized in this way as established cultural traditions, while the status of atheism is much more ambiguous. The connection between this modest non-religious identity and the powerful socio-economic position outlined above demonstrates how ambivalent non-religious identities—identifying oneself yet shying away from identifying oneself at the same time—can be bound up with power. At the same time, the absence of a tradition of cultural identification can make powerful positions invisible, even to those who occupy them. Thus, when people see their non-religious orientation as primarily defined by ambivalence, they may do so sincerely, albeit inaccurately.

This is not to suggest that all non-religious people in Britain speak from a position of power. A critical engagement with ambivalent atheist and non-religious cultures is called for only because this can be the case, not because there are no other non-religious socio-cultural positions or experiences. Indeed, while ambivalent identities may serve the interests of some non-religious people, their ability to dictate representations of non-religion can also deny those in less advantageous positions the opportunity to identify collectively. The politics of inauthentic ambivalence are, then, complex and culturally contingent—much more so than post-colonial critics of secularism typically allow.

The Politics of Authentic Ambivalence

This discussion has focused on the ways in which ambivalence toward explicit religious and non-religious stances may be associated with substantive perspectives, that is, with non-religious rationalism, relativism, and non-nominal identities and with secular neutrality and indifferentism. In these cases, categories such as 'not religious' and 'non-religious' are recast as salient, emic terms—items of self-description rather than academic designations that merely follow the logic of survey research (Pasquale 2007). In addition to these cases, however, other ambivalent non-religious identities are 'authentic', reflecting real uncertainty about how best to express or even understand one's own relationship to religion and non-religion. Some people in this study had spent considerable time thinking about their non-religious views and identity yet still struggled to express their position clearly or satisfactorily. Such experiences present another set of concrete phenomena to which ethnographers can give their attention.

There are at least two reasons underlying real ambivalence in relation to religion. The first of these relates to the diffuse way in which non-religious threads are interwoven throughout wider cultures. Like many alternatively spiritual cultures, non-religious cultures are not commonly expressed in dedicated institutions or centers of public discussion. This means that there are relatively few publicly available articulations of non-religion. In the UK today, an apparent proliferation of identity labels—atheist, agnostic, humanist, secular, rationalist, freethinker, skeptic, Bright, secularist—actually presents a fairly limited set of options: most of these terms are associated with organized and activist forms of non-religion and with intellectualist and rationalist understandings of non-religiosity (Lee 2014, forthcoming). For those for whom activist and rationalist forms of non-religion are not salient, there may be few alternative resources and reference points.

Over the course of this research, I met several people who believed that they had been able to articulate their non-religious identities better as a result of contact with New Atheist outputs, such as Dawkins's writings. I also met people who felt that they had no way of articulating their non-religious positions, sometimes because they felt distant from these same outputs and lacked other reference points and cultural touchstones. These contrasting experiences—of empowerment and relief, on the one hand, and of disempowerment and uncertainty, on the other—are positive and negative indications of the role that self-understanding and self-representation play for non-religious people in their personal and social lives. This is not only because they are stigmatized, as Smith (2010, 2013) discusses in relation to his US-based research, but because cultural forms are a de facto resource.

We might then look on the lack of ready non-religious categories in contemporary British public life as a cultural predicament. While this predicament may be less urgent when other cultural and economic resources are widely available, it may be problematic in other circumstances. As Gerd Baumann (1996) has shown with respect to some white groups in Southall (west London), intersectional configurations include the possibility of experiencing certain dominant positions (be it whiteness or atheism) and exclusion at the same time. Such deeply ambivalent socio-economic situations—in which the individual has no recourse to resources provided through collective identification available to more vulnerable groups—are precarious and frequently associated with social unrest and violence. This demonstrates that the issue of ambivalent non-religious identities may be a pressing one, bound up with social tensions that involve religious and non-religious groups alike.

On the other hand, authentic ambivalence can also be associated with the same positions of power discussed in relation to inauthentic forms of ambivalence. Bagg and Voas (2010: 108) speculate that contemporary Britons' ability to hold 'fuzzy' religious beliefs and identities "exists in large part because [those beliefs] are rarely used or challenged." This point might also apply to 'fuzzy' non-religious beliefs and identities, implying that poorly articulated non-religious positions reflect how deeply these positions are embedded. Even if this is the case, these dominant positions may still contain the seeds of their own disempowerment. If non-religiosity is commonly expressed in tacit forms because it is deeply embedded in some areas of British cultural life, this may lead to a state of non-religious illiteracy—similar to the religious illiteracy that has become a concern of sociologists and social commentators in recent years. Rather than interpreting the absence of a strong non-religious identification as indifference, seeing it instead as a form of non-religious illiteracy opens up new ways of thinking about non-religion in contemporary societies and about religious–non-religious relations. In both of these ways, then, ambivalent non-religious identities are also ambivalent in the sense that they simultaneously empower and disempower those who hold them.

Conclusion

Building on my work distinguishing between indifference and the performance of indifference or indifferentism (Lee 2014, forthcoming), this chapter has discussed the ways in which apparently ambivalent identities may express concrete positions. It also shows how indifferentist and other inauthentic identifications as ambivalent may gain momentum when used as mechanisms through which power is claimed or protected. In addition, the chapter draws attention to authentic experiences of ambivalence with regard to non-religious identity and demonstrates the ways in which this may be disempowering, relative to the experience of those who can draw upon more developed self-understandings and collective identities. It shows how these two modes of ambivalence and indifference—authentic and inauthentic—are bound up with one another, at once serving the interests of non-religious people and, by impoverishing non-religious cultures, undermining them as well. This is a cultural predicament that non-religious elites may be able to take for granted, but which may also constrain religious–non-religious relations and be felt more acutely by those whose positions are more vulnerable or precarious in other regards.

This analysis supports the idea that we need to engage critically with non-religious and atheist cultures, but it also shows that scholars should neither assume nor simplify the nature of the power relations at hand. In this way, all religious and non-religious identities can be viewed as ambivalent because they are seen to be fundamentally different from each another; each attains both strength and weakness from this arrangement. In some cases, non-religious identities are associated with dominant, normative positions, and the 'anti-practice' of failing to identify as non-religious may be seen as an attempt to maintain claims to superior, pure knowledge and to disempower others involved in this web of relations (see also Fitzgerald 2000). But non-religious people also struggle for representation in the public domain as a result of a wider 'illiteracy' about non-religious experience and culture. Even non-religious actors occupying elite socio-economic positions are to some extent disenfranchised because of this. As Seán McLoughlin (2005: 535) puts it: "To be sure, we all have multiple identities … However, we must also 'speak from somewhere'. 'Being heard' requires an act of prioritising, of naming oneself, of coming into representation, if only momentarily."

In some ways, establishing clear forms of self-representation is not the only means of being heard, because disclaiming representation is a method of naturalizing positions and thereby exerting power over other 'less natural' positions. Representation is nevertheless a significant method of being heard, and it can be singularly efficacious in particular contexts and scenarios. Hence, the absence of representational resources is simultaneously empowering and disempowering. Particularly when it comes to issues related to 'multi-faith society' (a term that both excludes and naturalizes 'non-faith' positions), it is likely that failing to understand practices of representation adopted by non-religious people, whether they are explicit or conspicuously and meaningfully absent, is an obstacle to faith–non-faith interaction. Regardless of whether non-religious interlocutors are in a position of relative power or relative weakness, the issue is that they are not level with religious parties that can call on cultural traditions to develop personal and shared identities. This, like all forms of inequality, is precarious, with the potential to bring about social tensions or to exacerbate them when they arise.

Ethnographers stand to make a particular contribution in response to this predicament precisely because it involves subtle cultural forms that are frequently invisible, even to those who experience and enact them. Already, Talal Asad (2003) and Fenella Cannell (2010) have called for the development of an anthropology of secularism, and Johannes Quack (2012) has made an early and pioneering contribution to the anthropology of organized non-religion. This research establishes the value of cultural approaches to the study of non-religion, including the study of everyday or lived forms. Building on these works, this chapter seeks to draws attention to a key contribution that anthropologists might make—that is, to analyze the diffuse, decentralized, and naturalized forms of non-religious culture that manifest in ambivalence. Certainly, the study of indistinct and ambivalent atheist cultures poses unique methodological challenges, requiring ethnographers to identify research sites that are not classified according to their atheism or their non-religion. But ethnographic methods are especially well-suited to navigating these challenges—to drawing out embedded and hidden socio-cultural formations. If the field of non-religious studies is something of an empty shell (Lee 2012b: 137), with so much empirical work remaining to be done, ethnographers are set to provide a crucial contribution.

Acknowledgments

I wish to thank the editors of this volume and the anonymous reviewers for their helpful suggestions and comments on earlier drafts of this chapter. This work is funded by the Economic and Social Research Council, the Blackham Fellowship, and the European Research Council (ERC) Grant No. 283867 on the topic "Is Religion Special?"

Lois Lee is a Research Associate at the Religion and Political Theory Centre, University College London, and has a PhD in Sociology from the University of Cambridge. She has authored many articles on non-religion and secularity, and her volume *Recognizing the Non-religious: Reimagining the Secular* is forthcoming with Oxford University Press. She is the founding director of the Nonreligion and Secularity Research Network (NSRN) and co-editor of the journal *Secularism and Nonreligion* and of the book series, Religion and Its Others: Studies in Religion, Nonreligion and Secularity, published by De Gruyter.

Notes

1. Reflecting the discursive context of this research, I focus on non-religious atheism and non-religious 'godlessness' in this chapter, rather than the experiences of atheism and godlessness that can occur—briefly, stably, lightly or profoundly—within religious traditions, experiences, and subjectivities. By 'non-religious' and 'non-religion', I refer to the concepts put forward by Lee (2012a, 2012c, forthcoming) and Quack (2014) in which non-religion is not merely an analytical conceptual container for anything we want to make distinct from religion, but is used in more concrete terms to describe all those phenomena—principles, practices, positionings, and so on—that are expressed or understood according to how they differ from religion. This definition expands on earlier notions of irreligion, in which the only phenomena of interest were hostility or indifference to religion (see, e.g., Campbell [1971] 2013), to include a range of distinctions from religion that may not be negative in nature (discussed further in the following pages). By first and second wave, I refer to the stirrings of social scientific interest in non-religion seen in the late 1960s to early 1970s and in contemporary research, respectively. See Bullivant and Lee (2012) for a short history of this research field. This intellectual history has informative differences and intriguing overlaps with the histories of the Soviet Union and Eastern Europe as presented in Sonja Luehrmann's contribution to this volume.
2. The socio-cultural Brights movement was founded to support a naturalistic worldview and a means to connect non-religious people. See http://www.the-brights.net/.
3. Data are from the 2008 British Social Attitudes survey (http://www.britsocat.com). This figure combines 13 percent who said that they "don't believe in God" and 15 percent who said that they "don't know if there is a God, and there's no way to find out." This is a combination of what can be called 'propositional atheism' and 'practical atheism', or 'positive atheism' and 'strong agnosticism'.

4. See http://www.britsocat.com. This compares to the 22 percent who communicated ambivalence between the two categories offered ("neither religious nor non-religious"). Interestingly, people self-classifying as "religious" were more likely than the "non-religious" to describe themselves as "somewhat" religious rather than "very or extremely" religious (30 and 7 percent, respectively). See also Lee (2014).

5. Stephen Bullivant (2010) has provided a useful sociological overview of this UK-US publishing and broadcast phenomenon. See also Taira and Illman (2012) and Tremlett and Shih (this volume).

6. Bender (2012) does not engage with recent work concerning non-religion directly and is unclear as to whether talking about religion is something internal or external to the religious field. She writes that the religious field "*includes* both religious practices and institutions (churches, religious groups, movements, and so on) and nonreligious ones (those that organize, regulate or impinge *upon* it)' (ibid.: 280–281; emphasis added). By being 'included' but also acting 'upon' it, talking about religion is simultaneously located inside and outside of the religious field. In this, Bender expresses some of the confusion that the ongoing theorization of non-religion hopes to resolve, but her discussion also makes space for considering how atheist subjectivities may be formed in conversations around other things than atheism itself.

7. For a longer discussion of this research methodology, see Lee (2012a: 10–14, 59–86).

8. Pseudonyms are used to preserve research participants' anonymity.

9. See also Tremlett and Shih's exploration of doubt in this volume.

10. See Hirschkind (2012: 636–638) for a helpful discussion of rationalism.

11. See Lee (2012a, 2014) for more examples and details concerning this phenomenon. Bullivant (2012) and Lee (2013) also discuss this finding. In addition, Christopher Cotter's (2011) qualitative study of non-religious orientations also finds that people disclaiming any significant non-religious identity have non-religious opinions readily at hand when these commitments are tested.

12. See Knott (2005) for an overview of Bourdieu's work on fields in reference to the religious and the non-religious.

13. I am grateful to Paul-François Tremlett for his suggestion that bicycle riding may be interesting as a spatial practice associated with and to some extent embodying elite positions in contemporary European urban centers.

References

Asad, Talal. 1993. *Genealogies of Religion: Discipline and Reasons of Power in Christianity and Islam*. Baltimore: Johns Hopkins University Press.

Asad, Talal. 2003. *Formations of the Secular: Christianity, Islam, Modernity*. Stanford, CA: Stanford University Press.

Bagg, Samuel, and David Voas. 2010. "The Triumph of Indifference: Irreligion in British Society." Pp. 91–111 in *Atheism and Secularity*, vol. 2: *Global Expressions*, ed. Phil Zuckerman. Santa Barbara, CA: Praeger.

Baumann, Gerd. 1996. *Contesting Culture: Discourses of Identity in Multi-ethnic London*. Cambridge: Cambridge University Press.

Bender, Courtney. 2012. "Practicing Religions." Pp. 273–295 in *The Cambridge Companion to Religious Studies*, ed. Robert A. Orsi. Cambridge: Cambridge University Press.

BHA (British Humanist Association). 2011. "The Census Campaign." http://census-campaign.org.uk/ (accessed 18 December 2011).

Bruce, Steve. 2002. *God Is Dead: Secularization in the West.* Oxford: Blackwell.

Bullivant, Stephen. 2010. "The New Atheism and Sociology: Why Here? Why Now? What Next?" Pp. 109–124 in *Religion and the New Atheism: A Critical Appraisal,* ed. Amarnath Amarasingam. Leiden: Brill.

Bullivant, Stephen. 2012. "Not So Indifferent After All? Self-conscious Atheism and the Secularisation Thesis." *Approaching Religion* 2, no. 1: 100–106.

Bullivant, Stephen. 2013. "Defining 'Atheism.'" Pp. 11–21 in Bullivant and Ruse 2013.

Bullivant, Stephen, and Lois Lee. 2012. "Interdisciplinary Studies of Non-religion and Secularity: The State of the Union." *Journal of Contemporary Religion* 27, no. 1: 19–27.

Bullivant, Stephen, and Michael Ruse, eds. 2013. *The Oxford Handbook of Atheism.* Oxford: Oxford University Press.

Campbell, Colin. [1971] 2013. *Toward a Sociology of Irreligion.* Rev. ed. London: Alcuin Academics.

Cannell, Fenella. 2010. "The Anthropology of Secularism." *Annual Review of Anthropology* 39: 85–100.

Cotter, Christopher R. 2011. "Toward a Typology of 'Nonreligion': A Qualitative Analysis of Everyday Narratives of Scottish University Students." MSc thesis, University of Edinburgh.

Cragun, Ryan T., and Joseph H. Hammer. 2011. "'One Person's Apostate Is Another Person's Convert': What Terminology Tells Us about Pro-religious Hegemony in the Sociology of Religion." *Humanity & Society* 35, no. 1–2: 149–175.

Cragun, Ryan, Barry Kosmin, Ariela Keysar, Joseph H. Hammer, and Michael Nielsen. 2012. "On the Receiving End: Discrimination toward the Non-Religious in the United States." *Journal of Contemporary Religion* 27, no. 1: 105–127.

Edgell, Penny, Joseph Gerteis, and Douglas Hartmann. 2006. "Atheists as 'Other': Moral Boundaries and Cultural Membership in American Society." *American Sociological Review* 71, no. 2: 211–234.

Engelke, Matthew. 2015. "Humanist Ceremonies: The Case of Non-Religious Funerals in England." Pp. 216–233 in *The Wiley Blackwell Handbook of Humanism,* ed. Andrew Copson and A. C. Grayling. Oxford: Wiley Blackwell.

Fitzgerald, Timothy. 2000. *The Ideology of Religious Studies.* Oxford: Oxford University Press.

Hirschkind, Charles. 2011. "Is There a Secular Body?" *Cultural Anthropology* 26, no. 4: 633–647.

Knott, Kim. 2005. *The Location of Religion: A Spatial Analysis.* London: Equinox.

Knott, Kim, Elizabeth Poole, and Teemu Taira. 2013. *Media Portrayals of Religion and the Secular Sacred: Representation and Change.* Farnham: Ashgate

Lee, Lois. 2011. "From 'Neutrality' to Dialogue: Constructing the Religious Other in British Non-religious Discourses." In *Modernities Revisited,* ed. Maren Behrensen, Lois Lee, and Ahmet S. Tekelioglu. IWM Junior Visiting Fellows' Conferences, vol. 29. http://www.iwm.at/publications/5-junior-visiting-fellows-conferences/lois-lee-2/ (accessed 23 June 2011).

Lee, Lois. 2012a. "Being Secular: Towards Separate Sociologies of Secularity, Nonreligion and Epistemological Culture." PhD diss., University of Cambridge.

Lee, Lois. 2012b. "Locating Nonreligion, in Mind, Body and Space: New Research Methods for a New Field." Pp. 135–158 in *Annual Review of the Sociology of Religion,* vol. 3: *New Methods in the Sociology of Religion,* ed. Luigi Berzano and Ole P. Riis. Leiden: Brill.

Lee, Lois. 2012c. "Research Note: Talking About a Revolution: Terminology for the New Field of Non-religion Studies." *Journal of Contemporary Religion* 27, no. 1: 129–139.

Lee, Lois. 2013. "Western Europe." Pp. 587–600 in Bullivant and Ruse 2013.

Lee, Lois. 2014. "Secular or Nonreligious? Investigating and Interpreting Generic 'Not Religious' Categories and Populations." *Religion* 44, no. 3: 466–482.

Lee, Lois. Forthcoming. *Recognizing the Nonreligious: Reimagining the Secular*. Oxford: Oxford University Press.

McLoughlin, Seán. 2005. "Religion and Diaspora." Pp. 526–579 in *The Routledge Companion to the Study of Religion*, ed. John R. Hinnells. London: Routledge.

Meek, James. 2011. "In Broadway Market." *London Review of Books*. 9 August. http://www.lrb.co.uk/blog/2011/08/09/james-meek/in-broadway-market/ (accessed 9 August 2011).

Pasquale, Frank L. 2007. "Empirical Study and Neglect of Unbelief and Irreligion." Pp. 760–766 in *The New Encyclopedia of Unbelief*, ed. Tom Flynn. Amherst, NY: Prometheus Books.

Quack, Johannes. 2012. *Disenchanting India: Organized Rationalism and Criticism of Religion in India*. New York: Oxford University Press.

Quack, Johannes. 2014. "Outline of a Relational Approach to 'Nonreligion.'" *Method & Theory in the Study of Religion* 26, no. 4–5: 439–469.

Sherine, Ariane. 2008. "All Aboard the Atheist Bus Campaign." *Guardian*, 21 October. http://www.guardian.co.uk/commentisfree/2008/oct/21/religion-advertising (accessed 21 February 2011).

Smith, Jesse M. 2010. "Becoming an Atheist in America: Constructing Identity and Meaning from the Rejection of Theism." *Sociology of Religion* 72, no. 2: 215–237.

Smith, Jesse M. 2013. "Creating a Godless Community: The Collective Identity Work of Contemporary American Atheists." *Journal for the Scientific Study of Religion* 51, no. 1: 80–99.

Taira, Teemu, and Ruth Illman. 2012. "The New Visibility of Atheism in Europe." *Approaching Religion* 2, no. 1: 1–2.

Turner, Bryan S. 2010. "Religion in a Post-secular Society." Pp. 649–667 in *The New Blackwell Companion to the Sociology of Religion*, ed. Bryan S. Turner. Chichester: Wiley-Blackwell.

Voas, David. 2009. "Who Are the Non-religious in Britain and Where Do They Come From?" Paper presented at the first conference of the Nonreligion and Secularity Research Network, Oxford, 11 December.

Voas, David, and Rodney Ling. 2010. "Religion in Britain and the United States." Pp. 65–87 in *British Social Attitudes: The 26th Report*, ed. Alison Park, John Curtice, Katarina Thomson, Miranda Phillips, Elizabeth Clery, and Sarah Butt. London: Sage/National Centre for Social Research.

Voas, David, and Siobhan McAndrew. 2012. "Three Puzzles of Non-religion in Britain." *Journal of Contemporary Religion* 27, no. 1: 29–48.

Chapter 2

GODLESS PEOPLE AND DEAD BODIES
Materiality and the Morality of Atheist Materialism

Jacob Copeman and Johannes Quack

In this chapter we seek to elucidate the practical, moral, and ideological dimensions of body donation[1] by professed atheists as an instance of their material culture par excellence. Professed atheists are by no means the only people who donate their bodies, yet the practice is strikingly prominent—widely promoted and enacted—in a variety of atheist circles across time and geographical region. With a particular focus on atheist activists in the Indian sub-continent, we consider how and why body donation has developed into such an act of concentrated significance for many, suggesting that this is due to its simultaneous fulfillment of a number of different purposes held to be important by such activists. Since the matter—the material composition—of what might be termed the quintessential 'atheist gift' is so central, our analysis of it cannot but be at the same time an analysis of the material culture of atheism. Our focus, in other words, is on the materiality of atheist materialism.

'Materialism' is treated here as a 'folk' term partly characterized by what it rejects, that is, belief in 'immaterial' entities such as God, soul, spirits, any kind

Notes for this chapter begin on page 57.

of miraculous materialization, and so forth. At its core lies a view similar to the conviction that Weber (1964: 317) described as central to processes of 'disenchantment', namely, that the world is—in principle—explainable and therefore controllable, and that there are no incalculable, mysterious, supernatural forces. But importantly, we do not treat materialism only as a mode of belief. We concentrate here on the vitality of materialism's material culture, arguing that material enactment and demonstration—professed materialists' engagements with materials—are as constitutive of materialism as 'belief' in it. Recent moves to reinvigorate study of the material culture of religion (e.g., Keane 2008; Morgan 2009) are to be welcomed, but must be extended to non-religion (Quack 2014) as a means of addressing the long-standing irony that sees scholars represent materialism as an abstract doctrine and, hence, as immaterial. Of course, a myriad of atheist intellectual engagements with materialism do exist—in India, our main focus in this chapter, and elsewhere—but the majority of atheists are not materialist philosophers. Indeed, a large number of atheists might not know what 'materialism' is (in doctrinal terms) and enact it only implicitly.[2]

Our principal examples derive from our fieldwork experiences among Indian rationalist, humanist, and atheist activists,[3] but we also draw on historical accounts of skeptical communities in nineteenth- and twentieth-century France and Britain. For clarity, we use the term 'atheist activists' to describe our fieldwork interlocutors, but the reticence with which activists use the term 'atheism', or *nastika*, in public must be noted.[4] While such terms are used privately, their public usage is sometimes discouraged since they have the potential to prevent activists from getting a sympathetic or fair public hearing. As one leader told us: "Yes, we are atheists and rationalists, but if we say we are atheists, we get into all kinds of trouble. So we don't say it always." As with rationalist organizations globally, there is an unequal representation of the sexes in the Indian movement. Roughly, active women constitute less than a quarter of the group's membership. The caste make-up of activists is quite diverse, but the movement's leaders tend to hail from upper-caste and -class backgrounds.[5]

The differentiated nature of non-religion is often overlooked in the contemporary "god debate" (Engelke 2012), as are its lived, practical dimensions (Quack 2012a: 221–244)—a state of affairs particularly ironic as far as the Indian situation is concerned, given atheists' concerted focus there on practical action (see Quack 2012c). Ethnography is an apt tool to counter such occlusions, allowing us instead to draw out "the experiential and embodied side of being non-religious" (Engelke 2012) and to pay heed to non-religious material culture. One might object that the generalizing nature of our chapter's title runs the risk of undermining our aim to highlight the differentiated nature of non-religion. However, this is precisely our point. We complement our principal Indian case study with examples from elsewhere in order to show that certain aspects of this 'atheist gift' are indeed held in common across divergent contexts of non-religion. Although in different times and places an atheist's body may be donated for autopsy, anatomy, or transplantation, its recipients are usually likely to include, in some form, 'knowledge' and 'progress' and, connected to this, those who are left behind ('the living'). We also consider how atheist body donation is in some ways a 'self-gift' to the atheist community, insofar as it enables the community to bypass the priests and rituals it finds so redundant while allowing it to display the 'moral' nature of its materialism. Yet the Indian case also speaks to a very specific present-day situation and possesses its own unique set of practical and ideological complexities—complexities that this chapter seeks to unpack.

The Matter of Disbelief

The Indian atheist activists with whom we have spent time—as opposed to those often characterized dismissively by activists as metropolitan-based 'talking shop' humanists or 'armchair atheists'—do not simply 'believe' in materialism. They seek to debunk or 'expose' what they consider to be pernicious supernatural beliefs via skilled deployments of materials.[6] In other words, the religious beliefs and practices they regard as both wrong and harmful are challenged by them, not only on the intellectual level, but also through hands-on activism, performances, and campaigns. For instance, the retooling of sacred objects for non-religious purposes forms a key part of the methodology at education programs conducted by atheist activists. They re-employ temple objects such as lamps, coconuts, and candles in order to reveal the irrational and fraudulent functions that these items are seen to serve in the sacred contexts from which they derive. "[Priests and gurus] use these things to cheat you, but we will use them to educate you," said one activist. An Indian rationalist leader, who undertakes nationwide 'miracle exposure' programs, carries with him a 'miracle bag' containing an array of chemicals, powders, and apparatuses in order to demonstrate the 'science behind miracles'. He begins his performances, usually in front of schoolchildren, teachers, or both,[7] by materializing 'from thin air' sacred ash (*vibhuti*), which he then distributes among amazed onlookers while stating, for instance, "Promotion milega" (You'll get a promotion). *Vibhuti* is commonly materialized by Indian *chamatkari baba*s (miracle men). Recently deceased guru Sathya Sai Baba famously designated the materialization of *vibhuti* as his 'calling card', while a CNN journalist described it as the guru's "signature illusion" (Marshall 2004). Given the guru's popularity and the extraordinary fetishization of this substance among his devotees (Srinivas 2010), *vibhuti* has taken on the stature, for activists, as the number-one superstitious substance and therefore figures prominently in their programs.

Having distributed the substance and successfully seized everyone's attention, the activist states: "But it is not a miracle. It is a trick." He then explains that the substance is in fact decompressed dried powder, which, via a sleight of hand, he has produced from between his fingers, making it clear that nothing can be materialized out of the blue. If a devotee is in the audience, he may have, in a reflex action, ingested the substance and so shouted something like "But it tastes and smells the same as Sai's!" To much laughter, the activist will then declare: "Of course! I bought it from the same shop at Sathya Sai Baba. It is actually cow dung roasted with sandalwood." To reinforce the point, and if the technology is available at the location, he might at this stage show slow-motion video footage of the guru performing exactly the sleight of hand he has just performed himself. The effect can be powerful.[8] Another standard declaration, made by the activist at this stage in the program, is delivered in an incredulous tone: "Engineers at IITs[9] believe in Sathya Sai Baba's materialization of *vibhuti*. We have [in India] twenty-first-century technology but a medieval mentality. This is very dangerous." This is the cue for a lesson in basic materialism: the law of nature that matter can be neither created nor destroyed, to which, distressingly, even the nation's leaders in science and technology do not fully subscribe.

Moreover, skepticism and exposé are embodied in a variety of ways. Activists ask audience members to check their pulse—it is not detectable, just like those yogis who claim they can stop their heartbeats. But the trick is simple and subsequently demonstrated. A small rubber ball, about the size of an eye, is pressed under the activist's armpit, causing his pulse to become undetectable. Rationalists challenge many other such instances of claims by 'god men'[10] to be able to control matter solely via mind power, for instance, offering large sums of money to anyone who is able to perform a miracle such as living without food and water for weeks under 'scientific conditions'. Yet the activists themselves also perform physically demanding 'miracles' and thereby use their own bodies in the service of supernatural exposé, in a not dissimilar manner to the ascetics whom they are challenging. Some activists have needles placed through their cheeks and hooks through muscles in their backs in order to demonstrate that it is quite possible to endure such bodily violations without the aid of any kind of supernatural power. Others bury their heads in holes in the earth, risking suffocation, or walk over burning coals. For atheists, the body is thus a key material and technique in what we might term the 'culture of proving'.[11] Indeed, if there is an 'atheist body', perhaps it is that which is placed in the service of exposé and the establishment of proof.[12]

Much more could be said about the technologies of exposé employed by Indian atheist activists. Our purpose in providing a sense of them here is simply to show that the 'matter of belief' is fought (or exposed) via the 'matter of disbelief'. This recognition is a necessary starting point for providing insights into the material culture of materialism. Yet the irony remains that materialism is more often than not dematerialized in its typical characterization, scholarly and otherwise, as an abstract tenet of atheist dogma. Among those with whom we worked, materialism is not just a belief.[13] It is something that is worked out— made manifest, reconfirmed, even constituted—via specific material practices. Morgan (2009: 12) argues that "materiality *mediates* belief, that material objects and practices both enable it and enact it." We would not object to this assessment but simply expand the point to include disbelief and unbelief, which are, after all, negatively defined forms of belief (in the non-supernatural, the definitiveness of the laws of nature, and so on). It is not a coincidence that the atheist activist's materialism is formulated and demonstrated via an array of materials and material practices. For instance, the activist's 'miracles bag' contains materials whose purpose, via techniques of performative demonstration, is, so to speak, to reclaim materials for materialism—not only compressed roasted cow dung and sandalwood powder, but also potassium permanganate and glycerin (for the 'spontaneous' lighting of fires), camphor (for burning on the hands and in the mouth with no pain, since heat rises), tablets of aspartame (for transferring 'divine sweetness' to audience members' hands), to name but a few of the chemicals and substances contained therein.

The material culture of atheism is not a wholly novel object of scholarly analysis. Lee (2012: 145–149) provides a valuable discussion of non-religious rituals of burying and memorializing, an area in which Engelke (2014) is also conducting important work. One also thinks of the 'atheist objects' that populated 'anti-religion museums' in the former Soviet Union (Paine 2009). In such museums, icons and relics were subjected to a "deliberate policy of sacrilege" and employed to "expose the tricks and the crimes of the clergy" (ibid.: 65). Further objects of exposé, strikingly similar to those used by atheists in India, can be found in books such as *The Discoverie of Witchcraft* ([1584] 1973), which was written in the sixteenth century by the English 'country gentleman' Reginald Scot to counter belief in witches. However, the situation is not entirely satisfactory, in part due to problems generated by recent publicly circulated "hyper-intellectualised version[s] of what it means to do without Him" (Engelke 2012). It remains necessary, therefore, to underscore the point that the recent foregrounding of the matter of belief as an indispensable object of study (Engelke 2005; Keane 2008; Morgan 2009) needs to be extended to the study of disbelieving and skeptical communities for exactly the same reasons that it was necessary in the former case. It should be seen as a corrective to prior analyses that reduced religious (or non-religious) lives to a 'state of mind' and discounted those 'material manifestations' that were necessary for the establishment of these systems' social existence, making them "available to, interpretable by, and, in most cases, replicable by other people: bodily actions, speech, the treatment of objects, and so forth" (Keane 2008: S114).

We suggest that the atheist's dead body may be considered an exemplary instance of the matter of disbelief and a key atheist material artifact. If *vibhuti* is thought of by activists as a 'useless' materialization and religious offerings as a waste of resources, the dead body that is not offered or donated, from a rationalist point of view, is similarly a waste of resources. Yet the cadaver that remains undonated embodies a double tragedy, since the cadaver could so easily, if it were donated, epitomize a righteous utility. Unlike the materializations of ash that rationalists criticize so acerbically, which moreover mystify and exploit those who witness them, the matter of disbelief is pressed into the service of progress and demystification. And, of course, in the province of death and dying, the 'usefully' donated body serves, by contrast, to reveal the undonated cadaver as a site of illusion and destruction.

We now turn to a further exploration of these matters, drawing on interviews and writings that disclose what Indian rationalists consider an ideal-typical approach toward issues of dying and death. While these statements do not represent the common practices of all members of the rationalist movement, they illustrate the 'official' perspective and some practical dilemmas as outlined by both leaders and lay members in the larger movement.

Creative Refusal

It hardly needs to be said that life-cycle rituals figure prominently in everyday life in India. The official Indian rationalist worldview rejects all religious beliefs and practices connected with such rituals, including those associated with death. For instance, observances that concern the soul, rebirth, or any other conceptions of afterlife or non-material life substances, including Hindu rituals such as *antyesti* (last sacrifice) or *śraddha* (ancestral rites), are all repudiated. The rites that follow the death of a person help to deal with one of the most polluting and inauspicious occurrences in classical Hinduism. Family members of the deceased are separated from normal social life until they are reintegrated through the performance of the appropriate rituals. Families are usually concerned about the heightened danger of being attacked by malevolent spirits until *śraddha* are performed. These rites also allow the spirit of the deceased to travel on its way (see Flood 1996: 207). Only after the soul of the deceased has reached the realm of the *pitr-loka* (ancestors) can the family be certain that the deceased will not return as a ghost to haunt the living. For atheist activists, such conceptions underscore the status of the domain of death and dying as one of concentrated superstition. By tackling superstitions in this domain, the understanding is that they are challenging these beliefs where they are most strongly rooted in society.

The booklet *Mrutyu Tane Manavta* (Humanity at the Time of Death) (Desai 1996), published by Satyasodhak Sabha, the Gujarat Rationalist Association, features standard rationalist criticism of death rituals, excoriating their illogicality, their furtherance of Brahminism, and the financial burden that they place upon families. Both irrational and harmful, these rituals are to be rejected on epistemological as well as moral grounds: "Satyasodhak Sabha has strongly stated that the soul or spirit does not go anywhere after death—no event takes place after death. After the death, relatives gather for a meal on the 12th–13th day [and] on the first death anniversary … [T]hey feed Brahmins on every death anniversary, and conduct *shraddha* rites (a ceremony performed in honor of a dead ancestor). But all these rituals and beliefs are unscientific, unnecessary and create a financial burden. This should be stopped immediately and boldly" (ibid.).

Such aversion to lining the pockets of ritual specialists via death rituals is by no means a uniquely Indian phenomenon. André Lefèvre, a French freethinker, willed all his useful body parts to the School of Anthropology of Paris, adding the stipulation that all matters of death should be taken care of "without the interference of any priest or any church" (Hecht 1997: 714). Eugène Véron expressed a more specifically anti-clerical attitude. "I do not want," he explained, "after my death, to contribute, even a little, to the accumulation of the wealth of the clergy, against which I have combated all my life and which never ceases to do to France and to the Republic all the evil in its power" (ibid.: 715–716).

Rationalist societies not only denounce and reject religious rituals but also promote alternatives—that is to say, they engage in 'creative refusal' (Graeber 2013). This is an important point. Activists who debunk miracles and expose fraudulent gurus are generally believed, within the movement, to be performing an important service. But at the same time, there is some discomfort with the 'negative' agenda that these campaigns seem to embody. Such activities instantiate what eminent twentieth-century Indian atheist activist and leader Goparaju Rao, known simply as Gora, termed 'negative atheism', which he defined in opposition to his own concept of 'positive atheism' (Rao 1978).[14] His son, Dr. Vijayam, who heads the Atheist Centre in Andhra Pradesh,[15] explained to us that "negative atheism is where you are always finding fault with others. It is a historical necessity. But though a doctor will give you an electrical shock, that's not the therapy. Exposing superstitions is not the end in itself. It is an entry point. We must expose superstitions, but we must also emphasize an alternative way of life." Dr. Vijayam thus follows his father in underscoring the need for a 'positive atheism' that moves beyond criticism of religion by proposing 'human-centered' alternatives to the practices it would replace.

Echoing this, the aforementioned Gujarat Rationalist Association booklet, under the heading "Adopt Best Last Ritual," proposes the following alternatives: "Deceased person's unfinished work or ideas can be taken forward. Give donations to the organizations working for the welfare of the poor and needy. Tree plantings can be carried out in the memory of the dead. Support various voluntary organizations in their work." One Maharashtrian rationalist told us that one of the most important tasks of the atheist activist is to engage in "rational substitution" with regard to the practices they combat. To employ his term, then, we suggest that the atheist's gift of his/her dead body is a rational substitution of particular ideological and practical significance. This is so because it appears to productively bridge positive and negative atheism. Body donation is no doubt a 'negative' rejection of prior forms, with the cadaver, like roasted cow dung and sandalwood powder in the hands of the atheist activist, retooled as an object of exposé or matter of disbelief that casts the undonated cadaver, in contrast, as an embodiment of destruction and hopeless mystification. Yet it also asserts a positive atheism that contributes a 'human-centered' alternative to the practice it would replace. In fact, the contrast could not be more plain, for in a reversal of the idea that the non-pacified dead may cause difficulties for the living, Dr. Vijayam states that atheists, "in recognition of the fact that there's no life after death, pledge for organ, eye, and body donation" and devise ceremonies that "try to improve the quality of life here on earth."[16] That is to say, the dead may, via body donation, not disrupt but instead assist the living.[17]

As was mentioned above, the Satyasodhak Sabha rejects the feeding of Brahmins associated with mourning ceremonies. The present-day pan-Indian rationalist movement had its origins in late-nineteenth-century- and early-twentieth-century reformist opposition to caste inequities and Brahminical hegemony, and contemporary Indian rationalism is similarly invested in undoing the ritual authority traditionally embodied in the Brahmin priest. Indeed, caste is defined as profoundly superstitious—as *the* paramount superstition—by many atheist activists.[18] Not only is the mortuary gift of food or money to a Brahmin non-productive in Indian rationalist terms, it perpetuates one of the country's biggest evils—the dominance of the 'priestly class'. In rationalist hands, the mortuary gift persists, but only insofar as it is turned on its head.

Thus, when the body of Jyoti Basu, the former Marxist chief minister of West Bengal, was donated upon his death in January 2010, anti-caste rationalist campaigners lavished praise upon him. As one obituary put it:

> Claiming to die for the masses, we have seen our political class like to be cremated among weeping people and amidst the chant of Vaidik Mantras by aristocratic Brahmins ... The cremation of a political leader is again an opportunity for greedy priestly class to pontificate us on greatness of religious virtues for the purpose of spreading their virus ... The racist brahmanical philosophy has preached us that donating your eyes and body is dangerous.[19] Jyoti Basu ... has saved us from priestly pontification ... In the villages, people offer their income to Brahmins in hope the dead person would get it. If we have to make the brahmanical priestly class redundant, we must follow what Jyoti Babu did, by donating our bodies and shunning the rituals, we are so fond of, in the name of our culture. One hope, our political class will learn a lesson from this that life is meant to serve the people and it end[s] here, there is no point in getting yourself purified by the priestly class which has cheated the people for centuries in the name [of] death and birth.[20]

By eliminating the mediation of the grasping Brahmin priest, the mortuary gift, as reconstituted by rationalist activists, perpetrates an attack on the caste system itself. It should be noted that this is hardly the first attempt to bypass the mediations of Brahmin priests—reformist anti-Brahmin movements have endeavored to do so for centuries (see Copeman and Reddy 2012). What is new here is the method.

Moral Materialism, Positive Atheism

As was noted above, body donation serves a number of different purposes for Indian atheists. Let us now consider body donation in terms of the practical and ideological value it holds for Indian atheist activists. Daniel Miller (2008) maintains that value is to be found via processes of commensuration. In contrast to what he calls 'bottom-line' (or foundational) understandings that seek to locate the origin of value in definite sources—most famously, of course, in labor (Marx 1990)—for Miller (2008: 1129), value is to be found where competing factors are brought to a complex resolution. As we have suggested, the atheist's dead body embodies a similar bridging function. Part of its value for Indian atheists lies in the way it represents a combination of 'negative' rejection of unscientific and destructive death rituals and 'positive' atheist agenda setting. In a dazzling reversal that retains the form of a mortuary offering, the gift is now one that assists the living and contributes to science. In this way, the atheist's dead body bridges a tension within Indian atheist activism. It is a practice to which both those whose principal goal is to expose superstition and those whose main goal is to outline constructive alternatives are happy to subscribe.

Vital here is what we have been calling the materiality of atheist materialism. As is often remarked, atheists are wont to express their identity 'negatively' in opposition to religious beliefs and practices. As was seen above with reference to *vibhuti*, staunch atheists may well make fun of religious practices and the matter of belief; indeed, much of their material culture is structured in such a way. One thinks, for instance, of the atheist parody of the ichthys symbol, which features a fish with emerging feet enclosing the name 'Darwin', and of T-shirts such as the one featuring the word 'fiction' spelled out using religious symbols. The material culture of comedic debunking is a particular feature of Indian miracle exposé campaigns. The South Indian guru Mata Amritanandamayi, who famously hugs her devotees in what are usually tearful encounters, makes grown men faint, not because of her *shakti* (divine energy), according to the atheists, but because she presses them to her 'big jugs'. An Indian rationalist film depicts a swami in a rocket going around the earth to show what would happen if swamis could *really* levitate (their weight would need to be less than the weight of the gravitational force of the earth). In imitation of one famous guru's 'signature illusion', a schoolgirl, having rubbed together in her hands a tablet of aspartame, causes the skin of those she touches to become 'miraculously' sweet. Amid much laughter, her fellow schoolchildren are made to touch her feet and chant "Oh Mata Ji Apki shakti!" (Oh Divine Mother, your power!). Thus, a substance of mystification is retooled as matter of disbelief. Integrated into the canon of 'atheist substances' through the comedic practices of atheist materiality, another material is reclaimed for materialism.

However, the material culture of mockery exacerbates the tension, to which we earlier referred, that exists between negative and positive projections of disbelief, providing a striking instance of the former. The atheist's dead body and organ donation, on the other hand, provide a compellingly different material culture element—one that is positive and lacks the ridicule evinced in the examples just given. In each case, materials are reclaimed for materialism, but the atheist promotion of body donation suggests an austere atheist materiality that goes beyond the comedic. In several respects, then, this is a material culture to be taken seriously.

Body donation also plays a positive role with respect to what might be called atheist impression management, that is, atheists' body donations act to counter the claim to moral superiority made by those who are god fearing. Indeed, the accusation that atheists are lacking in compassion and moral sense is prevalent in India, as it is elsewhere. For instance, one Hindu right organization, Hindu Jagruti, cites the Upanishads[21] in support of its assertion that "a righteous code of conduct" is dependent on fearing God, while also claiming that "Ego" is "Low" among "Seekers" and "High" among "Rationalists."[22] A particularly shrill instance from elsewhere is found in Pasquini's (2009: 61) *Atheist Personality Disorder*: "What little atheists do for the needy is virtually always done for self-aggrandizement [and] self-promotion ... Put my name on it, and I'll donate! ... Atheists give less to charity than any group in the world." Sensitivity to this kind of criticism is acute among Indian atheist activists, and the publication of Greg Epstein's (2009) *Good without God*, which as its title suggests confronts such accusations head on, was greeted enthusiastically and with much discussion at pan-Indian rationalist conferences—much more so than, for instance, Dawkins's (2006) *The God Delusion*.

The very first sentence of the aforementioned Gujarat rationalist text (Desai 1996) emphasizes the moral dimension of rationalists' position toward death and dying: "We want to inform the Gujarat community that a rationalist attitude will not only make life meaningful and enjoyable but also helpful to others even after death." For one prominent South Indian rationalist, "the most human way" to deal with the death of his mother was to arrange for the transplantation of her organs. "I went from hospital to hospital with the liver of my mother," he told us. "That was my passion and what I had to do. I see this as a tribute to the principle of life." For this atheist activist, as for many others, "the donation of one's body is a moral thing to do. In fact, I consider it to be the most moral thing you can do."

Such donations reverse the typical argument concerning atheist egoism: they show that atheists can be moral (by donating their bodies to other humans), while religion is egoistic (not only does cremating or burying the body foreclose the possibility of its humane donation, mortuary gifts to the deceased are self-serving insofar as a primary aim is to avoid the unwanted attentions of the non-pacified departed). Moreover, it is atheist materiality that performs this reversal. The atheist's donated body provides a kind of 'material report' (Ssorin-Chaikov and Sosnina 2004) or objectification (Miller 2010) of the atheist's godless morality. In this way, 'moral materialism' is both achieved and made evident.[23]

Avoidance of Ritual and Setting an Example

We have thus far sought to show how body donation contributes to the fulfillment of a number of prevalent atheist objectives: not only has it developed into a key feature of atheist impression management, it successfully bridges different poles of the movement, while circumventing the pecuniary grip of the Indian atheist's traditional foe, the Brahmin priest. We consider now in greater detail the issue of circumvention, for at a very basic level, body donation is compellingly attractive to atheists because it bypasses the conventional mortuary rituals they find so objectionable. In our interviews with activists, although they tended to be spoken of in the same breath, evading the ritual impulse was frequently posited ahead of medical science as a reason to donate. For Pune-based Suman Oak: "There are two good reasons to donate: first, it is useful for medics, and, second, you can avoid useless ceremonies." N. Pancholi, a Ghaziabad-based lawyer and the secretary of the India Renaissance Institute,[24] told us: "We donate to avoid ritual, but also to promote medical research."

But, of course, things do not always proceed smoothly, for, as Jennifer Hecht (2003: 21) puts it, even the "best-laid plans are … difficult to carry out after one's own demise"—as in the famous case of Indira Gandhi ignoring the unambiguous request in the will of her father and India's first prime minister, Nehru, that that no religious ceremonies be performed after his death (Zachariah 2004: 257). As Suman Oak explained to us, "While alive, [rationalists] make an affidavit to donate, but their family members sometimes do not respect this. The family thinks *atma* [soul] will linger if ceremonies are not completed. Only after cremation will it be free, or take rebirth. If the funeral does not happen, then the *atma* will become a ghost, roaming about. And ghosts punish the people who don't do ceremonies for them." It is rare that all of one's close family members will be fellow atheists, and acute tensions can and do arise. Having pledged his/her body, the matter of the future facilitation of one's gift may well cause the would-be donor some anxiety. The concern is that donors will be dragged into rituals at some point when they have no control over their lives. This is reflected in advice offered to the would-be body donor in the aforementioned *Mrutyu Tane Manavta* (Desai 1996): "If possible, prepare the person mentally to whom the authority is given [to enact the post-mortem donation], and whatever their personal beliefs are, make sure that they will act according to the authority given to them. (Satyasodhak Sabha has had a number of experiences where the dead person has informed their close relatives, or stated in writing, their intention to donate their eyes or body, but where the relatives, after the person's death, because of their emotions, do not act accordingly.) Identify the right person to avoid this."

The problem of familial disobedience is by no means unique to the Indian case. For example, in late-nineteenth-century France, members of the atheist Society of Mutual Autopsy faced similar difficulties. Members willed their brains to one another for dissection, which they believed would conclusively disprove the existence of the soul while providing valuable phrenological insights. Hecht (2003: 21) provides examples in which the problem of relatives' reluctance to enact such donations was met head on: should family members contest this aspect of the donor's will, they were to be disinherited.

Indian atheist leader Narendra Nayak also took a staunch approach to his family members' desire to perform death rituals for his mother. He narrated his experience to us:

> My mother died in 1995 from cancer. It was not unexpected. By the time, she died she also had become an atheist. Her and my beliefs grew together. She told me, "Well, I know you are not going to perform any ceremonies to send my soul to heaven, but don't donate my body to the medical college, please just cremate me." I went ahead and cremated. My family tried to force me to do all the rituals for sending [her] soul to heaven, but I resisted. In our ancestral home, near Mangalore, my relatives said there were lots of problems. This was three years after my mother's death. So they summoned some astrologers to do a big expensive ceremony, during which they said because the ghost of my mother has not been sent to heaven, her soul is coming here and causing problems. They asked me to do the ceremonies so she would go to heaven, and I said no. Instead, they did the next best thing ... they did some ceremonies to make her spirit go to other houses, not our ancestral house. So my mother is still roaming around, although she can't go to our ancestral home because of the protective rituals. So that's the sorry fate of the mother of a rationalist!

Although they concern a refusal to perform rituals rather than body donation, the events recounted by Nayak, are nevertheless emblematic of the family tensions that an atheist's unbending attitude toward death and dying frequently generates. Not all atheist activists are as uncompromising as Nayak (see Quack 2012a: 240). However, in resisting his family's admonitions on multiple occasions, Nayak presents an exemplary narrative of the unwavering rationalist. Indeed, the events related above are also described in Nayak's (2007) book *Battle Against Supernatural* and in numerous skeptic newsletters for the edification of readers. We now consider the matter of setting an example in greater detail.

As was noted above, Indian atheists view death and dying as a particularly high-density locus of superstition. Persuading people to pledge their bodies is to persuade them to accede to much more besides: the act comes to stand for a kind of richly symbolic renunciation of superstition. In this way, body donation (and to some extent donations involving blood and organs) has come to be defined as an iconic rationalist practice that has been pressed into service as an instrument of pedagogy. Body donation is thus afforded a status, similar to that of the dissection of cadavers in the early colonial era,[25] as metonymic of a much wider liberation from superstition. The exemplary atheist death is mobilized as an instrument of what Hecht (2003) has called 'evangelical atheism'. If miracles are good public relations for an aspiring religion (Strmiska 2000: 113), the good atheist death is also important for bringing the tenets of rationalist activism to the attention of a wider public. Since, as we have mentioned, activists try to spread their worldview by challenging superstition and religion where they perceive it to be most strongly rooted (i.e., in the domain of death and dying), it is necessary for rationalists to make their body donations public; all the potential for 'propaganda' is lost if they donate privately. As David Nash (1995: 159) puts it in reference to nineteenth-century British freethinkers, who were similarly concerned to avoid typical death rituals, death becomes a key "ideological event" with explicit instructional value—a situation in which activists have to "lie down to be counted" (McManners 1981: 107). If the Indian tradition of 'lives as lessons' (Arnold and Blackburn 2004) offers up exemplary life narratives for purposes of emulation, atheist activists enact a tradition that is similar yet thoroughly their own—atheist '*deaths* as lessons'. Similar to the role of last words in the Western literary *ars moriendi* tradition, the good atheist death functions didactically as "a lingering exhortation" to those left behind (Faust 2008: 11).

The deaths of noted atheist activists, through the pledging of their bodies and the enactments of these pledges, are held up as exemplary. An article in the Maharashtra-based rationalist newsletter *Thought & Action*, for instance, recounts the contribution of pivotal twentieth-century rationalist Abraham Kovoor,[26] who died in 1978. "'I am not afraid of death and life after death', Kovoor wrote in his will. '*To set an example*, I don't want a burial.' He donated his eyes to an eye bank and his corpse to a medical college for anatomical study, with instructions that his skeleton eventually be given to the science laboratory of Thurston College. All of these wishes were honoured" (Rationalist 2008: 18; emphasis added). Noted rationalist Basava Premanand, a figure of comparable stature to Kovoor in twentieth- and twenty-first-century Indian atheist activism, became extremely concerned after being diagnosed with cancer. In anticipation of his death, he did all that was needed to facilitate the successful donation of his body, including relocating to a place where the necessary amenities would be available. In an interview first published in March 2009, seven months before his death, Premanand declared his intention to move from the small town in Tamil Nadu where he resided, since "it might be difficult to do what I want to be done with my body," to the metropolitan center of Bangalore, "where the facilities are better ... I want all the parts of my body to be donated to others so that they can be put to use. I don't want to be buried or cremated. I would like my remains to be used for study or research" (Nayak 2009: 22). Republished in a special issue of the journal *Bangalore Skeptic* upon his death, the interview evinces his exemplary dedication. The lessons elaborated in his life are reaffirmed in his dying commitment to the donation of his body; his death is rendered instructional. Ideal-typical cases such as these receive a degree of media attention and thus connect with a public beyond fellow rationalists. At the same time, they place pressure on common members to follow the lead of the righteous ones.

The most high-profile recent atheist death was that of Jyoti Basu, mentioned earlier. When the former chief minister of West Bengal died in 2010 at age 95, his death became the stimulus for a major media campaign to boost body donation.[27] Indeed, the Bengal media took on a role similar to the one it had assumed after the death of religious leader Balak Brahmachari in 1993. Faced with a mass of devotees who refused to accept that Brahmachari had died—they insisted instead that he had gone into a state of *nirvikalpa samadhi*, a reversible coma-like state achievable only by those who possess the utmost spiritual prowess—the media turned the death into a "fight for rational values in public life and against obscurantist beliefs and practices" (Chatterjee 1999: 111). It should be noted that the extent to which the media can be termed rationalist 'fellow travelers' is extremely limited, and the relationship between atheist activists and media agencies is in many respects a difficult one. In certain cases, however, collaborations are possible, and by making Basu's death visible as an ideological event, the media's coverage was something of a publicity coup for the rationalists. The atheist's dead body, as one activist put it, "should carry his message" (Quack 2012a: 236), and indeed the materiality of atheist materialism as a vital strategy of persuasion is as evident in instances of public body donation as in cases of miracle demonstration.

This brings us back to the question of evidence, discussed briefly earlier, for the visibly donated body takes on the status of a crucial evidential fact. Mumbai-based secular leader V. K. Sinha stated to us that the three major transformations in life—birth, marriage, and death—are critical "tests for atheism," while Narendra Nayak quoted Albert Camus' observation that "society judges a man by what he does when his mother dies," in reference to his own actions on the deaths of his parents. Death is seen here as the decisive test for atheism in several key respects: first, because of the assumption that many people facing the end of their lives are prone to turn to religion; second, because religious beliefs and practices related to death are rooted so strongly in India's culture and everyday life; and third, because the way that the body is treated is seen as confirmation and verification of the true position that one held in life. The fate of the atheist's dead body is thus invested with significance as being key to defending and/or 'proving' the enduring constancy of the atheist worldview. By producing valuations of lives lived in this way, the atheist's body forms an intensely biographical moment. Rather than a passive object amid the "fuss" of "religious rites or prayers,"[28] the body now becomes both a material signifier and an enactment of materialism. In several senses, it is therefore an object of evidence—it evidences the truth of materialism itself as well as the donor's ethical consistency. There is thus a double moral aspect to the death of the atheist activist. We have seen how, as a 'helpful' action, body donation allows the atheist to enact a moral materialism. Yet these are also times of moral peril, for if one fails to make arrangements for a good atheist death, or if one's atheism is recanted in one's dying moments, the ethical consistency of a whole life may be called into question.

There is a long-standing tradition of accusation and counter-accusation in this respect. As David Hume neared his death, "[i]t is said that the rabble of Edinburgh congregated around his house demanding to know when the atheist would recant" (Hacking 1986: 238). In nineteenth-century France, the importance of a good materialist death was recognized as a means of countering priests' taunts concerning atheist deathbed conversions (Hecht 2003: 31). In England, a "staple tactic used by the Christian apologists to discomfort the infidel was to discredit the deathbed of the movement's own past heroes. Much ink and paper was spent in describing the deathbed of Thomas Paine who was supposed to have recanted and spent his last days in torment consuming improbable quantities of brandy and instructing those around him to burn copies of *The Age of Reason*" (Nash 1995: 164). It is thus not difficult to understand why a notion of "the 'good [atheist death]' was popularized as a supreme test of belief … That persistent attempts were still made to undermine these 'good deaths' was itself instrumental in making them of still further importance. This in part explains the longevity of the classic set-piece, stage-managed secularist death" (ibid.: 167). Let us detail, then, a contemporary Indian variant of the stage-managed atheist death.

When the rationalist leader Premanand was dying from cancer early in October 2009 at the age of 79, his close colleague Narendra Nayak sought to secure his message by taking his signature and fingerprint on a "Declaration of attitude and temperament." The editor of *Bangalore Skeptic* then sent an e-mail message to a rationalist list that was also posted online, detailing Premanand's deteriorating health and asserting that while "his vital organs have been affected," his "brain and his ideology remain intact, and we wanted the world to know about it and to make a declaration on his behalf that it remains so." This was important because there was apparently a rumor circulating that, on his deathbed, this noted atheist had "started believing in god and supernatural powers." A scanned copy of Premanand's declaration was attached to the message. It stated:

> It is common for the purveyors of superstitions and such anti rational forces to start spreading rumors about rationalists turning to god and other supernatural forces at the end of their lives and becoming devotees of gods and god men of

various types ... It is also claimed that at times of crises ... we staunch rationalists ... turn to spiritualism and religion ... I wish to clarify that as on today the
twentieth of September 2009 I remain a staunch rationalist and wish to place
on record the following: a. I continue to be a rationalist of full conviction. b.
I do not believe in any supernatural power. All the powers that we encounter
are in the realm of nature and nothing exists beyond that. c. I do not believe in
the existence of the soul or rebirth. d. I have not turned to any religion, god or
any sort of spiritual pursuits. e. When I pass away I shall be leaving only my
body which is to be donated to a medical college and no spirit or soul to cause
problems for the living.

This critical reassertion of a commitment to body donation in Premanand's
rejoinder to the rumor seems to confirm emphatically the status of body donation as a special indicator of self-consistency and steadfastness. Premanand's
atheism transparently endures, and the lesson elaborated in his life is reaffirmed in his dying commitment to the donation of his body. Nonetheless,
despite the best efforts of his atheist colleagues and friends, rumors were
spread on the Internet after Premanand's death that cast aspersions on the
state of his atheism at the end of his life. As Premanand was a particularly
vehement critic of Sathya Sai Baba during his life and authored the voluminous
Murders in Sai Baba's Bedroom (2001), it is perhaps unsurprising that a website
that exists in order to "expos[e] critics' smear campaigns against Bhagavan Sri
Sathya Sai Baba" was the main source of these rumors.[29]

Yet there is a twist involved that makes this episode somewhat different
from those reported in nineteenth-century England and France. Tsing (2000:
352) notes that "the cultural processes of all 'place' making and all 'force'
making are *both local and global*, that is, both socially and culturally particular and productive of widely spreading interactions." Premanand, of course,
responded to and sought to debunk local superstitions, miracles, and gurus.
He targeted, in particular, Sathya Sai Baba, some of whose devotees in turn
sought to debunk the debunker—not unlike those nineteenth-century priests
who were reviled and feared by atheists "for the taunting public spectacle they
made of any well-known atheist's deathbed conversion" (Hecht 2003: 31). This
resulted in Premanand's "Declaration of attitude and temperament" as a way
of nullifying the anticipated attempt to render his dying dispositions suspect.
Global connectivity may be nothing new (Bayly 2003), but the Internet enables
a new instantaneity and so caused the declaration to achieve a near-immediate
global audience.[30] Hence, just a few days afterward, a US atheist living in
Kentucky was able to take inspiration from Premanand's declaration in a blog
titled "Ensuring a Rational Death": "As an out, loud and proud atheist with
freakazoid relatives, one of my great fears is that my godbot family members
will try to turn my eventual death into a last-second conversion victory for
their invisible sky wizard. So I think I will borrow from Basava Premanand's
rationalist living will."[31] Then follows the declaration, and the comment: "I
wish I'd known the man. He's leaving us one small story from what must
have been a life of reason, and is dying as a free man, free in thought." If the
declaration itself borrowed from the kinds of deathbed testaments innovated

in nineteenth-century France and Britain (Hecht 2003; Nash 1995), it quickly traveled back to Euro-America, inspiring atheists there as well.

Recent studies of digital media have drawn attention to its potential for evangelical outreach and visions of a globally connected religiosity (Miller and Horst 2012; Oosterbaan 2011). Atheist activist communities that are engaging combatively in their own local situations also gain inspiration from and share experiences with other globally dispersed atheist web users. To reiterate, connections across boundaries are hardly novel phenomena, yet new articulations of 'godlessness', combining and recombining online, are facilitated and made visible in myriad web forums. Just as consideration of the matter of belief should not preclude the matter of disbelief, neither should the new and significant attention paid to religion and media (Meyer 2011) preclude recognition of non-religion and media. But that is another article.

Conclusion

While for some, the Book of Nature is a way of studying God's revelation to humankind, for others, the natural sciences are a thoroughly secular undertaking. We have no wish to present atheism as a monolith, nor do we desire to dichotomize the varieties of religious and non-religious positions. There are conservative and progressive religious and non-religious approaches within biomedical ethics, and both atheists and theists may have many reasons to donate their bodies—or to refrain from doing so. It is interesting to note that in eighteenth-century England, public anatomy teaching was considered by some to reveal the work of the Creator and thus "offered an argument *against* atheism" (Bates 2008: 3; emphasis added). Of course, body donation is not the same thing as anatomy instruction, although the former of course exists to facilitate the latter (in present times also potentially offering up a supply of transplantable organs). In spite of such differing perspectives, we have argued in this chapter that body donation can be described as an instance of atheist material culture *par excellence*. The philosopher and atheist Jeremy Bentham, who, upon his death in 1832, famously had his body preserved for display at University College London, understood the donation of his body as a means of helping to combat mischievous superstitions concerning the corpse (Collings 2000). Rather than reveal the work of the Creator, Bentham hoped that public lectures performed over his body would provide a forceful demonstration "that the primitive horror at dissection originates in ignorance" (Marmoy 1958: 80).

The case of Bentham and the other examples discussed in this chapter—principally from India, but also France and England—show the remarkable extent to which the atheist's body, donated for autopsy, instructional, and/or transplantation purposes, recurs across time and space. The atheist's dead body may thus be considered the 'atheist gift'. Held in common across the differing contexts of non-religion discussed in this chapter is the notion that the dead body makes possible the gift of knowledge and progress, that is, it is a gift given to an "anticipated future … envisioned as the outcome of an immanent process of development" (Langlitz 2006: 245). Such an act contributes to this development and thereby helps to bring it about. It is moreover a gift to the living—to those who will benefit from it. It is also a 'self-gift' to the atheist community, enabling its members, in theory, to avoid the rituals they abhor while at the same time rendering their materialism 'moral'. Lastly, body donation is a gift of morale to remaining atheists, confirming the deceased's materialist constancy and thereby helping to nullify in advance rumors of recantation.

Remarkable though the spatio-temporal recurrence of this 'atheist gift' is, the Indian variant possesses certain unique features that need to be acknowledged. Hecht's (2003) study of the Mutual Autopsy Society frames nineteenth-century French atheism in essentially negative terms: here atheism amounts to a lack that the Society and its body donations helped to ameliorate. Suffering the "emotional distress" of living "without belief in God" and "bereft" without prayers and processions (ibid.: 40), atheists were both given something to believe in (scientific materialism) and allowed to 'live on' via membership in the Society and the donation of their bodies. In the Indian case, however, body donation bridges 'negative' rejection (of unscientific and destructive death rituals) and 'positive' atheist agenda setting (being a gift to the living, not the dead, and a material report of moral materialism). Moreover, if in Bentham's case the display of his dead body was for purposes, in part, of "delicious profanation … a kind of sly joke against contemporary prejudice and outraged opinion" (Collings 2000: 124), Indian body donation is constitutive of a more austere atheist materiality that goes beyond the comedic (although Indian atheist material culture is not averse to 'delicious profanation' in other contexts, as we have seen).

This chapter has sought to give an account of lived materialism in India and to prepare the ground for its more substantial analysis at the present time and in the future. In characterizing body donation as a means of providing material reports of atheist activists' moral materialism, our account connects with Keane's (2010: 82) concern to explore how "people and their relations to other people are mediated by semiotic forms." Particularly pertinent is Keane's emphasis on ways in which "ethical actions" become subject to "palpable objectifications" (ibid.: 74) that enable a person's (ethical) character to become available for inspection or evaluation, using the example of an account book. The account book—as a material form—gives 'ethical shape' to commercial actions and makes them available for evaluation. An atheist's donated body is his/her account book in this sense: it is the material form that makes manifest the moral nature of an atheist's materialism. Indeed, the reflexive nature of atheist body donation—the way in which the gesture is presented to the self and others as 'ethical'—makes it 'meta-ethical' in the sense proposed by Lambek (2010a: 32). Although body donation is only one of the ways in which Indian atheist activists have sought to reclaim materials for materialism, this chapter has suggested reasons why the atheist's donated body has attained a particularly important stature in the material culture of materialism.

Acknowledgments

We would like to thank Lydie Fialova, Nayanika Mathur, and the editors of this volume for their helpful comments on drafts of this chapter. We would also like to recognize the translation of the book *Mrutyu Tane Manavta* (Humanity at the Time of Death) by Percy Patrick. Finally, we acknowledge that the work of Johannes Quack was funded by the German Research Council (DFG) as part of the Emmy Noether-Project (QU 338/1-1), "The Diversity of Nonreligion."

Jacob Copeman is a Lecturer in Social Anthropology at the University of Edinburgh. He is the author of *Veins of Devotion: Blood Donation and Religious Experience in North India* (2009), the editor of *Blood Donation, Bioeconomy, Culture* (2009) and *South Asian Tissue Economies* (2013), and the co-editor of *The Guru in South Asia: New Interdisciplinary Perspectives* (2012, with Aya Ikegame) and *Social Theory after Strathern* (2014, with Alice Street).

Johannes Quack is an Assistant Professor in Social Anthropology at the University of Zurich. He is the author of *Disenchanting India: Organized Rationalism and Criticism of Religion in India* (2012) and the co-editor of *The Problem of Ritual Efficacy* (2010, with William Sax and Jan Weinhold), *Religion und Kritik in der Moderne* (2012, with Ulrich Berner), and *Asymmetrical Conversations: Contestations, Circumventions, and the Blurring of Therapeutic Boundaries* (2014, with Harish Naraindas and William Sax).

Notes

1. Here we are examining body donation for the immediate purposes of autopsy, medical training (i.e., anatomy instruction), and/or extraction of organs for transplantation.
2. To avoid confusion, we note here that we are not talking about 'materialism' in any Marxist sense of the term and that 'materialism' and 'being materialistic' are not the same thing. One still encounters the assumption that all atheists are rampantly materialistic, which of course is not necessarily the case.
3. Quack has conducted ethnographic research among Indian rationalist societies since 2007, and Copeman since 2009. Although we carried out our respective stretches of fieldwork independently, in order to avoid unnecessary distraction we do not differentiate between ourselves when presenting ethnography in this chapter.
4. The difficulties connected to the use of the notion of atheism in Hindu contexts is discussed elsewhere. See Quack (2012b, 2013).
5. See Quack (2012a) for more on the socio-economic backgrounds of activists.
6. On the spectrum of atheist activists ranging from intellectuals or 'a-theologians' to down-to-earth social activists, see Quack (2012a: 208–211).
7. 'Catching them young' is considered to be vitally important. Teachers and students are thus particular targets of atheist activist campaigning.

8. Instead of such performances, some rationalist groups sell respective VCDs and DVDs that debunk the 'miracles'.
9. The acronym refers to the Indian Institutes of Technology, prestigious technology and engineering colleges.
10. 'God men' is a generic term for various kinds of religious specialists (e.g., *bābā, mullā, sādhu, maulavī, phakīr, tantrik, or mantrik*) and is often used by rationalists in a derogatory manner.
11. We draw this term from Livingstone's (1999) work on communities of mathematicians.
12. This observation may be considered a slightly oblique response to Hirschkind's (2011) recent question, "Is there a secular body?"
13. See also the chapter in this volume by Paul-François Tremlett and Fang-Long Shih, who argue against understandings of belief as "private, cognitive acts." Instead, they maintain that "believing and doubting are constituted socially."
14. Gora's distinction differs from Antony Flew's (1976) discussion of 'negative' and 'positive' atheism.
15. Further details about the Atheist Centre in Andhra Pradesh may be found in Quack (2012a: 89–91; 2012c).
16. http://www.iheu.org/atheist-ceremonies (accessed 14 June 2014).
17. In other historical and cultural contexts, cremation has been perceived to assist the living, certainly more so than (Christian) burial practices. For instance, in his book *Der Kreislauf des Lebens* (The Circle of Life), the freethinker and physiologist Jakob Moleschott (1852: 422) advocated cremation as a more rational and hygienic funeral practice, pleading that human remains should be used to fertilize fields and ought not to be wasted in tombs and graves. The underlying logic of Moleschott's proposal and that of atheist advocates of body donation is the same. The point is not necessarily to defend a certain practice but to consider what is most 'rational' in the circumstances and to avoid a waste of resources (meanwhile, attacking religious beliefs along the way). While cremation allowed this in mid-nineteenth-century Europe, body donation does so in India today.
18. For example, the name of the organization Satyasodhak Sabha explicitly refers to the 'truth seeking' (*satyasodhak*) ceremonies initiated by anti-untouchability campaigner Jyotiba Phule (1827–1890) to replace caste-entrenching religious rituals. See Quack (2012a: 64–67).
19. This is a reference to the idea that any organ taken from a person will be missing in that person's next birth; for example, an eye donor will be reborn without eyes or will be blind.
20. See http://www.countercurrents.org/rawat180110.htm.
21. The Upanishads are Hindu sacred treatises (ca. 800–200 BC) that expound the Vedas (texts originating in ancient India) in primarily non-dualist, mystical terms.
22. http://www.hindujagruti.org/hindusim/knowledge/article/why-is-it-important-to-understand-implied-meaning-in-spirituality.html#9 (accessed 14 June 2014).
23. The suggestive term 'moral materialism' is drawn from Joseph Alter's (2011) recent book in which it is used quite differently.
24. An organization propounding 'scientific humanism', the India Renaissance Society was founded by M. N. Roy in 1946. For more on Roy, see Quack (2012a: 83–85).
25. Local negative attitudes toward dissection were viewed by colonial commentators as evidence of the superstition over which colonial rule would prevail. Dissection "was seen to be a necessary, even exemplary, part of nineteenth-century Western medical practice" (Arnold 1993: 5). Heavily freighted with taboo and stigma, the project of fostering a cluster of eager trainee dissectors was representative of the wider civilizing mission invoked by the British as justifying their presence in the sub-continent.

26. For more on Kovoor, see Quack (2012a: 96–97).
27. Having elaborated on the circumstances of Basu's death elsewhere (Copeman and Reddy 2012), we will not discuss it further here.
28. These are the words of N. I. Chacko, a member of the Indian Rationalist Association, who died in 1978. See Quack (2012a: 242) for a full account.
29. http://www.saisathyasai.com/baba/Ex-Baba.com/Premanand/b-premanand-deception.html (accessed 14 June 2014).
30. Premanand's declaration was published on the pan-Indian rationalist website Nirmukta. See http://nirmukta.com/2009/09/22/premanand-in-abhirami-hospital-coimbatore/.
31. See http://blueinthebluegrass.blogspot.com/2009/10/ensuring-rational-death.html.

References

Alter, Joseph. 2011. *Moral Materialism: Sex and Masculinity in Modern India*. New Delhi: Penguin Press.

Arnold, David. 1993. *Colonizing the Body: State Medicine and Epidemic Disease in Nineteenth-Century India*. Berkeley: University of California Press.

Arnold, David, and Stuart Blackburn. 2004. "Introduction: Life Histories in India." Pp. 1–28 in *Telling Lives in India: Biography, Autobiography, and Life History*, ed. David Arnold and Stuart Blackburn. Bloomington: Indiana University Press.

Bates, Alan W. 2008. "'Indecent and Demoralising Representations': Public Anatomy Museums in Mid-Victorian England." *Medical History* 52, no. 1: 1–22.

Bayly, C. A. 2003. *The Birth of the Modern World, 1780–1914: Global Connections and Comparisons*. Oxford: Blackwell.

Chatterjee, Partha. 1999. "Modernity, Democracy and a Political Negotiation of Death." *South Asia Research* 19, no 2: 103–119.

Collings, David. 2000. "Bentham's Auto-icon: Utilitarianism and the Evisceration of the Common Body." *Prose Studies* 23, no. 3: 95–127.

Copeman, Jacob, and Deepa S. Reddy. 2012. "The Didactic Death: Publicity, Instruction and Body Donation." *HAU: Journal of Ethnographic Theory* 2, no. 2: 59–83.

Dawkins, Richard. 2006. *The God Delusion*. Boston, MA: Houghton Mifflin.

Desai, Babubhai, ed. 1996. *Mrutyu Tane Manavta* [Humanity at the Time of Death]. Surat: Gujarat Rationalist Association.

Engelke, Matthew. 2005. "Sticky Subjects and Sticky Objects: The Substance of African Christian Healing." Pp. 118–139 in *Materiality*, ed. Daniel Miller. Durham, NC: Duke University Press.

Engelke, Matthew. 2012. "What Is a Good Death? Ritual, Whether Religious or Not, Still Counts." *Guardian*. 14 May. http://www.theguardian.com/commentisfree/belief/2012/may/14/good-death-ritual-religious (accessed 14 May 2012).

Engelke, Matthew. 2014. "The Coffin Question: On the Material Culture of Non-religious Funerals." Paper presented at Social Anthropology Seminar Series, University of Edinburgh, 14 February.

Epstein, Greg M. 2009. *Good without God: What a Billion Nonreligious People Do Believe*. New York: William Morrow.

Faust, Drew G. 2008. *This Republic of Suffering: Death and the American Civil War*. New York: Knopf.

Flew, Antony. 1976. *The Presumption of Atheism and Other Philosophical Essays on God, Freedom, and Immortality*. London: Elek.

Flood, Gavin. 1996. *An Introduction to Hinduism*. Cambridge: Cambridge University Press.

Graeber, David. 2013. "Culture as Creative Refusal: Heroic and Anti-heroic Politics." *Cambridge Anthropology* 31, no. 2: 1–19.

Hacking, Ian. 1986. "Self-Improvement." Pp. 235–240 in *Foucault: A Critical Reader*, ed. David C. Hoy. Oxford: Blackwell.

Hecht, Jennifer M. 1997. "French Scientific Materialism and the Liturgy of Death: The Invention of a Secular Version of Catholic Last Rites (1876–1914)." *French Historical Studies* 20, no. 4: 703–735.

Hecht, Jennifer M. 2003. *The End of the Soul: Scientific Modernity, Atheism, and Anthropology in France*. New York: Columbia University Press.

Hirschkind, Charles. 2011. "Is There a Secular Body?" *Cultural Anthropology* 26, no. 4: 633–647.

Keane, Webb. 2008. "The Evidence of the Senses and the Materiality of Religion." *Journal of the Royal Anthropological Institute* 14, no. S1: S110–S127.

Keane, Webb. 2010. "Minds, Surfaces, and Reasons in the Anthropology of Ethics." Pp. 64–83 in Lambek 2010b.

Lambek, Michael, ed. 2010a. "Introduction." Pp. 1–38 in Lambek 2010b.

Lambek, Michael, ed. 2010b. *Ordinary Ethics: Anthropology, Language, and Action*. New York: Fordham University Press.

Langlitz, Nicolas. 2006. "Review of *The End of the Soul: Scientific Modernity, Atheism, and Anthropology in France* by Jennifer Michael Hecht." *American Anthropologist* 108, no 1: 244–245.

Lee, Lois. 2012. "Locating Nonreligion, in Mind, Body and Space: New Research Methods for a New Field." Pp. 135–158 in *Annual Review of the Sociology of Religion*, vol. 3: *New Methods in the Sociology of Religion*, ed. Luigi Berzano and Ole P. Riis. Leiden: Brill.

Livingstone, Eric. 1999. "Cultures of Proving." *Social Studies of Science* 29, no. 6: 867–888.

Marmoy, C. F. A. 1958. "The 'Auto-icon' of Jeremy Bentham at University College London." *Medical History* 2, no. 2: 77–86.

Marshall, Andrew. 2004. "Hoax-Busters." CNN Traveller. http://157.166.226.119/2004/issue3/india (accessed 16 January 2013).

Marx, Karl. 1990. *Capital*. Vol. 1: *A Critique of Political Economy*. Trans. Ben Fowkes; intro. Ernest Mandel. London: Penguin Books.

McManners, John. 1981. "Death and the French Historians." Pp. 106–130 in *Mirrors of Mortality: Studies in the Social History of Death*, ed. Joachim Whaley. London: Europa Publications.

Meyer, Birgit. 2011. "Mediation and Immediacy: Sensational Forms, Semiotic Ideologies and the Question of the Medium." *Social Anthropology* 19, no 1: 23–39.

Miller, Daniel. 2008. "The Uses of Value." *Geoforum* 39, no 3: 1122–1132.

Miller, Daniel. 2010. "Anthropology in Blue Jeans." *American Ethnologist* 37, no. 3: 415–428.

Miller, Daniel, and Heather A. Horst. 2012. "The Digital and the Human: A Prospectus for Digital Anthropology." Pp. 3–35 in *Digital Anthropology*, ed. Heather A. Horst and Daniel Miller. Oxford: Berg.

Moleschott, Jakob. 1852. *Der Kreislauf des Lebens*. Mainz: Zabern.

Morgan, David. 2009. "Introduction: The Matter of Belief." Pp. 1–17 in *Religion and Material Culture: The Matter of Belief*, ed. David Morgan. London: Routledge.

Nash, David S. 1995. "'Look in Her Face and Lose Thy Dread of Dying': The Ideological Importance of Death to the Secularist Community in Nineteenth-Century Britain." *Journal of Religious History* 19, no. 2: 158–180.

Nayak, Narendra. 2007. *Battle Against Supernatural*. Podanur: B. Premanand.

Nayak, Narendra. 2009. "An Interview with Basava Premanand." *Bangalore Skeptic* 2, no. 10: 21–22. http://nirmukta.com/2009/01/27/an-interview-with-basava-premanand/.

Oosterbaan, Martijn. 2011. "Virtually Global: Online Evangelical Cartography." *Social Anthropology* 19, no 1: 56–73.

Paine, Crispin. 2009. "Militant Atheist Objects: Anti-religion Museums in the Soviet Union." *Present Pasts* 1: 61–76.

Pasquini, John J. 2009. *Atheist Personality Disorder: Addressing a Distorted Mindset.* Bloomington, IN: AuthorHouse.

Premanand, Basava. 2001. *Murders in Sai Baba's Bedroom: Who Murdered the Six? A Critical Analysis of the Records.* Podanur: B. Premanand.

Quack, Johannes. 2012a. *Disenchanting India: Organized Rationalism and Criticism of Religion in India.* New York: Oxford University Press.

Quack, Johannes. 2012b. "Hinduism, Atheism, and Rationalism." Pp. 626–632 in *Brill's Encyclopedia of Hinduism*, ed. Knut A. Jacobsen. Leiden: Brill.

Quack, Johannes. 2012c. "Organised Atheism in India: An Overview." *Journal of Contemporary Religion* 27, no. 1, 67–85.

Quack, Johannes. 2013. "India." Pp. 651–664 in *The Oxford Handbook of Atheism*, ed. Stephen Bullivant and Michael Ruse. Oxford: Oxford University Press.

Quack, Johannes. 2014. "Outline of a Relational Approach to 'Nonreligion.'" *Method & Theory in the Study of Religion* 26, no. 4–5: 439–469.

Rao, Goparaju R. (Gora). 1978. *Positive Atheism.* Vijayawada: Atheist Center.

Rationalist. 2008. "Abraham Kovoor." *Thought & Action* (October–December): 17–19. http://www.thoughtnaction.co.in/abraham-kovoor/.

Scot, Reginald. [1584] 1973. *The Discoverie of Witchcraft, Wherein the Lewde Dealing of Witches and Witchmongers Is Notablie Detected.* Reprint, edited with explanatory notes, glossary, and introduction by Brinsley Nicholson. Totowa, NJ: Rowman & Littlefield.

Srinivas, Tulasi. 2010. *Winged Faith: Rethinking Globalization and Religious Pluralism through the Sathya Sai Movement.* New York: Columbia University Press.

Ssorin-Chaikov, Nikolai, and Olga Sosnina. 2004. "The Faculty of Useless Things: Gifts to Soviet Leaders." Pp. 277–300 in *Personality Cults in Stalinism*, ed. Klaus Heller and Jan Plamper. Göttingen: Vandenhoeck & Ruprecht.

Strmiska, Michael. 2000. "Ásatrú in Iceland: The Rebirth of Nordic Paganism?" *Nova Religio: The Journal of Alternative and Emergent Religions* 4, no. 1: 106–132.

Tsing, Anna. 2000. "The Global Situation." *Cultural Anthropology* 15, no. 3: 327–360.

Weber, Max. 1964. *Soziologie: Weltgeschichtliche Analysen.* Stuttgart: Kröner.

Zachariah, Benjamin. 2004. *Nehru.* London: Routledge.

Chapter 3

ATHEIST POLITICAL CULTURES IN INDEPENDENT ANGOLA

Ruy Llera Blanes and Abel Paxe

One of the reasons why godlessness, non-religion, and atheism often appear as hard to pin down in contemporary theory may be due to their constant reformulation in the spheres of discourse and ideology. Recent efforts have attempted to go beyond the layer of presentation and debate in order to locate their philosophical roots and upbringings (Geroulanos 2010; Watkin 2011) and their translations and effects into particular 'cultures' or 'traditions' with the same epistemological value as any given religious movement or institution (see, e.g., Hecht 2003; Luehrmann 2011). However, it is only very recently that atheism has become, academically speaking, something more than a mere ethereal, abstract aspect of circulating worldviews. For the most part, it has been defined as a negation of something much more substantial—a "conscious, articulated credo against God's existence" (see the introduction to this volume).

However, the fact that atheism often remains a political issue, negotiated at the ideological and discursive level, is also telling. If there are intellectual trends that determine the political character of religion (see Strenski 2010) or the religious character of politics (Vries and Sullivan 2006), atheism, in turn, has historically been approached in terms of its political content and consequences. Obviously, historically speaking, there have been many pretexts for this association of ideas, namely, in what concerns religion and its negation in state politics, for example, in the Soviet Union, Cuba, China, Vietnam, and Ethiopia (see Crahan 1979; Donham 1999; Froese 2004; Luehrmann 2011; Toan 2010). From this perspective, and incorporating such conceptual legacies, one can easily acknowledge that 'identifying' or 'locating' atheism becomes an exercise in defining what 'politics' means. In this chapter, we will work with a restricted, pragmatic understanding of politics as a 'translation of theory into practice', when certain levels and regimes of discourse become 'agent', or effective, and have an impact on people's lives through processes of governance. Such moments of translation may include diverse pragmatic stances, ranging from juridical initiatives and education programs to police repression and political speeches. In such cases, anti-religion, irreligion, and godlessness become in many ways agent and materialized.

But this exercise in distinction is not intended to disconnect atheism from its political element—in fact, quite the opposite. In this chapter we propose to look at the political ideology of atheism as it developed in one specific context and historical moment: the first years of independent Angola, starting in 1975. We will examine how atheism, as a key term in this period's political manual, was translated within one specific political culture—that of Angola's ruling party ever since independence, the MPLA[1]—into specific policies and actions that had repercussions on its citizens' daily lives, namely, those practicing religion. Similar to many other African countries at the end of the colonial era, Angola was experiencing thriving ideological debate, coupled with dramatic political shifts and further acts of violence. Within such movements, atheism often appeared, underscoring wider ideologies of nationalism, modernity, and social transformation—many of which continue to resonate to this day. In the following pages, we will be charting this political history, adding an ethnographic depiction of how atheism became materialized in certain stances of post-independence Angolan social life.

Tracing Atheism in Africa

'Africa' and 'religion' seem to be two inevitably paired tropes nowadays. Most theories of secularization usually represent the African continent as the 'counter-paradigm' against which (especially) Europe is configured as a place of non-belief. This is the case with Grace Davie's (1999) suggestion of 'European exceptionalism', Philip Jenkins's (2006) theories of 'Christian southernization', and Charles Taylor's (2007) depiction of the 'secular age'. Works such as these often highlight the historical distinctiveness of Europe vis-à-vis formations of atheist and/or secularist currents, indirectly perpetuating the Weberian paradigm of Eurocentered modernist rationalization and disenchantment. Such meta-narratives of Western faith are coupled with the ever-thriving field of African religion studies, which ceaselessly charts the dynamic, stimulating religious phenomena in this continent.[2]

Several recent polls seem to confirm such theories, placing non-religion and atheism in Africa in the extreme minority (see Zuckerman 2006). In most countries, the figure was under 1 percent, while the figure for atheists registered 1.5 percent in Angola (Johnstone 1993). Regardless of how such surveys were conducted, these minimal figures contribute to the depiction of religion as a preponderant, pervasive aspect of life in Africa (Ellis and ter Haar 2004: 178ff.).

However, such a framing often obscures the fact that Africa has important and multiple atheist histories that were decisive in its political and social history and still have specific currencies in the continent. An example is the influence of socialist utopias in the transition from colonialism to independence. As in other regions of the continent, post-independence Lusophone Africa was a geopolitical region where ideas of the 'modern man' circulated within political, intellectual, and cultural circles. These ideas were influenced by translations of Marxist and Marxist-Leninist political manuals, which included definitions of religion and its place in society. In such cases, there was an explicit connection between the historical revisionism promoted by the processes of revolution, nationalism, and emancipation, on the one hand, and an ideal of progressive modernity that was inherently utopian (secular, enlightened, future-oriented, libertarian), on the other. Such an objective would be, in theory, achieved with the implementation of the Marxist manual, that is, through the organization of the forces of production. Such was certainly the case in post-independence Mozambique and Angola, where the hegemonic parties—FRELIMO[3] and the MPLA, respectively—explicitly engaged in anti-religious campaigning amid encompassing theories and policies of individual and collective transformation, for the most under the framework of utopian ideas of renewal, progress, and modernity (see, e.g., Morier-Genoud 1996).

But these were not just autochthonous ideological constructs; instead, they were a consequence of decades of intense circulation of ideas among late-colonial African intellectuals, leaders, and militaries, who progressively probed theories of resistance and liberation (Bragança and Wallerstein 1982; Rotberg and Mazrui 1970), as well as ideologies of societal transformation. Within this perspective, the historical influence of communism—more specifically, the Soviet version of communism—in some countries was decisive. Several authors have discussed the specific markers behind the differentiated installation of socialist regimes in newly independent countries such as Kwame Nkrumah's Ghana, Julius Nyerere's Tanzania, and Léopold Senghor's Senegal (see, e.g., Brockway 1963; Friedland and Rosberg 1964; Mazrui and Wondji 2010). This 'African version' of socialism took on different expressions and pragmatist developments within diverse ideologies of collectivism and Pan-Africanism (Mazrui and Wondji 2010). It also acquired philosophical character, as reflected in Nkrumah's (1970) famous thoughts on 'consciencism' (see also Biney 2011). In countries like Angola, this implied the ideological/pragmatic importation and adaptation of Soviet (mainly Leninist) models of governance. Associated with a conflictual, militarized post-independence period, these models have produced what has been called a 'Sovietization of the social' (see below). From this perspective, there was an intense debate concerning the role of communism in the emergence of libertarian, independentist associations in late-colonial Africa.

In this historical moment, the spread of Marxist ideas among African intellectuals and politicians had, as a focal point, African students who were able to pursue higher education in Europe—especially in France, England, and Portugal—where they were able to have contact with leaders of the European Communist parties before becoming prominent political leaders in their countries of origin. With independence, however, socialism met an ambiguous situation: the new countries engaged, often pragmatically, in policies that oscillated politically between the East (communism) and the West (democracy). Apparently, leaders such as Nkrumah, Nyerere, and Jomo Kenyata of Kenya adopted socialist ideology only to obtain political support for the ideological processes of emancipation they conducted. The socialist ideology therefore served as a political factor of mobilization and unity in these countries, helping to avoid rifts between traditional societies and ethnic and religious strains.

In the case of Ghana, for instance, the program of social transformation adopted by Nkrumah saw in religion a resource to explore in order to contain potential problems. For him, the new political ideology would assert itself in a philosophical definition, without necessarily renouncing the fundamental values of traditional religions, Islam, and Christianity (see McClendon 2012). Unlike Nkrumah, the revolutionary Angolan intellectuals saw religion as a problem to be contained and did not discern any need to consider its potentialities (Tshishiku et al. 2010). This may perhaps be related to the particular place of religion in colonial Angola and the consequent process of translation of Leninist ideology, which we will describe below.

In any case, the emergence of Angolan leftist nationalism established religion (and its negation) as a politically agent element. This policy had its maximum impact in the 1976–1979 period, during the office of the first president of Angola, Agostinho Neto, but it would have a long-lasting influence in the subsequent decades. Eduardo dos Santos (1966: 42), for instance, debated the connections between communism, which he defined as a non-religion but nevertheless a form of 'faith', and indigenous (and more specifically Bantu) tribalism. As a Portuguese academic involved in the colonial enterprise, he sought to prove the discrepancy and 'danger' behind the adoption of non-religious (or, more specifically, non-Catholic) worldviews—the backdrop being, obviously, the defense of the Catholic roots behind the Portuguese colonial endeavor, which he defended (see Blanes 2014), as well as the definition of 'righteous' autochthonous beliefs. His argument was in many ways an ideological response to the increasing recognition of the role played by different religious movements—Protestant, independent, and also grassroots Catholic—in the development of independentist Angolan ideologies (Blanes 2014; Péclard 1998; Rocha 2003; B. Schubert 1999).

Militant Atheisms in Pre- and Post-independence Angola

The debate above situates us within a specific temporality and geography, that is, late-colonial and independent Angola. In counterpoint to 'culturalist' speculations like those of Santos, we propose that to understand atheism in Angola, we must look into the individual trajectories that brought about the moment—the agents of transformation of theory into praxis. Following a recent suggestion by Sonja Luehrmann (2011), we argue that the 'personal reproduction' incorporated in these individual trajectories allows us to understand the mediation between individual experiences and the production of collective utopias, including the creation of a 'militant atheism' in Angola.

From this perspective, the history of Angolan independence is fraught with interesting paradoxes. One most immediate example is the role played by religion in the process. Historically a colony of Catholic implantation (mostly in the coastal and northern regions), and a focus of Protestant missionary work in the hinterland since the late nineteenth century, there is some debate regarding the role played by Protestant missions in what is referred to today as the 'formation of national consciousnesses' during the liberation wars (1961–1974) and then the post-independence period (see, e.g., Birmingham 1992; Freston 2001; Henderson 1990; Rocha 2003; B. Schubert 1999). This speculation is based on the fact that the Protestant missions—generally, Baptists in the north, Methodists in the center, and Congregationalists in the south—provided education to the future leaders throughout the territory (Freston 2001: 119–120). In such educational projects, the missionaries imparted ideals of organization and administration that were more democratic and therefore clashed with the colonial project (ibid.).

Interestingly, the leaders of the three most important politico-military movements during this period, Agostinho Neto (MPLA), Jonas Savimbi (UNITA),[4] and Holden Roberto (FNLA),[5] shared a common biographical aspect: all were sons of local Protestant pastors and/or studied in Protestant missions before leaving to obtain higher education in Europe and eventually adopting non-religious convictions. On the other hand, despite their common background, the three leaders eventually placed themselves in different (ultimately opposing) areas of political influence and engaged in diverse socio-historical activities marked by differing ethno-political backgrounds.

Agostinho Neto, for instance, was born in Catete, a small village about 30 kilometers east of Luanda, into a family of Protestant (Methodist) pastors of Mbundu origin, his father having been a well-known pastor in Angola in the 1930s and 1940s. He soon moved to Luanda, where he was exposed to an urban Luso-African *assimilado* (assimilated) culture as a student in the Salvador Correia High School and the Liga Nacional Africana.[6] He later worked in the public health sector and became active in the local scene, writing pieces for local newspapers such as the *Estandarte* and the *Farolim*. After completing his secondary education, he eventually moved to Coimbra, Portugal, to obtain a degree in medicine with a scholarship granted by the local Methodist church. In Portugal, he engaged in political and partisan activities, becoming part of the board of the Casa dos Estudantes do Império[7] and a militant of the youth section of the MUD.[8] In 1952, he was arrested by the Portuguese political police (PIDE)[9] for collecting signatures to support the "Movimento para a Paz" (Movement for Peace). He was released seven years later and completed his university career, returning to Angola in 1959 to pursue medical practice as well as political activities.

Through such activities, Neto's initial Protestant background gradually evolved into a Marxist praxis. Influenced by the pro-Soviet Portuguese Communist Party, he began to engage in an ideology of a free, independent Angola, fighting against the development of privileged social classes that would contribute to new forms of discrimination. Within this framework, his main proposition—the cornerstone behind his socialist project—would be the struggle against imperialism. After his return, he joined the MPLA political party, the outcome of the merger of different political associations such as the PLUA[10] and the Angolan Communist Party, founded by Viriato da Cruz (see Bittencourt 1997). In 1960, Neto was arrested by the PIDE once again and sent into exile, later fleeing to Morocco and Zaire. He eventually became the main protagonist behind the proclamation of Angolan independence in 1975 and its first president (Bittencourt 2010; Reis 2010; Rocha 2003; Serrano 2008; Tali 2000).

Holden Roberto, in turn, was born into a family of descendants of the Kingdom of Kongo monarchy. He grew up in Baptist missions that eventually supported his studies in Leopoldville, where he began to engage in political activities after working for several years in the Belgian colonial administration. His political ideals were marked by a strong ethnic (Bakongo) consciousness that later evolved into an Angolan, multi-ethnic independentism. In 1954, he was one of the founders of the UPNA (Union of Peoples of Northern Angola), which was later renamed the UPA (Union of Peoples of Angola).

His trip to the United States in the 1950s allowed Roberto to connect with Protestant missions, African diasporic communities, and politicians. His Belgian-Congolese education, his connections with Congolese political circles, and his North American experience contributed to his classification as being politically 'influenced by America'. Despite his friendship with Frantz Fanon, Kwame Nkrumah, and Patrice Lumumba, he was seen as an anti-communist and culturally connected to Protestants and North Americans. Nevertheless, when he was chased by the Belgian police due to his political activities, he fled to Ghana, where he was employed by Nkrumah's cabinet. In the late 1950s, Roberto integrated the Ghanaian delegation of the All-African Peoples' Conference into several United Nations meetings, where he denounced the situation in Portuguese territories. He became an avid reader of Nkrumah and Ghandi. The support that he had received from the missionaries had a strong impact on his nationalist ideas, revealing a syncretism of African and Christian values (Marcum 1969; Rocha 2003).

In March 1961, Roberto organized the first guerrilla incursion into northern Angola, a particularly violent moment that kick-started the militarization of the liberation process. Not long afterward, his party would join the PDA[11] to form the FNLA, which would become one of the main contenders of the liberation and post-independence periods.

Jonas Savimbi, of Ovimbundu ethnicity, was the son of an evangelical pastor from Moxico (Benguela). Fred Bridgland's (1986) more or less consensual historiographical version of Savimbi's life describes his trajectory from the missionary stations in the Dondi to his studies in Lisbon. In Europe, Savimbi would take part with Neto in the same movements and institutions before traveling to Lausanne and Freiburg, where he completed his university studies.

He would eventually join the FNLA, where he was appointed foreign affairs representative of the self-styled Revolutionary Government of Angola in Exile (GRAE), founded by Holden Roberto. Savimbi eventually left the organization and founded the UNITA, due to strong ideological divergences (ibid.; see also Marcum 1969; Reis 2010). He would then become a protagonist of the liberation war, acting mostly in the southeastern areas.

These biographical sketches of political leadership reveal the process of transition from an initial religious background into a secularized political theology conceptually rooted in axes such as ideas of emancipation, independence, and reconstruction. Although it was part of a recurring dialogue, the idea of unification remained destabilizing (see Chicoadão 2002), inasmuch as each political leadership found diverse inspiration and would evolve, in post-colonial Angola, into significantly opposed partisan and ideological configurations (Messiant 2008; Reis 2010).[12] But if there is a coincidence in these processes, it is that the role of religion in the story of Angolan independence, which was not at all insignificant (see Marcum 1978; Pélissier 1978; B. Schubert 2000), became subsumed and obfuscated by other, de-religionizing social ontologies.[13] We can therefore trace the historical and political moments that transformed eventual religious utopias into confirmed political utopias. The transformation, we argue, is directly related to a specific 'victorious history' (Benjamin 1968), that of the party that assumed almost exclusive control after 1975: the MPLA and its leaders and ideologists, who imposed their agenda over the other parties while implementing a straightforward communist agenda. In other words, the political transition observed in Angola followed a specific process whereby an 'Angolanized' version of Soviet governance was rehearsed. In this rehearsal, religion would play a particular role (see Paredes 2011; Rocha 2003). Hence, there is a need to look at the particular histories and protagonists that configured the 'atheist cultures' under scrutiny.

From this perspective, the history of atheism in Angola cannot be understood without a deeper look into the MPLA's individual and ideological history. As the academic and former MPLA activist Margarida Paredes (2011) suggests in her analysis of the trajectory and literary production of Deolinda Rodrigues,[14] the process of ideological configuration of the MPLA, marked by a centralizing ideal of 'unity' that merged party (partido) and nation (nação) into a socializing slogan—"MPLA é o Povo, o Povo é o MPLA" (MPLA is the people, the people are the MPLA)—was in fact inspired by both the Marxist praxis and a Methodist background. This association may be explained by the coincidence of the ethnic/regional profiling of the Protestant mission in Angola, which made the Methodists prevalent in the region from which several protagonists of the MPLA's 'victorious history' emerged.[15] For many MPLA militants, Methodism was, to use Feuerbach's semantics, a kind of 'atheist religion' to be assumed and manipulated in the process of constructing the New Man. As we will argue below, Methodism also exemplified how the government's religious policy was very nearly even in its application.

But, as we also see in Rodrigues's story, this was an outcome of a process of intellectual transformation, in many ways connected to recognition of the 'colonial situation' (Balandier 1955), contact with socialist ideologies, and increasing political confrontation, which led to a context of enmity (see Blanes 2012). Thus, what seemed to be a paradox—the religious roots of Angolan atheism—was in fact the outcome of leadership trajectories that, in the course of establishing political careers, embarked on intellectual formations that replaced religious with socialist utopias.

Furthermore, it was no secret that the intellectual transformation experienced by such leaders, which took place mostly abroad (e.g., among the Portuguese communist movement that resisted the Estado Novo dictatorship), established the ontological replacement. As it was known that these leaders were affiliated with the Portuguese Communist Party, the immediate ideological references were evident. Works by Lenin, Nkrumah, and Fanon were looked on as required reading by many political leaders and adepts in this period. Very soon, Angola entered the international scene, backed by the USSR and Cuba. In any case, the most important reference was the Marxist-Leninist manual and its revolutionary theses.[16]

In 1975, in the aftermath of the liberation war in Angola and during the polemical process of installing an MPLA cabinet led by Neto, the local political field was marked by two concomitant actions. On the one hand, there was the escalation toward a fratricidal confrontation between the independentist political parties (the MPLA, UNITA, and FNLA) over disagreements concerning the constitution of the first independent government. On the other hand, there was the unstable construction of national sovereignty, marked by the presence of Cuban armed forces supporting the MPLA and by attempted invasions by South African and Zairian troops (allegedly in support of UNITA and FNLA, respectively), which would be repelled by Neto with the support of the Cuban troops. The first days of Angolan independence were thus marked by violent internal strife and a related process of intense ideological imposition of Angolan nationhood (J. Schubert 2014).

Within this framework, the Angolan government had no room to accommodate religion, which was highlighted as an example of what was not 'intended' to be included within the constructivist project. During this period, there was an intense circulation of modernist ideas among several intellectuals, politicians, and activists engaged in debating the process of decolonization and the version of a post-colonial state that was to be created. Seen in this light, modernism and modernity were expectations managed by the protagonists of independence regarding the construction of the state. Here, ideas of the New Man, free of the inherited flaws of colonialism, affected ideologies of culture, economy, religion, and so on. This was directly inspired by what was known at the time as *marxismo sovietizante* (Sovietizing Marxism). Along with a materialist rewriting of African and Angolan history (see MPLA 1975), the translation of ideology into praxis implied a *sovietização do social* (Sovietization of the social), which produced what would be generally known as *ateismo militante* (militant atheism) (see Messiant 2008; Paredes 2011).[17] In other words, the MPLA jargon of nationalist revolution and emancipation categorized religion as an instrument of hegemony that perpetuated a tradition deemed harmful for the revolutionary project. A report from the MPLA's Central Committee in 1977 was quite explicit in these terms: "Religion has always been, throughout history, one of the instruments used by the exploiting classes to dissuade the exploited classes from the revolutionary struggle for their liberation" (Neto 1977: 35; our translation).

Thus, considering the revolutionary context of the time, there was an expectation of "liquidating the sequelae of regionalism and tribalism" and thus a promotion of a "true national culture enriched by the revolutionary cultural conquests," which would become crystallized at the MPLA's congress in 1977.[18] In the party's first theses and resolutions, one can see that religion was not a central subject in the debates. Nevertheless, its negation appears in several forms, for example, in connection with education and instruction. This became evident in the party's use of scientific and historical materialism to counteract notions of faith within the idealization of Angola's 'new society' (J. Schubert 2014). In a report written after the first congress of the MPLA, Neto (1977: 30–31) recalled how it was important that all militants learn "revolutionary theory," describing "agitation" and "propaganda" as fundamental actions for the diffusion of libertarian and nationalist ideas among the Angolan peoples. This had begun through clandestine pre-independence literacy programs, which were to be continued after independence with the so-called escolas de formação de quadros (corps training schools), where all those who were committed to the revolutionary ideals would receive adequate theoretical training.

In this new context, the goal was to legitimize the hegemony of the newly installed power. One of the necessary steps to achieve such a situation was to establish the laicity (e.g., secularity) of the state. This had become effective in the November 1975 Constitution (Art. 7), which defined a boundary between the state and religious institutions. The Constitution reads: "The Popular Republic of Angola is a laic state, with a complete separation between the State and religious institutions. All religions will be respected and the State will protect churches, cult places, and property, as long as they conform to the State laws." The singular importance of this position is that the party and the state do not forbid religion, following Lenin's proposition of state neutrality and distancing concerning religious affairs. But other MPLA directives produced contradictions between the 'ideal' and 'practice'.

When it was stated that all ideas suggesting a concession on behalf of the state with regard to its positions concerning religious affairs should be combated, this established a guideline that marked the factual, pragmatic relationship between the state and churches for the MPLA. On the one hand, it was about "the relationship with churches and organizations formed around certain religious movements; and about the relationships with the citizens who profess those religious beliefs"; on the other hand, it was about "the attitude to take concerning religion as an ideology, a misrepresented reflection of reality in the people's mentality" (Neto 1977: 36). Regarding the first aspect, we highlight the guarantee that religious postulates would not be used to combat the socialist revolutionary process. Regarding the second aspect, the emphasis is given to the promotion of practices that allow for religious believers to engage in the tasks of the revolution. So despite the recognition of freedom of conscience for Angolan citizens and the hypothetical role of religious worldviews in the debate, it was also recognized that the construction of the 'new society' (one in which 'man would no longer exploit man') should be actively promoted by the secular, laic, atheist state, which would in turn define the terms of such a promotion. As Neto (1977: 36) put it: "This policy must be subordinated to a persistent and systematic diffusion among the masses concerning the scientific conceptions about the world and society. It should also be noted that the struggle to reinforce National Unity is incompatible with segregation and repudiation of believers. In fact, the Party will establish a policy that will attract and engage believers in the tasks of the Revolution."

The Materializations of Political Atheism

What was the outcome of such political and legislative actions? How were these ideologies translated into the practical reality of everyday life? In this section we will explore such translations in post-independence Angola through the repression exerted upon religious groups and individuals, as well as, and especially, through the education policies enforced during the revolutionary period.

One sign of active state repression against religious movements was the existence of *campos de re-educação* (re-education camps) throughout the territory. A notorious example was the Campo de São Nicolau, located in the Namibe province in southern Angola. Previously used by the Portuguese colonial regime for political prisoners, it continued to be used after independence by the MPLA to imprison individuals considered to be 'subversive', 'lackeys of imperialism', 'antagonists', or 'counter-revolutionaries'. Such camps were but one of the possible destinations for dissentient religious protagonists. There was also the mass imprisonment of mostly Tokoists and Jehovah's Witnesses during the first years of independence when foreign missions were closed, subsequently becoming 'Angolanized'. Concomitantly, the Catholic Church's Radio Ecclesia was shut down, and the Church's estate was confiscated. In June 1976, in a rally promoted in Luanda by the OMA,[19] the protesters urged that Lopo do Nascimento, who was prime minister at the time, undertake drastic measures against movements such as the Jehovah's Witnesses and the Tokoist and Kimbanguist churches, whose followers should be sent to such political re-education camps. Many of those present held signs that read "CIA equals Jehovah" or "Toko equals FNLA" (Paxe 2009).

Within this framework, the most important religious institutions at the time suffered some sort of active persecution. Perhaps the most striking case was the Tokoist Church, led by the prophet Simão Toko. Founded in Leopoldville in 1949, it became a symbol of anti-colonial resistance due to its followers' endurance under state repression and its leader's criticism of the colonial venture (Blanes 2011, 2014; Grenfell 1998; Paxe 2009). However, despite his charisma and ability to rally Angolans, Toko refused to take part in the military upheaval and often publicly accused the UPA, the MPLA, and other groups of being assassins. After independence and the installation of the militant atheism regime, Toko's stance triggered an active repression of the movement, resulting in a ban on its public manifestation and the constant imprisonment of Toko and other main leaders of the church. A few years later, in 1979, when Tokoists refused to prolong the mourning period for Agostinho Neto, the police and army took revenge on them, with several narratives of arrests and torture.[20]

Apart from the imposition of an anti-religious policy, Angolan atheism also materialized through active enforcement in educational settings. Schools and other public organizations thus became ideal channels through which such ideologies were conveyed. These included the OPA[21] and the army, which cultivated slogans that depicted Angolan citizens as revolutionaries. In this framework, murals in public institutions (hospitals, schools, factories, warehouses) and military units were instruments of a pedagogical campaign that sought to popularize revolutionary slogans. Today, one can still appreciate this, for instance, in the murals of the Hospital Militar in Luanda (fig. 1).

Indeed, the constant elevation of the political and ideological engagement of activists, intellectuals, and Angolans in general, through the dissemination of the guidelines and objectives of the MPLA, became a priority in the party and the government. It is in this context that the escolas do partido (party schools) were created to replace both the centros de instrução revolucionária (revolutionary instruction centers), which were initiated during the liberation struggle in the maquis (areas of refuge occupied by the revolutionaries during the liberation war), and the escolas de formação de quadros, which were established shortly after independence. The escolas do partido were intended to train and equip the militants using the revolutionary principles of Marxist-Leninist ideology and to shape political activists (Neto 1977; Paxe 2009), as well as to instruct staff members of the party and the government on the principles of scientific socialism and proletarian internationalism. In the opinion of MPLA ideologues, these frameworks would ensure the structuration of the party and the purity of Marxism-Leninism thought against any misrepresentations. The party schools thus became new models of schooling that refashioned the colonial educational system that had been implemented in the 1960s (Soares 2002). The goal was to elevate forward-thinking political-ideological and cultural knowledge while combating manifestations of reactionary ideologies, such as tribalism, religion, regionalism, and racism. In this vein of reproduction of 'social ontology', information was identified as a key element in the formation of the militants' socialist consciousness. Complementing the political activity of the MPLA, and under its guidance, radio broadcasts, television programs, and the press were charged with mobilizing, training, and educating the Angolan people concerning the objectives of the socialist revolution.

The content and practice of the educational system resulting from the education policy established by the MPLA, whose guidelines corresponded to its project of social change, seem to be the locus of such processes of translation. The 'people's school' that stemmed from this policy quickly became an instrument of ideological homogenization of ethnic, racial, and social differences (see Vieira 2007: 109). Every educational activity was developed amid revolutionary fervor, in remembrance of Ngangula,[22] and the New Man

FIGURE 1 Murals in the Hospital Militar in Luanda

resulting from this schooling would be someone who cultivated values such as *amor à patria* (love of one's country) and "fidelity to the principles of the revolution" (ibid.: 110). In this way, socialism would be effectively built through instruction. We cite as an example a letter addressed to the board of the *Jornal de Angola*, the official national newspaper. Written by a school-teacher, the letter indignantly questions the incongruence between what was reproduced in official and religious education in Angola: "How will we create a man to serve the people and the revolution with false religious ideas? If I agree with the church, will I not be contradicting the history of Angola? Will I not be lying to our children?" Such a concern (and disconcertment) over the pragmatics and practicalities of atheist didactics also reveals, however, the mobilizing strength behind the MPLA's project of personal and collective transformation in 1970s Angola.

Thus, we observe a straightforward conjunction between the MPLA's onto-logical project and the rejection of religion. Militant atheism became a 'test' over the level of commitment and sincerity of Angolan intellectuals. Aware that not all partisan militants were totally 'free' from religion, the MPLA simultane-ously promoted an ethics of self-exigency—hence the well-known motto "É do MPLA quem merece e não quem quer" (You must deserve to be MPLA, want-ing is not enough)—and a pragmatic selectivity whereby only those religions whose ideology did not incorporate references to the project of constructing the New Man and the socialist society were to be repressed (Neto 1977; Paxe 2009). Such was the case, for instance, with the Tokoists and Jehovah's Wit-nesses, but not the Methodist churches.

Conclusion: Atheist Legacies in Contemporary Angola

Despite the active anti-religious stances described above, today it seems that atheism has somewhat disappeared from the Angolan public sphere. In its place are new vocabularies that point to a reappropriation of the religious phenom-enon (i.e., coll]aboration, partnerships, strategic collaboration, etc.). There is also a conformation of religious ideals to political ideals, where both state and churches actively work together to promote peace building and other social welfare activities (Comerford 2005). This is not the product of a sudden change but instead a prolonged 'pragmatic turn' initiated in the 1980s, after the current president, José Eduardo dos Santos, assumed office in September 1979. Santos sponsored a politico-juridical revision that progressively recognized religious movements and eventually granted them social control, producing what has been described as a situation of 'religious proliferation' (Fernando 2010; Viegas 2007), in which religious practice and discourse now occupy a significant place in the media and landscape.

This proliferation, however, has occurred not simply as a consequence of the juridical revision associated with the Santos leadership's pragmatic and centralizing governance (J. Schubert 2014). It has also come about due to an acknowledgment that the state-sponsored atheism of the late 1970s was not entirely successful in its objective to repress religious activity. In fact, it produced divergent ways of 'being religious' in Angola. Some people aligned with the political project, while others became martyrs as a result of their resilient and confrontational stance toward the atheist policy (Blanes 2014).

In any case, this pragmatic turn, also framed by the demise of the Soviet bloc and the introduction of important legislative changes in 1992,[23] has seen not only the retreat of explicit anti-religious policies but also the waning of a specific atheist, anti-religious jargon in the political sphere. However, one thing that is evident in Angola today is the continuation of the progressive, modernizing New Man discourse and the strong ideological investment in education as an instrument for the formation of collective consciousnesses, with an outlook toward a nationalist utopia. If one can argue that Angolan politics has become post-ideological, as in the Soviet case (Luehrmann 2011), in the aftermath of the Angolan revolution and war one can still observe certain legacies in action. These legacies, we argue, have been subsumed within a wider framework of post-war, forward-looking modernist utopias (Jameson 2005) and have become the grounds upon which those goals are nurtured. From this perspective, the ontological quality of atheist thinking that was promoted in post-independence Angola has become the narrative substance for a new configuration of nationhood in which religion is no longer viewed as a vestige of colonialism but as a space of potentiality.

This transition exemplifies how the story of atheism and godlessness in Angola is very much a product of the historical and political moment, where certain trajectories informed its ideological formation and consequent transformation into specific practices. Within this recognition, one can speculate that, as part of the political sphere, atheism emerges mostly as a narrative construction, inserted within wider processes of political thinking governance.

Acknowledgments

The authors would like to thank the elders Avelino Paxe, Cordeiro, Pedro Sozinho, Mateus, Antônio, A. Paxe, M. Paxe, Silva, Almeida, Antônio e Sousa, Neves Álvaro, Maturino Nzila, Benção Kitunga, and Paracleto Mumbela.

Ruy Llera Blanes, who received his PhD from the University of Lisbon in 2007, is a Ramon y Cajal fellow at the Spanish National Research Council (CSIC). His current research site is Angola, where he is working on the topics of religion, mobility (diasporas, transnationalism, the Atlantic), politics (leadership, charisma, repression, resistance), temporalities (historicity, memory, heritage, expectations), and knowledge. He is also co-editor of the journal *Religion and Society: Advances in Research*.

Abel Paxe received his MA from the Center of African Studies, ISCTE-IUL, Lisbon, in 2009. His MA thesis was on social resilience in northern Angola. He is also a researcher for the project titled "Reconciliation and Social Conflict in the Aftermath of Large-Scale Violence in Southern Africa: The Cases of Angola and Namibia," funded by the Volkswagen-Stiftung, Germany. He is currently a researcher at the Institute of Social Sciences and International Relations in Luanda. He has been conducting research on Angolan religion since 2005.

Notes

1. Movimento Popular de Libertação de Angola (MPLA, Popular Movement for the Liberation of Angola).
2. Although the list of references could be lengthy, on the topic of African Christianities see Kollman (2010a, 2010b). Interestingly, much of the recent literature on religion in Africa has focused on its political components (e.g., Ellis and ter Haar 2004; Marshall 2009; Mudimbe 1997). We propose that the reader keep this in mind for what remains of this chapter.
3. Frente de Libertação de Moçambique (FRELIMO, Mozambique Liberation Front).
4. União Nacional para a Independência Total de Angola (UNITA, National Union for the Total Independence of Angola).
5. Frente Nacional de Libertação de Angola (FNLA, National Liberation Front of Angola).
6. The Liga Nacional Africana (National African League) was a socio-cultural association created in Luanda in the 1920s for the colonial and native elites of the colony (see Castelo 2005; Rodrigues 2003).
7. The Casa dos Estudantes do Império (House of Students of the Empire) was a government-sponsored organization based in Lisbon that provided housing and served as a meeting point for the minority of African students who had Portuguese citizenship. It was closed in 1965 by the Portuguese government after being pronounced subversive.
8. The Movimento de União Democrática (MUD, Movement of Democratic Union) was a political organization that fought Salazar's Estado Novo regime in Portugal starting in 1945.
9. Polícia Internacional de Defesa do Estado (PIDE, International Police for the Defense of the State).
10. Partido da Luta Unida dos Povos Africanos (PLUA, Party for the United Struggle of the African Peoples).
11. Partido Democrático de Angola (PDA, Angolan Democratic Party).

12. In 1975, after 14 years of military combat and the retreat of the Portuguese troops (motivated by the April 1974 Carnation Revolution that took place in Lisbon), Angola finally achieved independence. This opened a round of negotiations between the main parties involved in the liberation campaigns—the MPLA, UNITA, and FNLA. But the agreements settled with the Portuguese government in Alvor on 15 January 1975 did not translate into a peaceful change of regime. Soon after, the three parties began a civil war that lasted until 2002.

13. Both authors of this chapter have made this argument concerning the Tokoist Church (Blanes 2014; Paxe 2009).

14. Deolinda Rodrigues, a cousin of Agostinho Neto, was a guerrilla and an activist who fought against the Portuguese regime for the MPLA. She was murdered in 1968, allegedly in a prison run by the FNLA, and is remembered today as one of the great martyrs of the independence struggle.

15. Another case in point is Roberto de Almeida, who was a member of the Departamento de Informação e Propaganda (DIP, Department of Information and Propaganda), the agency in charge of conceiving and applying the anti-religious policies.

16. These publications include Lenin's April Theses, a series of directives published in 1917 in the Bolshevik newspaper *Pravda*, and other books produced in the wake of the Russian Revolution.

17. One particular episode marked the development of state affairs in what concerned, among many other things, religion. Known as *fraccionismo* (fractionism), it was an attempted (and failed) coup d'état led by one of the MPLA leaders, Nito Alves, against Neto on 26 May 1977, after which a significant and violent purge took place within the MPLA, ending in the expulsion or disappearance of the party's main ideologues (see, e.g., Mateus and Mateus 2007; Tali 2010). This resulted in an ideological shift that introduced a pragmatic, literalist appropriation of the Marxist-Leninist theses, including the concept of 'privatized religion' and its consequent removal from partisan ideology.

18. People's Republic of Angola Constitutional Law, Articles No. 5 and No. 13.

19. Organização da Mulher Angolana (OMA, Organization of the Angolan Woman), a civil organization connected to the MPLA.

20. Personal histories are also involved here. As a historical curiosity, both Toko and Neto were fellow students in their high school days in the Liceu Salvador Correia in 1930s Luanda (see Kisela 2004). A gifted student in the Kibokolo mission where he grew up, Toko was sent by the Baptist missionaries to Luanda to complete his secondary schooling. During this period, he stayed in Neto's father's house. This, however, did not prevent the two leaders from becoming estranged during the process of independence, when Toko was seen as a public leader who did not convey the same version of nationalism as proposed by the MPLA.

21. Organização do Pioneiro Angolano (OPA, Organization of the Angolan Pioneer), known after 1991 as Organização do Pioneiro Agostinho Neto (Organization of the Pioneer Agostinho Neto).

22. Augusto Ngangula, a young boy killed by Portuguese troops, is remembered today as a martyr and pioneer of Angolan nationalism (see Tuta 2011).

23. The most important of these legislative changes include the introduction of a multi-party political system and the diversification of economic and diplomatic networks (see, e.g., Chabal and Vidal 2007; Messiant 2008, 2009).

References

Balandier, Georges. 1955. *Sociologie actuelle de l'Afrique noire*. Paris: Presses Universitaires de France.

Benjamin, Walter. 1968. *Illuminations: Essays and Reflections*. New York: Schocken Books.

Biney, Ama. 2011. *The Political and Social Thought of Kwame Nkrumah*. New York: Palgrave Macmillan.

Birmingham, David. 1992. *Frontline Nationalism in Angola and Mozambique*. London: James Currey.

Bittencourt, Marcelo. 1997. "A Criação do MPLA." *Estudos Afro-Asiáticos* 32: 185–208.

Bittencourt, Marcelo. 2010. *Estamos Juntos: O MPLA e a Luta Anticolonial*. 2 vols. Luanda: Kilombelombe.

Blanes, Ruy L. 2011. "Unstable Biographies: The Ethnography of Memory and Historicity in an Angolan Prophetic Movement." *History and Anthropology* 22, no. 1: 93–119.

Blanes, Ruy L. 2012. "O Tempo dos Inimigos: Notas para uma antropologia da repressão no século XXI." *Horizontes Antropológicos* 18, no. 37: 261–284.

Blanes, Ruy L. 2014. *A Prophetic Trajectory: Ideologies of Place, Time and Belonging in an Angolan Religious Movement*. New York: Berghahn Books.

Bragança, Aquino, and Immanuel Wallerstein, eds. 1982. *The African Liberation Reader*. Vol. 1: *The Anatomy of Colonialism*. London: Zed Press.

Bridgland, Fred. 1986. *Jonas Savimbi: A Key to Africa*. Edinburgh: Mainstream Publishing.

Brockway, Fenner. 1963. *African Socialism*. London: Bodley Head.

Castelo, Claudia. 2005. *Passagens para África: O Povoamento de Angola e Moçambique com Naturais d Metrópole (1920–1974)*. Porto: Afrontamento.

Centro de Estudos Angolanos. 1965. *História de Angola*. Porto: Edicoes Afrontamento.

Chabal, Patrick, and Nuno Vidal, eds. 2007. *Angola: The Weight of History*. New York: Columbia University Press.

Chicoadão. 2002. *Angola Ontem! Cronologia de Passos a Caminho da Libertação*. Luanda: Nzila.

Comerford, Michael. 2005. *O Rosto Pacífico de Angola: Biografia de um Processo de Paz*. Luanda: Edição de Autor.

Crahan, Margaret E. 1979. "Salvation through Christ or Marx: Religion in Revolutionary Cuba." *Journal of Interamerican Studies and World Affairs* 21, no. 1: 156–184.

Davie, Grace. 1999. "Europe: The Exception That Proves the Rule?" Pp. 65–83 in *The Desecularization of the World*, ed. Peter Berger. Grand Rapids, MI: Eerdmans.

Donham, Donald. 1999. *Marxist Modern: An Ethnographic History of the Ethiopian Revolution*. Berkeley: University of California Press.

Ellis, Stephen, and Gerrie ter Haar. 2004. *Worlds of Power: Religious Thought and Political Practice in Africa*. London: Hurst.

Fernando, Manuel. 2010. *As Religiões em Angola: A Realidade do Período Pós Independência (1975–2010)*. Luanda: INAR.

Freston, Paul. 2001. *Evangelicals and Politics in Asia, Africa and Latin America*. Cambridge: Cambridge University Press.

Friedland, William, and Carl G. Rosberg, Jr. 1964. *African Socialism*. Stanford, CA: Stanford University Press.

Froese, Paul. 2004. "Forced Secularization in Soviet Russia: Why an Atheistic Monopoly Failed." *Journal for the Scientific Study of Religion* 43, no. 1: 35–50.

Geroulanos, Stefanos. 2010. *An Atheism That Is Not Humanist Emerges in French Thought*. Stanford, CA: Stanford University Press.

Grenfell, F. James. 1998. "Simão Toco: An Angolan Prophet." *Journal of Religion in Africa* 28, no. 2: 210–226.

Hecht, Jennifer M. 2003. *The End of the Soul: Scientific Modernity, Atheism, and Anthropology in France.* New York: Columbia University Press.

Henderson, Lawrence. 1990. *A Igreja em Angola.* Lisbon: Editorial Além-Mar.

Jameson, Fredric. 2005. *Archaeologies of the Future: The Desire Called Utopia and Other Science Fictions.* London: Verso.

Jenkins, Philip. 2006. *The New Faces of Christianity: Believing the Bible in the Global South.* Oxford: Oxford University Press.

Johnstone, Patrick. 1993. *Operation World.* Grand Rapids, MI: Zondervan.

Kisela, Joaquim A. 2004. *Simão Toco: A Trajectória de um Homem de Paz.* Luanda: Nzila.

Kollman, Paul. 2010a. "Classifying African Christianities: The Anthropology of Christianity and Generations of African Christians." *Journal of Religion in Africa* 40, no. 2: 118–148.

Kollman, Paul. 2010b. "Classifying African Christianities: Past, Present, and Future: Part One." *Journal of Religion in Africa* 40, no. 1: 3–32.

Luehrmann, Sonja. 2011. *Secularism Soviet Style: Teaching Atheism and Religion in a Volga Republic.* Bloomington: Indiana University Press.

Marcum, John. 1969. *The Angolan Revolution: The Anatomy of an Explosion (1950–1962).* Cambridge, MA: MIT Press.

Marcum, John. 1978. *The Angolan Revolution: Exile Politics and Guerrilla Warfare (1962–1976).* Cambridge, MA: MIT Press.

Marshall, Ruth. 2009. *Political Spiritualities. The Pentecostal Revolution in Nigeria.* Chicago: University of Chicago Press.

Mateus, Dalila, and Álvaro Mateus. 2007. *Purga em Angola.* Lisbon: ASA.

Mazrui, Ali, and Christophe Wondji, eds. 2010. *História Geral da África.* Vol. 8: *África desde 1935.* Brasília: UNESCO.

McClendon, John H., III. 2012. "Nkrumah's Consciencism: Philosophical Materialism and the Issue of Atheism Revisited." *Journal on African Philosophy* 4. http://www.africaknowledgeproject.org/index.php/jap/article/view/1644.

Messiant, Christine. 2008. *L'Angola postcolonial.* Vol. 1: *Guerre et paix sans démocratisation.* Paris: Karthala.

Messiant, Christine. 2009. *L'Angola postcolonial.* Vol. 2: *Sociologie politique d'une oléocratie.* Paris: Karthala.

Morier-Genoud, Eric. 1996. *Of God and Caesar: The Relation between Christian Churches and the State in Post-colonial Mozambique, 1974–1981.* Basel: Klauspeter Blaser.

MPLA (Popular Movement for the Liberation of Angola). 1975. *História de Angola.* Porto: Edições Afrontamento.

Mudimbe, Valentin. 1997. *Tales of Faith: Religion as Political Performance in Central Africa.* London: Athlone Press.

Neto, Agostinho. 1977. *Relatório do 1º Comité Central do MPLA.* Lisbon: Edições Avante.

Nkrumah, Kwame. 1970. *Consciencism: Philosophy and Ideology for Decolonization.* New York: Monthly Review Press.

Paredes, Margarida. 2011. "Deolinda Rodrigues, da Família Metodista à Família MPLA, O Papel da Cultura na Política." *Caderno de Estudos Africanos* 20: 11–26.

Paxe, Abel. 2009. "Dinâmicas de Resiliência Social nos Dircursos e Práticas Tokoistas no Icolo e Bengo." MA thesis, ISCTE-IUL.

Péclard, Didier. 1998. "Religion and Politics in Angola: The Church, the Colonial State and the Emergence of Angolan Nationalism, 1940–1961." *Journal of Religion in Africa* 28, no. 2: 160–186.

Pélissier, René. 1978. "A la recherche d'un dieu anti-colonialiste." Pp. 159–189 in *La colonie du minotaure: Nationalismes et révoltes en Angola (1926–1961)*. Orgeval: Éditions Pélissier.

Reis, Fidel. 2010. "Das Políticas de Classificação às Classificações Políticas (1950 1996): A Configuração do Campo Político Angolano. Contributo para o Estudo das Relações Raciais em Angola." PhD diss., ISCTE-IUL.

Rocha, Edmundo. 2003. *Contribuição ao Estudo da Génese do Nacionalismo Moderno Angolano: Período de 1950–1964: Testemunho e estudo documental*. Luanda: Kilombelombe.

Rodrigues, Eugénia. 2003. *A Geração Silenciada: A Liga Nacional Africana e a representação do branco em Angola na década de 30*. Porto: Afrontamento.

Rotberg, Robert, and Ali Mazrui, eds. 1970. *Protest and Power in Black Africa*. New York: Oxford University Press.

Santos, Eduardo dos. 1966. "Sobre o Comunismo e Tribalismo Banto." *Boletim do Instituto de Angola* 24–25: 41–62.

Schubert, Benedict. 1999. "Os protestantes na guerra angolana depois da independência." *Lusotopie*: 405–413.

Schubert, Benedict. 2000. *A Guerra e as Igrejas: Angola, 1961–1991*. Bern: P. Schlettwein.

Schubert, Jon. 2014. "'Working the System': Affect, Amnesia and the Aesthetics of Power in the 'New Angola.'" PhD diss., University of Edinburgh.

Serrano, Carlos. 2008. *Angola: Nascimento de uma Nação: Um estudo sobre a construção da identidade nacional*. Luanda: Kilombelembe.

Soares, Amadeu C. 2002. "Levar a Escola à Sanzala: Plano de Ensino Primário Rural em Angola 1961-2." *Episteme* 4, no. 10–11–12: 133–164.

Strenski, Ivan. 2010. *Why Politics Can't Be Freed from Religion*. Oxford: Wiley-Blackwell.

Tali, Jean-Michel M. 2000. *O MPLA Perante Si Próprio (1962–1977): Ensaio de História Política*. Vol. 1. Luanda: Nzila.

Tali, Jean-Michel M. 2010. *O MPLA Perante Si Próprio (1962–1977): Ensaio de História Política*. Vol. 2. Luanda: Nzila.

Taylor, Charles. 2007. *A Secular Age*. Cambridge, MA: Belknap Press.

Toan, Tran van. 2010. "A Breath of Atheism in Religious Vietnam." *Social Compass* 57, no. 3: 311–318.

Tshishiku, Tshibangu, Ade Ajayi, and Lamin Sanneh. 2010. "Religião e Revolução Social." Pp. 605–629 in Mazrui and Wondji 2010.

Tuta, Francisco. 2011. *A História do Pioneiro Heróico Augusto Ngangula*. Luanda: Edição de Autor.

Viegas, Fátima. 2007. *Panorama das Religiões em Angola: Dados Estatísticos 2007*. Luanda: Instituto Nacional para os Assuntos Religiosos.

Vieira, Laurindo. 2007. *Angola: A Dimensão Ideológica da Educação 1975–1992*. Luanda: Nzila.

Vries, Hent de, and Lawrence Sullivan, eds. 2006. *Political Theologies: Public Religions in a Post-Secular World*. New York: Fordham University Press.

Watkin, Christopher. 2011. *Difficult Atheism: Post-Theological Thinking in Alain Badiou, Jean-Luc Nancy and Quentin Meillassoux*. Edinburgh: Edinburgh University Press.

Zuckerman, Philip. 2006. "Atheism: Contemporary Numbers and Patterns." Pp. 47–68 in *The Cambridge Companion to Atheism*, ed. Michael Martin. Cambridge: Cambridge University Press.

Chapter 4

FORGET DAWKINS
Notes toward an Ethnography of Religious Belief
and Doubt

Paul-François Tremlett and Fang-Long Shih

This chapter has been written to engage with the phenomenon of New Atheism, here treated as a discourse (Foucault 1981). We assume that New Atheism constitutes a series of discrete strategies and styles of argument and refutation that have proliferated across a range of media for talking about religion.[1] Initially associated with a certain limited corpus of semi-academic and polemical writings by Richard Dawkins (2006), Daniel Dennett (2007), Christopher Hitchens (2007), and Sam Harris (2005), there is already talk of a 'New New Atheism' (Beha 2012). In this chapter, when we use the term 'New Atheist discourse', we will be referring exclusively to the initial texts by Dawkins, Dennett, Hitchens, and Harris.

New Atheist discourse is marked by a binary logic that opposes religion to science, belief to doubt, and a pre-modern past to a modern present. It is suggestive of a temporal sensibility and attitude toward being modern that strike us as something of a 'survival' or remnant of late-nineteenth-century anthropology, where religious belief and a pre-modern past were sutured together in

Notes for this chapter begin on page 94.

opposition to science and a modern present. We will problematize this binary logic of New Atheist discourse as a point of departure for a critical analysis of the manner in which New Atheist discourse stages belief and doubt. In particular, we will counter the New Atheist assumption that doubt and belief represent private, cognitive acts. By way of a response, we offer two ethnographic vignettes—one from the Philippines and another from Taiwan—to argue that religion is not a matter of private or mental belief or doubt but rather a matter of public action and practice in which believing and doubting are constituted socially and dialogically.

The Timeliness of Being Modern

Classical social theory was fabricated around a series of binary oppositions that contrasted the despotic and irrational mire of cultural and religious authority with the emergence of a new rational, knowing subject, heroically overcoming illusion to free itself (indeed, *him*self) from the fossilized accretions of tradition, culture, and religion. This evolutionist narrative of progress, which purported to describe the incremental accumulation of knowledge, freedom, self-mastery, and control, was constitutive of late-nineteenth- and early-twentieth-century accounts of religion. From Tylor (1903) to Freud ([1913] 2001), a concept of human development emerged in which religion was a strange belief that had grown in the midst of humanity's savage origins and groping attempts to understand the world (see Brickman 2003; Needham 1972; Stocking 1987). A fundamental feature of this kind of thinking about religion was its confidence that religious beliefs would be fatally undermined by the advance of science. The best part of a century later—although without reference to their esteemed forebears or to the critiques that saw Tylorean and Freudian evolutionary analyses of religion shelved by the social sciences—New Atheists seem intent on reviving this evolutionist approach. In a review of Dawkins's (2006) *The God Delusion,* Terry Eagleton (2006) concludes that Dawkins "turns out to be an old-fashioned Hegelian ... believing in a zeitgeist (his own term) involving ever increasing progress, with just the occasional 'reversal.'"[2]

In common, then, with earlier precedents, New Atheist discourse approaches religion in terms of a quaint notion of progress and as beliefs about events and entities that contradict the best accounts of the world delivered by several centuries of scientific discovery. To be sure, even though evolutionist accounts of religion have fallen from anthropological grace, the interest in belief—and specifically in religious belief as a representation (or not) of a state of affairs in the world—continues as a rich vein of ethnographic inquiry. This is best exemplified today by the work of Pascal Boyer (2001), which, it should be added, is cited approvingly by Dawkins (2006: 206–207) and Dennett (2007: 105–107) (see also Luhrmann 1994; B. R. Wilson 1970). A key feature of this approach, as it is articulated in New Atheist discourse, is that just as a scientific claim must stand or fall by virtue of its correspondence with a 'real' world 'out there', the same must apply for a religious claim. It is on this basis that Dawkins (2006: 24) states that belief in God, or what he calls 'the God Hypothesis', "is a scientific hypothesis about the universe," which suggests that the "reality we inhabit ... contains a supernatural agent who designed the universe and—at least in many versions of the hypothesis—maintains it and even intervenes in it with miracles, which are temporary violations of his own otherwise grandly immutable laws" (ibid.: 81–82). For New Atheist discourse, religious beliefs are, in effect, theories or hypotheses about the world. Therefore, to believe in God or an associated entity or event is to believe something about the world. According to Harris (2005: 63):

> It should be clear that if a person believes in God because he has had certain spiritual experiences, or because the Bible makes so much sense, or because he trusts the authority of the church, he is playing the same game of justification that we all play when claiming to know the most ordinary facts. This is probably a conclusion that many religious believers will want to resist; but resistance is not only futile but *incoherent*. There is simply no other logical space for our beliefs about the world to occupy. As long as religious propositions purport to be about the way the world is ... they must stand in relation to the world, and to our beliefs about it. And it is only by being so situated that propositions of this sort can influence our subsequent thinking or behavior. As long as a person maintains that his beliefs represent an actual state of the world (visible or invisible; spiritual or mundane), he must believe that his beliefs are a *consequence* of the way the world is. This, by definition, leaves him vulnerable to new evidence. Indeed, if there were no conceivable change in the world that could get a person to question his religious beliefs, this would prove that his beliefs were not predicated upon his taking any state of the world into account. He could not claim, therefore, to be *representing* the world at all.

Although the above provides a sense of how New Atheist discourse sets up religious claims so that they can be treated as scientific claims and therefore be subject to rigorous critical scrutiny, there are three things it does not capture: first, the New Atheist conviction that religion can be defined solely in terms of beliefs about special entities and miraculous events; second, the more general representation of religion as uncritical belief and scientifically informed atheism as critical doubt; and, third, the idea that doubt about religion can only come from outside religion because religious belief is the antithesis of the reflexive, critical, rational spirit that lies behind all genuinely scientific inquiry. Let us take each of these in turn.

The 'defining religion in terms of belief' debate has been around in the study of religion at least since Tylor and has rumbled on ever since. One of the reasons for maintaining that religion really does refer to specific, private mental events called beliefs is to ensure that the word 'religion' denotes a specific class of cognitive acts about deities, ghosts, or demons. Unfortunately, while the positivists are happy with this solution because it preserves the sense that the word 'religion' actually designates a distinctive class of phenomena, it obscures the fact that a great deal of religion has absolutely nothing to do with beliefs, deities, ghosts, or demons—or ontological claims at all (Laidlaw 2007: 222–225).

In short, defining religion substantively in terms of belief is all very well, but most scholars of religion would agree that there are numerous possible types of definition, including substantive, functional, and polythetic (B. C. Wilson 1998), and these are usually deployed strategically to open out particular research questions about religions rather than because anyone actually thinks a definition of religion is a plausible or even desirable objective.

Nevertheless, New Atheist discourse goes to considerable lengths to characterize religious belief as a particularly powerful class of mental events. "A belief," says Harris (2005: 12), "is a lever that, once pulled, moves almost everything else in a person's life." Hitchens (2007: 5), distinguishing between science and religion, states: "And here is the point, about myself and my co-thinkers. Our belief is not a belief. Our principles are not a faith. We do not rely solely upon science and reason, because these are necessary rather than sufficient factors, but we distrust anything that contradicts science or outrages reason. We may differ on many things, but what we respect is free inquiry, open-mindedness, and the pursuit of ideas for their own sake. We do not hold our convictions dogmatically." A contrast is set up between 'open-minded', science-informed, and evidence-based reason, on the one hand, and 'dogmatic' religion, on the other. New Atheist doubt thus appears as a kind of polar opposite to the default cognitive disposition of the religious to believe. But what kind of doubt does New Atheist discourse in fact set in motion? And what kind of belief?

According to Dennett (2007: 17), "The spell that I say *must* be broken is the taboo against a forthright, scientific, no-holds-barred investigation of religion as one natural phenomenon among many." In his discussion of Descartes' ([1637] 1968: 53–54) method of doubt, Pelkmans (2013: 7) describes it as "artificially staging doubt" because this is doubt where the consequences of its initiation are already known in advance, just as it was for Descartes ([1637] 1968: 95), who, despite claiming that "I shall apply myself seriously and freely to the general destruction of all my former opinions," in fact only used doubt to prove what he already (thought he) knew. Furthermore, if New Atheist discourse sets up doubt as a private and heroic cognitive act, it does exactly the same for belief. Belief and doubt turn out not to be opposed but mutually implicated cognitive acts that are reduced by New Atheist discourse to a matter of a 'rational choice' between competing and mutually exclusive arguments.

We would contend that neither religion nor science-inspired atheism are much like the caricatures generated by New Atheist discourse. Too much is omitted. For example, there is no Thomas Kuhn or Paul Feyerabend or Bruno Latour in New Atheists' representations of science, its histories, and the debates about methods, and there is little or no apparent familiarity with over a century of rigorous, empirical study of religions by philologists, sociologists, historians, and anthropologists, among others. In particular, we argue that because New Atheist discourse takes the rational, cognizing individual as its point of departure, its critique of religion is seriously blunted, if not fatally undermined, by myriad forms of historical and ethnographic evidence. For example, the matter of modernity and its relationship to religion and the secular has never involved a simple choice between different propositions and competing evidence. If for

Tylor, Freud, and the New Atheists 'progress' means more accurate, scientific knowledge about the world, for Edward Said (1995) the narrative of progress was in fact a convenient ideological prop for Empire, legitimating the West's sense of itself as superior while framing the rest of the world as clients of its self-proclaimed munificence (see also King 1999). For Max Weber, "the narrative of modernity" envisioned "the increasing subordination of social life to the calculations of instrumental reason" (Tremlett 2011: 291) and unsettlingly signaled the eclipse of meaning by disenchantment and of freedom by the "iron cage" of capitalism (Weber [1905] 2002: 181).

Being modern and its consequences—for these debates and discussions have always been about what it means to be modern—remain uncertain and contested. And although the above is hardly a comprehensive overview of classical or post-colonial social theory or New Atheist discourse and the anthropology of religion, it serves to make the point that modernity does not simply describe a straightforward historical journey marked by progress in rationality and science and the emergence of the free and rational, heroic and probably gendered subject from the stupefying mire of religion. Rather, modernity is a complex network of layers and webs of meaning that intersect debates in sociology, political science, anthropology, religious studies, philosophy, and economics about the possibility of establishing enduring social relationships.

Both the Philippines and Taiwan underwent profound and protracted processes of economic, political, and cultural reform as a result of interventions by foreign powers that led to the embedding of what Talal Asad (2003: 25) describes as secular "behaviors, knowledges, and sensibilities." The rationalizations of Japanese and Chinese Nationalist Party colonialisms in Taiwan—like those of the Spanish and the Americans in the Philippines—were certainly instrumental in urbanizing and thereby recomposing previously dispersed rural populations and replacing environments of forest, coast, river, mountain, and plain with ones of brick, glass, concrete, and metal. But these new modern environments, with their accompanying dispositions, skills, virtues, knowledges, habits, and post-metaphysical justifications, were hardly accompanied by any major perturbations about religion (see, e.g., Shih 2006; Tremlett 2012). States and economies were bureaucratized, while exchange was monetized and education universalized. But atheism did not catch on, as one might have supposed it should have done if the New Atheists are right about history's hidden hand—reason. In what follows, we offer brief ethnographic accounts from the Philippines and from Taiwan that point not to belief and doubt as private acts but to their public constitution in debate, argument, and even struggle.

Astral Journeys, Possession, and Healing in the Filipino Countryside

Mount Banahaw is an extinct volcano widely known by Filipinos as a center and repository of spiritual power and potency. Since about 1840, it has been a center of pilgrimage and healing and a home to nationalist religious movements who venerate the country's 'national hero', José Rizal. Revolutionaries fighting both the Spanish and the Americans sheltered there, and in more recent years it has been associated with Communist/Maoist insurgents. More recently still, it has been linked to encounters with UFOs and to the so-called New Age religion. From 1999 to 2000 and in 2003, I (Tremlett) conducted fieldwork in and around Mount Banahaw with a *samahan* (association) located on its western lower slopes that called itself the Association of International Healers. Every Saturday evening they would congregate together at the home of their leader, Ka Erning, to engage in various 'spiritual' practices in preparation for the arrival of patients the following morning. These practices included 'astral journeys', possession, and prayer, as well as much discussion—over numerous cups of coffee, *merienda* (light meals), and cigarettes—about their spiritual experiences. News and gossip from members and guests alike touched on ailments, diseases, and conditions and what could be done to 'heal' or alleviate them.

The focus of the discussion in the first instance is on spiritual practices and the conversations that these precipitated. It is worth noting that these practices were constantly being revised and in some cases were abandoned and replaced with new ones. The ad hoc nature of these practices—which might be better formulated as 'exercises', given that they were designed to facilitate the group's accumulation of spiritual power and potency (*kapangyarihan*) for the purposes of healing—indicates one aspect of the group's reflexivity, although prayer and the moment at which Ka Erning would, as it were, distribute the power to his followers by pressing the tips of his fore- and middle fingers on specific parts of their bodies remained constant.

During my first stay with Ka Erning's *samahan*, I was invited to participate in an experiment to test the hypothesis that the Bible is a 'living' book. The experiment, a variation of the group's astral practice, involved sitting, randomly opening the Bible and resting it on one's legs, placing one's hands palms down on its pages, closing one's eyes and emptying one's mind of specific thoughts, and, essentially, 'seeing' what happened. The experiment, practice, or exercise lasted five minutes or so and was then repeated after a short interval. At the end, I, like the other group members, had to report back on what I had 'seen'. These reporting sessions generated important questions about subjective experience and its epistemological validity. For example, members typically reported a range of experiences from *wala* (nothing) to complex visions of biblical personages and landscapes, as well as journeys by air, over land, and underground. Perhaps taking a cue from me, one member even began bringing a notebook to record these experiences. The point was that while all the reports were regarded as having been offered with sincerity, they were not all necessarily believed to be factual accounts on a par with a statement like "your cigarettes are under your chair." Rather, the exercises were taken to point, somewhat loosely, toward the agency of the Bible—as a living book—to generate sometimes uncanny experiences but, more importantly, to aid the group in its accumulation of power for the purposes of healing. Ka Erning and his followers ascribed to subjective experiences layers of meaning rather than a series of correspondences leading from mental acts to words to actual states of affairs in the world. Moreover, belief in the power of the Bible was not so much belief in the specific, individual propositions or hypotheses it might be said to contain but instead a more generalized belief in the Bible's spiritual potency—its *kapangyarihan*. In short, this alleged object of power and its situatedness in the webs of relationships of the *samahan* authorized not any specific claim about the structure of reality but rather a set of relationships between Ka Erning and his followers and the *samahan* as a whole with the patients who sought healing.

These issues took on even greater significance with regard to another regular feature of the group's Saturday night meetings. On most weekends, Ka Erning's youngest son would go into trances during which he would become, for a short while, a channel for an entity such as the Santa Niño. These trances, which were often sudden, dramatic, and disturbing, were occasions when the group received knowledge, advice, and also admonishment. However, these performances also provoked considerable debate. Were they real or were they faked? Belief and doubt circled each other, not as heroic, private mental acts challenging potential deceptions and illusions, but as part of a social process of coming together to debate and engage in spiritual practices for the purposes of healing.

In the end, the healers of course had one very obvious means of measuring or testing their power and success—by keeping a tally of all those whom they had healed and all those for whom treatment had not been successful. But they kept no such records. Ka Erning and his followers understood very well that people get sick and die and that no amount of treatment, whatever the source, can stop it. Most of the patients who came to be healed had chronic conditions such as arthritis or renal or cardio-vascular problems, and most if not all of the patients were on prescription drugs of various kinds for their conditions. Healing was never thought about or understood—by either the healers or their patients—in miraculous terms or as a zero-sum game. Nobody expected to be cured in the sense of complete and immediate recovery. Everyone, however, expected to spend time with a healer, his family, and followers—sharing rice, tilapia, rambutan, coffee, *merienda*, and conversation—to be prayed for, and perhaps thereby to receive some small amelioration of his or her condition.

At the center of the kind of religiosity that is more or less ubiquitous in the Filipino countryside, in the doubtless hundreds of small undocumented *samahans* (see Love 1977) where the same or similar kinds of practices described above carry on, a key concept is *bisa* (efficacy), expressed pointedly as "Does it work?" This very practical and pragmatic point of departure highlights underlying currents of belief and doubt, including, for example, doubt about the epistemological validity of subjective experience and acknowledgment that the power to heal is severely constrained. Yet while doubt occasioned collective reflection on the limits of human reason and the implacability of the world to apparently good but nevertheless so often ill-fated human intervention, it remained, much like the spiritual practices and indeed its friend belief, ad hoc; that is, doubt was never tied down to any specific act or event. Rather, doubt and belief existed as elements of social interactions, not as individual cognitive acts. Thus, a notion such as *kapangyarihan* is not simply an ontological concept that implies a specific truth claim about the way the world is. *Kapangyarihan* means power and potency and implies relationships between persons and persons, persons and places, persons and objects, and persons and entities (Cannell 1999: 229–230). Those relationships are socially and culturally structured and thereby reproduce prevalent norms and values about power—how it should be displayed, the way that it should be exercised, the appropriate behavior in its presence, and so forth. Moreover, there is significant overlap, if not identity, between these norms across religious and secular domains. The point is that in the Philippines religion cannot be conceptualized persuasively in terms of private assent to or dissent from any particular series of hypotheses or propositional claims about the world. It is a social practice that implies instead co-embeddedness within certain socially and culturally encoded norms and structures of conduct.

Predicting the Future of the Fourth Nuclear Power Plant in Taiwan

Religion in Taiwan is deeply embedded within society. It is not so much a matter of individuals or belief as it is of practice and *ling* 靈, the power of efficacy possessed by spirits and gods/goddesses. These deities are typically anthropomorphic in form and identified as the spirits of former human beings who lived notable lives (Shih 2010: 237). However, while *ling* does indeed imply a particular idea of reality, it is rarely if ever discussed in this way. *Ling* or efficacious power is instead recognized through its social dimensions, because power is always about social relationships and it is through relationships that power articulates and circulates. According to P. Steven Sangren (1987: 131), *ling* underlies "the logic of relations among religious symbols" and is "both a product and a generator of the social relations reproduced in ritual activity." The question is, if religion in Taiwan is primarily about practice and fundamentally social in character, where does that leave concepts such as belief and doubt?

The ethnographic example examined here relates to the *ling* of the 'anti-nuclear power goddess Mazu' 反核媽祖 in Ren-he Temple 仁和宮 and her relationship with the anti-nuclear power campaign. Ren-he Temple is situated adjacent to the site of Taiwan's fourth nuclear power plant, which is located on the northeast coast of Taiwan at a place known to local people as Yanliao 鹽寮 in Gongliao District 貢寮區. This nuclear plant has only recently been built after three decades of controversy. By contrast, Mazu, as goddess of the sea, has been the patron deity of the people of Gongliao for almost 200 years. Gongliao neighborhood is patterned mainly by fishing networks, which have further affected the cultural construction of Mazu worship: the goddess is asked for aid when fishermen are lost at sea or at times of similar distress. Ren-he Temple was built in 1821, and its continuous expansion implies that Mazu's *ling* has been efficacious in responding to the requests of individual villagers as well as the community as a whole (Ren-he Temple Management Committee

2004). In the past 30 years, the people of Gongliao have looked to Mazu's *ling* to empower their campaign against the fourth nuclear power plant. My (Shih's) field research was conducted in and around Ren-he Temple in the autumn of 2010 and in the summers of 2011 and 2012.

Following the lifting of martial law in Taiwan in 1987, pro- and anti-nuclear campaigning was consolidated along political party lines: the ruling Chinese Nationalist Party (KMT) favored nuclear power, while the new opposition party, the Democratic Progressive Party (DPP), opposed it. The Yanliao Anti-Nuclear Self-Defense Association 鹽寮反核自救會, created in 1988, worked closely with the DPP in a way that mutually empowered their political ambitions. However, after achieving presidential office in 2000, the DPP reneged on its electoral promise to shut down work on the plant, citing economic and legal reasons and the extreme expense that would be involved.[3] This resulted in the end of what might in retrospect be identified as the first stage of the Gongliao anti-nuclear campaign (1988–2000), described by Ming-Sho Ho (2003: 683) as a "party-dependent movement." After the KMT returned to presidential office in 2008, construction on the fourth plant was speeded up, and the work was completed in early 2010.

At the time of my first visit in 2010, the Gongliao anti-nuclear campaign had come back to life after almost a decade of inaction. Through my interviews I could tell that, over the previous 10 years, discussions of the anti-nuclear issue had turned to the DPP's perceived manipulation of the situation. Local people felt to various extents that they had been deceived or even betrayed by the DPP during its control of the presidency (2000–2008), and consequently they had become demoralized. It was difficult for Gongliao people to revive their campaign after the harmful political developments of 2000 and 2001, and they were now campaigning without support from any of Taiwan's political parties. I discovered that an alternative resource was being accessed by the local people to generate the power they needed—that is, their local goddess, Mazu of Ren-he Temple. In fact, Mazu had played a role in the anti-nuclear campaign from the very beginning, but it was not until its recent revival that she came to the forefront of the struggle (Shih 2012).

The focus of the discussion was the doubting—or, more precisely, the disbelieving—of a prediction made by Mazu at Ren-he Temple in 1988. Six days after the launch of the Yanliao Anti-Nuclear Self-Defense Association, members and villagers assembled in the yard of the Ren-he Temple to consolidate their campaign. However, prior to this assembly, the Association's committee, which was uncertain about the future of its anti-nuclear campaign, sent its three most senior members, who were also the most senior members of the Temple's committee, to consult the goddess Mazu. On behalf of the whole community, Mr. Wu Tian-fu, who was in his eighties, together with two assistants in their seventies, communicated with Mazu by casting *poe* 卜筊, also known as divination by using 'moon blocks'.

These divination blocks are cut into the shape of a crescent moon, rounded on one side and flat on the other. The procedure is explained in notices displayed at various temples: the diviner should hold out the blocks and raise them up to his or her forehead. He or she should make a proposition and then drop the blocks onto the floor. At the same time, the diviner should ask the deity for confirmation of the statement, saying, "If this is correct, please give me a *siu-poe* 顯筊." *Sui-poe* (affirmative *poe*) is one flat side down and one rounded side up, and it is taken to indicate agreement. The two other possible combinations are regarded as disconfirmations, although one is more emphatic than the other. If both blocks land flat side down, their lack of movement is understood to mean that the deity strongly disagrees with the proposition, and this position is called *im-poe* 陰筊 (disaffirmative *poe*). If both blocks land rounded side down, the way that they rock on the floor before coming to rest means that the deity is giving an equivocal answer because the statement was unclear, and this position is called *chhio-poe* 笑筊 (laughing *poe*). As such, the last two positions leave room for ambiguity in interpreting disagreement and thus are not taken very seriously. The process of casting the blocks therefore continues until a proposition is formulated that the deity will confirm as being the correct statement of point of view (see also Jordan 1972).

The three committee members involved had passed away before my field-work started, so I instead interviewed Mr. Wu Wen-tong, who was then the head of the Association and had witnessed the divination and the consequent announcement to the campaigners. The story I was told about the prediction made in 1988 can be summarized as follows:

> The first question that Mr. Wu Tian-fu asked was whether construction of the fourth plant would not be completed. This question did not receive an affirmative response for several castings. Mr. Wu then asked if the fourth plant *would* be built, and this time he obtained three affirmative responses.
>
> When this occurred, the committee members were dumbfounded, but Mr. Wu, who was very experienced in this kind of situation, then rephrased the question by asking whether the fourth plant would come into operation to generate electricity. This time, he did not receive an affirmative response for several castings. He then put the question in a different way, asking whether the plant would *not* be able to generate electricity. This time, he obtained three affirmative responses. (Compiled from several interviews; my translation)

After the divination, Mr. Wu Wen-tong was outside in the Temple's yard. He recalled that at the moment when Mr. Wu Tian-fu first announced Mazu's indication that the plant would be built, they were all shocked and subdued. However, when they further heard that the fourth plant at Gongliao would never be operated to generate electricity, they were relieved and became excited. Mr. Wu Wen-tong emphasized that at this time they did not take Mazu's indication as the basis for their campaign, and, after a few moments of excitement, they then moved on, as planned, to burn a truckload of free calendars in front of the main statue of the goddess Mazu. These calendars had been given out by the Taiwan Power Company, which was in charge of the construction of the fourth plant. This ritual burning was a public vow by the people of Gongliao that they would not be bribed by any agency with an interest in nuclear power.

It is interesting to note that the relationship of the campaigners to Mazu is not one of conforming to a religious authority, as is assumed in the New Atheist understanding of religion (Dawkins 2006: 27). Rather, the divination process of question and answer was a kind of playful back and forth between 'no' and 'yes', between disbelief/doubt and belief. Through this process, they were able to get the goddess to confirm an outcome that they wanted to believe in, while simultaneously believing that the fall of the *poe* was governed by the goddess's will. Whenever they received an answer they did not want, they experienced dismay and were reluctant to believe the goddess's prediction, and so they tried again and again by rephrasing the question until they received proof of the 'yes' confirmation they needed. In the 1988 divination, Mazu seemed to be indicating that the fourth plant at Gongliao would eventually be built, but that it would never be operated to generate electricity. Although this prediction offered encouragement, at that early stage it was not particularly relevant to the campaign, which had set stopping construction as its target and was working closely with the DPP to achieve this aim. Although at the time the campaign relied more on the political power of the opposition party, the goddess remained a part of it. For example, every year since the Association was founded, its members have participated in the annual Mazu pilgrimage, carrying a collection box that invariably receives enough donations to keep up the campaign during the coming year. The people of Gongliao say that the money raised is due to Mazu's blessing.

Furthermore, statues of the goddess Mazu have several times been carried by people from Gongliao around Taiwan as part of their demonstrations. One incident in particular is most often recalled among campaigners. This is the story of an event that occurred on 21 June 1993, during the KMT administration, when a statue of Mazu was brought by protestors from Ren-he Temple to the government's Parliament. The protestors broke through a police cordon, forced open the iron entrance gate, and made their way to the Parliament hall. Here, the statue was placed on a chair behind the speaker, so that the goddess could monitor the parliamentarians as they discussed increasing the budget for the fourth plant. The vote was disputed by the protestors and DPP parliamentarians and was nullified. However, the KMT later rescheduled the vote, and the funding for the fourth plant was subsequently passed on 10 July.[4] Interviewees during my field research emphasized that the budget had passed because the goddess was not present. They further stated that it was the goddess's *ling* that got them through the police cordon and the iron gate and that had initially nullifed the vote. It is worth noting in this context the importance of the public demonstration of Mazu's *ling* in the reassertion of her power.

At that time, the anti-nuclear power movement remained reliant on the DPP for support, and it went into decline when the DPP failed to halt construction of the fourth plant in 2000. In 2010, however, local people began to recall the first part of the prediction made in 1988, namely, that the fourth plant would eventually be built. This is the situation that is now being faced: the plant has been built, and once the safety tests have been completed, it could be operational. Technicians have been performing preliminary tests, resulting in a string of minor accidents, such as a fire, a power cut (see Guan and Mo 2010), some flooding, and even a small explosion. Moreover, in March 2011, the Fukushima earthquake, tsunami, and consequent nuclear disaster took place in Japan. These events contributed to a sense of anxiety about the safety of nuclear power and prompted a revival of the campaign to prevent the fourth plant from becoming operational. Many more campaigners have since begun to recall the second part of Mazu's prediction—that the fourth plant will never be operated to generate electricity. This is the hope and belief that is now being consolidated and spread via the new, current campaign. The post-2010 recall of the 1988 prediction suggests that Mazu's power—her *ling*—was recognized only once the social and political dimensions of her prediction had shifted. In contrast to the model of belief adopted by New Atheist discourse, belief in Mazu's prediction—or indeed disbelief or doubt about it—has emerged from social circumstances rather than from the mental acts of individual persons.

People in Gongliao are now turning back to the power of their patron goddess, thus recalling her words and *ling* as a resource to sustain their protest (Shih 2012). It is worth noting that a further dimension to this is the rumor and gossip currently circulating in the Gongliao community and within the plant itself. The examples of this that I collected can be productively treated as local discourses. I was told that technicians at the plant were themselves now aware of Mazu's prediction and were becoming increasingly anxious that they would never be able to get the plant operational. It is rumored that the excessive delays in the construction have meant that some of the parts needed are now out-of-date or have been discontinued, that some of the senior nuclear scientists involved in the project have retired or even died, and that ongoing tests have one after another failed or revealed additional problems.

Mr. Wu Wen-tong told me that he had recently been selected as a representative of the community and, in that role, had had a number of meetings with technicians inside the plant that had been organized by the Taiwan Power Company to demonstrate its purported safety and benefits. He said that the meetings had been tense and polarized. However, he added that, during the breaks, he had twice been approached by a couple of technicians asking whether Mazu had really predicted that the plant would never become operational. These technicians had also asked whether this had been predicted just one or two years previously, and he had replied that it had in fact been predicted more than 24 years ago. Given that most of the plant workers and technicians are not local to the area, Mr. Wu speculated that when temporary local workers at the plant saw the problems revealed or caused by the tests, they may have been prompted to blurt out, "Our goddess Mazu has already predicted this." He later discovered that other members of the community had been asked the same questions by plant workers and technicians.

Rather than representing the two worlds of religious belief and scientific doubt as existing in opposition, as in New Atheist discourse, in the local discourse of Gongliao, as expressed through gossip and rumor, science and religion are not opposed, and doubt and belief co-exist within religious practice. Local gossip and rumor suggest that some technicians have lost confidence in the plant and that they have begun to doubt their ability to make it operational. Some of them have even apparently turned to Mazu's *ling* and are taking note of her prediction about the fate of the nuclear plant. Although the technicians are scientists and non-local, they were born into and interact socially within the religious culture in which Mazu's *ling* is recognized. Their concern about the timing of Mazu's prediction implies that if the prediction had been made in the past two or three years, it could be interpreted as having been made up by locals after observing the failure of the recent tests. However, because the prediction was made more than 24 years ago, it is more believable. Actually, the fourth nuclear power plant is currently mothballed. This is further due to massive protests, a hunger strike, and the consideration of the risks of explosion.

Conclusions

In this chapter we have argued that New Atheist discourse needs to develop a far more nuanced and subtle account of religions beyond the current strategy of simply reducing religion to private mental events called beliefs. The evidence we have offered suggests that belief and doubt belong as much to social worlds as to individual, mental acts. Historical and ethnographic evidence points to an understanding of religion (or science) not as the private contemplation of ontological claims but rather as embodied, performed, and socialized patterns of interaction in which doubt and belief are constituted through historically situated socio-cultural structures of dialogic interaction. It is only as a result of careful and astute materialist analysis of such structured complexes that the real resonances of religious belief and doubt can be found.

Acknowledgments

A version of this chapter was presented at the Nonreligion and Secularity Research Network conference, held at the University of London in July 2012. We would like to thank Lois Lee and Katie Aston for giving us the opportunity to present this material at the conference. We would also like to take this opportunity to thank Ruy Llera Blanes, Galina Oustinova-Stjepanovic, and Mathijs Pelkmans. We would particularly like to thank the Taiwan Foundation for Democracy for its generous grant to support our fieldwork. All errors in fact and interpretation are, of course, our own.

Paul-François Tremlett received his PhD from the School of Oriental and African Studies. His thesis focused on local religion and national identity in the Philippines at the extinct volcano Mount Banahaw. His research interests include contemporary East Asian religiosities and spiritualities; spatialities, geographies, and place-making practices; modernities and secularisms; cognitive theory of religion; and Marxism and classical and contemporary social theory. A Senior Lecturer at the Open University, he is currently part of an international interdisciplinary research project titled "Reassembling Democracy: Ritual as Cultural Resource," which is funded by the Norwegian Research Council, and is carrying out research on Occupy London and Occupy Hong Kong.

Fang-Long Shih is a Research Fellow in the Asia Research Centre at the London School of Economics and Co-director of the LSE Taiwan Research Programme. She regards religion as being always embodied in political, social, and economic processes, and her publications address topics such as practices around maiden death and modernity, religion and identity, and religion and environmentalism. She edits the journal *Taiwan in Comparative Perspective* and is a co-editor, with Stuart Thompson and Paul-François Tremlett, of *Re-Writing Culture in Taiwan* (2009). She has also contributed chapters on religion and gender to the *New Blackwell Companion to the Sociology of Religion* (2010) and the *Routledge Handbook of Religions in Asia* (2014).

Notes

1. A note on the use of pronouns is in order. In the introductory and concluding sections of this chapter, the pronoun 'we' denotes both authors. In the ethnographic sections, the pronouns 'I' and 'my' refer to Paul-François Tremlett in the case of the Philippines and to Fang-Long Shih in the case of Taiwan.
2. Cannell (2010: 88) has also noted the strong connection made in New Atheist discourse between modernity and secularization, as if atheism—or something like it—is or ought to be the logical consequence of becoming modern.
3. For more details on the controversy over closing the fourth nuclear power plant, see Jacobs (2012: 175–180).
4. See "Nuclear Power Plant Issue Flares Up Again," *Taiwan Communiqué* 59 (1993): 21–22, http://www.taiwandc.org/twcom/tc59-int.pdf.

References

Asad, Talal. 2003. *Formations of the Secular: Christianity, Islam, Modernity*. Stanford, CA: Stanford University Press.

Beha, Christopher R. 2012. "Reason for Living: The Good Life without God." *Harper's Magazine*, July, 73–78.

Boyer, Pascal. 2001. *Religion Explained: The Evolutionary Origins of Religious Thought*. New York: Basic Books.

Brickman, Celia. 2003. *Aboriginal Populations in the Mind: Race and Primitivity in Psychoanalysis*. New York: Columbia University Press.

Cannell, Fenella. 1999. *Power and Intimacy in the Christian Philippines*. Cambridge: Cambridge University Press.

Cannell, Fenella. 2010. "The Anthropology of Secularism." *Annual Review of Anthropology* 39: 85–100.

Dawkins, Richard. 2006. *The God Delusion*. New York: Bantam.

Dennett, Daniel C. 2007. *Breaking the Spell: Religion as a Natural Phenomenon*. Harmondsworth: Penguin.

Descartes, René. [1637] 1968. *Discourse on Method and the Meditations*. Trans. F. E. Sutcliffe. Harmondsworth: Penguin.

Eagleton, Terry. 2006. "Lunging, Flailing, Mispunching." *London Review of Books* 28, no. 20: 32–34. http://www.lrb.co.uk/v28/n20/terry-eagleton/lunging-flailing-mispunching (accessed 5 May 2015).

Foucault, Michel. 1981. "The Order of Discourse." Pp. 48–78 in *Untying the Text: A Poststructuralist Reader*, ed. Robert Young. London: Routledge & Kegan Paul.

Freud, Sigmund. [1913] 2001. *Totem and Taboo*. Trans. James Strachey. London: Routledge.

Guan, Yu, and Yun Mo. 2010. "Anti-nuclear protests: Yesterday, Today, and Tomorrow." [In Chinese.] http://www.taiwangoodlife.org/story/20100909/2559.

Harris, Sam. 2005. *The End of Faith: Religion, Terror, and the Future of Reason*. London: Free Press.

Hitchens, Christopher. 2007. *God Is Not Great: How Religion Poisons Everything*. London: Atlantic Books.

Ho, Ming-Sho. 2003. "The Politics of Anti-Nuclear Protest in Taiwan: A Case of Party-Dependent Movement (1980–2000)." *Modern Asian Studies* 37, no. 3: 683–708.

Jacobs, J. Bruce. 2012. *Democratizing Taiwan*. Leiden: Brill.

Jordan, David K. 1972. *Gods, Ghosts and Ancestors: Folk Religion in a Taiwanese Village*. Berkeley: University of California Press.

King, Richard. 1999. *Orientalism and Religion: Postcolonial Theory, India and 'The Mystic East'*. London: Routledge.

Laidlaw, James. 2007. "A Well-Disposed Social Anthropologist's Problems with the 'Cognitive Science of Religion.'" Pp. 211–246 in *Religion, Anthropology, and Cognitive Science*, ed. Harvey Whitehouse and James Laidlaw. Durham, NC: Carolina Academic Press.

Love, Robert S. 1977. "The Samahán of Papa God: Tradition and Conversion in a Tagalog Peasant Religious Movement." PhD diss., Cornell University.

Luhrmann, T. M. 1994. *Persuasions of the Witch's Craft: Ritual Magic in Contemporary England*. London: Picador.

Needham, Rodney. 1972. *Belief, Language, and Experience*. Oxford: Basil Blackwell.

Pelkmans, Mathijis, ed. 2013. "Outline for an Ethnography of Doubt." Pp. 1–42 in *Ethnographies of Doubt: Uncertainty and Faith in Contemporary Societies*, ed. Mathijis Pelkmans. London: I.B. Tauris.

Ren-he Temple Management Committee. 2004. *Introduction to Ren-he Gong*. Taipei: Ren-he Temple Management Committee.

Said, Edward W. 1995. *Orientalism: Western Conceptions of the Orient*. Harmondsworth: Penguin.

Sangren, P. Steven. 1987. *History and Magical Power in a Chinese Community*. Stanford, CA: Stanford University Press.

Shih, Fang-Long. 2006. "From Regulation and Rationalization, to Production: Government Policy on Religion in Taiwan." Pp. 256–283 in *What Has Changed? Taiwan before and after the Change in Ruling Parties*, ed. Dafydd Fell, Henning Klöter, and Chang Bi-yu. Wiesbaden: Harrassowitz Verlag.

Shih, Fang-Long. 2010. "Women, Religions and Feminisms." Pp. 221–243 in *Blackwell Companion to the Sociology of Religion*, ed. Bryan S. Turner. Oxford: Blackwell.

Shih, Fang-Long. 2012. "Generating Power in Taiwan: Nuclear, Political and Religious Power." *Culture and Religion* 13, no. 3: 295–313.

Stocking, George W., Jr. 1987. *Victorian Anthropology*. New York: Free Press.

Tremlett, Paul-François. 2011. "Weber-Foucault-Nietzsche: Uncertain Legacies for the Sociology of Religion." Pp. 287–303 in *Sects and Sectarianism in Jewish History*, ed. Sacha Stern. Leiden: Brill.

Tremlett, Paul-François. 2012. "Two Shock Doctrines: From Christo-Disciplinary to Neo-liberal Urbanisms in the Philippines." *Culture and Religion* 13, no. 4: 405–423.

Tylor, Edward B. 1903. *Primitive Culture: Researches into the Development of Mythology, Philosophy, Religion, Language, Art and Custom*. Vols. 1 and 2. London: John Murray.

Weber, Max. [1905] 2002. *The Protestant Ethic and the Spirit of Capitalism*. Trans. Talcott Parsons. London: Routledge.

Wilson, Brian C. 1998. "From the Lexical to the Polythetic: A Brief History of the Definition of Religion." Pp. 141–162 in *What Is Religion? Origins, Definitions, and Explanations*, ed. Thomas A. Idinopulos and Brian C. Wilson. Leiden: Brill.

Wilson, Bryan R., ed. 1970. *Rationality*. Oxford: Basil Blackwell.

Chapter 5

ANTAGONISTIC INSIGHTS
Evolving Soviet Atheist Critiques of Religion and Why
They Matter for Anthropology

state-sponsored atheism of socialist states as an example of the stubborn blind-ness of secularist regimes to the reality of religious persistence (Froese 2008).

The commitment of entire states and their ruling parties to enforcing atheism and ostracizing religious believers certainly led to much suffering, bloodshed, and injustice, especially in the initial phases of destroying the institutional power of religious organizations. In the Soviet Union in the 1920s and 1930s, whole families of priests, imams, rabbis, lamas, and devout lay people were exterminated. During the height of persecution in 1921–1922, 1929–1930, and again in the late 1930s, putting down one's name on the list of 20 lay members required for the registration and legal functioning of a religious congregation was virtually a death sentence. At the outbreak of World War II, only three senior hierarchs of the Russian Orthodox Church were alive and not imprisoned in a labor camp (Mitrofanov 2002).

Atheist campaigns during those decades focused on the destruction of sacred sites and buildings and the public humiliation of clergy and religious believers (Greene 2009; Husband 2000). Rapidly enforced new norms of time, behavior, and dress made people overstep traditional religious norms and prohibitions, such as the cycle of fasts and feasts of Orthodox Christianity, the wearing of veils and other forms of head coverings, and the avoidance of burial grounds, many of which were deliberately turned into public parks (Dragadze 1993; Northrop 2004; Rolf 2006). As in settings of rapid and state-enforced seculariza-tion elsewhere in the world, the requirement to publicly reject and ridicule old norms served to underscore the point that religious commitments were incom-patible with membership in the new society that was in the making (Bantjes 1997; Navaro-Yashin 2002; Copeman and Quack, this issue).

Those parts of Eastern Europe that came under socialist influence after World War II followed suit in their own battles between political regimes and institu-tional religion, although sometimes in less violent forms (Gärtner et al. 2003). The requirement to be atheist was so closely associated with Marxist politics that socialist parties in the Global South 'translated' it into their cultural con-texts (see Blanes and Paxe, this issue). In the Soviet Union itself, the initial open violence against religious believers was replaced by restrictions and intimidation during the post-war decades. Some members of younger generations grew up with little exposure to religion as a complex of practices and acquired the 'dis-positional atheism' described by Galina Oustinova-Stjepanovic (this issue). But for scholars and officials in socialist states, atheism always remained more than a heuristic stance toward the possibility or impossibility of religious experience. Anyone who gathered and disseminated information about religious traditions and practices had to present this work as actively contributing to religion's eventual disappearance.

Despite the political mandate to help exterminate religion, many Soviet atheists recognized empirical challenges to the expectation of inevitable secu-larization. The way that they dealt with these challenges has implications for current debates about the knowability of religion through the lens of the social sciences. After World War II, the communist parties of Eastern Europe to some degree resigned themselves to the persistence of religious institutions. With the exception of Albania, the world's only officially atheist state, all socialist governments offered religious organizations more or less restrictive conditions under which they could legally register and created specialized bureaucracies for monitoring religious life (Chumachenko 2002; Şincan 2010). By the 1950s and 1960s, the capacity of religious believers to adapt their dogmas and organizational structures to the requirements of a changing social world attracted the attention of officials and scholars alike.

For Marxists committed to the idea that being determines consciousness, the normative expectation remained that religious attachments would eventually disappear from the lives of socialist citizens. With the exception of institutions of theological learning, which passed on textual and liturgical knowledge with little comparative or theoretical research, 'scientific atheism' remained the only heading under which knowledge about religion could be gathered, analyzed, and discussed in public settings. In Soviet writings about religion from the post-war decades, one feels what Ranajit Guha (1988), referring to British descriptions of Indian peasant uprisings, has called the 'prose of counter-insurgency', that is, the definition of a social phenomenon as hostile and foreign to the values of those authoring the description, and the attempt to define the motivations of religious actors as irrational.

Looking at atheist debates from the Soviet Union, one sees that the obligatory hostile stance toward religion certainly limited the interpretive possibilities of scholars and officials. But the ideological puzzle of why religion was not going away also brought about increasingly complex inquiries into the religious practices of socialist citizens. Contrary to what critiques of secularism as a rigid and restrictive system of thought might lead us to expect,[2] there were significant innovations within Soviet atheist critiques of religion over the last decades of Soviet socialism, all growing out of the effort to understand what religion meant to citizens and how to replace it most effectively.

For contemporary anthropology, atheist scholarship on religion can be a useful antidote to an assumption that has gained ground in recent decades— the idea that a positive emotional attitude toward research subjects necessarily leads to deeper insights into their world than a critical or even neutral stance. Methodological discussions of ethnographic fieldwork acknowledge a range of affective responses by the researcher, oscillating between admiring identification and fearful withdrawal (Davies and Spencer 2010; Kleinman and Copp 1993). But as narratives for presenting fieldwork data, stories of overcoming doubt and distance through sharing emotional experiences seem convincing to many anthropologists and their readers, at least in North America.[3] As I outline below, a number of Anglophone scholars of religion and secularism have argued that normative equations between secularity, modernity, and academic rationality inhibit empathy with religious practitioners and diminish our capacity to understand contemporary religious dynamics. By contrast, the development of empirical studies of religious life in the Soviet Union in the 1960s and 1970s shows that the imperative to be critical can be as powerful (and limiting) a motivation for attentive observation and astute analysis as the quest for sympathetic understanding.

Ethnographic Empathy

The methodological stance of an empathetic sharing of the 'native's point of view' was implicit in the research methods of the first generation of participant observers in anthropology. Franz Boas, Bronislaw Malinowski, and lesser-known predecessors such as Nikolai Miklukho-Maklai and Frank Hamilton Cushing argued that it is only through leaving the detachment of the armchair and sharing people's lives and daily concerns that one comes to understand their view of the world (Clifford 2005; Kohl 1979). The claim to privileged understanding came under critique from a new generation of Anglophone anthropologists toward the end of the twentieth century (Asad 1973; Clifford and Marcus 1986). But the participatory and dialogical approaches championed by some members of this generation tended to place even more value on positive affect such as trust, friendship, and shared purposes between researchers and researched. If one needs to be bewitched in order to learn about witchcraft, or to befriend someone suffering from possession in order to write a rich account of this affliction, the premium placed on positive emotional connections is high (Crapanzano 1980; Favret-Saada 1977). In an early critical engagement with this trend toward empathy and suspension of disbelief, Ernest Gellner (1970) asserts that it sometimes turns the scholar's home society into the only legitimate object of criticism. This raises the problem of how to define what is one's home and how to separate it from the societies under study.

In the anthropology of religion, calls for methodological empathy often arise from just such a self-critical impulse. Some of the first challenges to the secularization thesis in anthropology came from studies of evangelical Christians, following the urge to demystify what had become the 'repugnant cultural other' (Harding 1991) of American liberal intellectuals. More recently, the post–Cold War and post-9/11 image of politicized Islam has prompted anthropologists to challenge the assumptions about proper politics and proper religion that underlie the demonization of certain religious movements as 'extremist' or 'fundamentalist' (Bilgrami 1992).

In her contribution to a forum on secularism, Saba Mahmood (2008: 448–449) repeatedly describes the public discourse on religion in the public sphere since September 11 as "shrill," framing anthropology's responsibility as one of inquiring into and rethinking "normative conceptions of the subject, law and language" and of laying bare "the epistemological and ontological assumptions" of self-described secular discourses. Her argument follows that of Talal Asad (2003, 2006), who has described liberal secularism as the outcome of a complex history of theological and political developments in Western Europe—a history that has also profoundly shaped the discipline of anthropology. Dissecting and critiquing secularism, in this interpretation, is an exercise in anthropological self-criticism that is a necessary step toward overcoming the Eurocentrism of the discipline.

As anthropologists Sherry Ortner (1995) and Webb Keane (2003) have noted, such self-critical stances toward histories of 'othering' and 'objectification' in anthropology have had paradoxical consequences for the discipline's empirical commitment to describing and theorizing other people's lives. When Harding (1991) and Mahmood (2001) reflect on the paradoxes of the 'repugnant cultural other' and the 'docile agent', respectively, their central question concerns what the discourses about such fundamentalist others reveal about the ontological certainties of secular society. In a kind of 'ethnographic refusal' (Ortner 1995), they do not probe the interpersonal dynamics and social shifts that lead people to adopt or abandon religious orthodoxies. Rather, their focus is on tracing the genealogies of secularist myths about religious others. In Mahmood's (2005: 37) words, her own "repugnance" against the practices of the conservative Muslim Egyptian women she worked with led her to explore "the depth of discomfort [that] the pietistic character of this movement evokes among liberals, radicals, and progressives alike." Although several of the women had grown up in more secular families (ibid.: 176, 185), Mahmood offers little discussion about the changes in Egyptian society that accompany these shifts from more secular to more religious ways of being.

A second aspect of 'ethnographic refusal' in the anthropology of secularizing or post-secular societies is the dearth of ethnographic studies that include committed, secularist research subjects who are worthy of empathy. With the exception of some exploratory texts that begin to analyze ways in which secularism is lived (Farman 2013; Hirschkind 2011), Asad and his students approach the study of secularism as a way to develop a critique of liberalism. They focus their attention on clashes between religious and secularist stances in Western Europe, North America, and regions formerly colonized by Western Europe, such as the Middle East and India. The state-sponsored atheism of socialist Eastern Europe and northern Eurasia remains outside of their view, as does the broader question of how the militantly secularist movements of the twentieth century—in the Soviet Union and China, but also in Kemalist Turkey and Nehru's India—took Western ideas about normative historical development to build specific versions of modernity on the ruins of multi-ethnic, multi-religious empires (cf. Bhargava 1998b; Goossaert and Palmer 2011; Khalid 2006).

Considering the history of claims about anthropology as an 'atheist' discipline explored by Galina Oustinova-Stjepanovic (this issue; see also Blanes 2006), it may be that atheists in the field do not seem exotic enough to warrant ethnographic empathy. In a recent, critically acclaimed ethnography of evangelicals in the United States, Tanya Luhrmann (2012: xvi) sets out to build "a bridge across the divide" between unbelievers and believers. For her, this only involves explaining how believers learn to believe in God. She appears to assume that her readers know how non-believers think. When an anthropologist as a "professional infidel" (Faubion 2001: 30, 71) encounters unbelief in the field, it still seems to be hard to see it as a cognitive stance and cultural way of life in need of explanation and investigation.[4]

In some ways, studying atheism in the Soviet Union is a convenient way out of the dilemma of the overly familiar. Although once imposed and promoted by an impressive apparatus of repression and propaganda, public avowals of atheist convictions have gone out of fashion since the collapse of the Soviet Union in 1991, giving atheism the exotic appeal of a relic of past political moments.

My archival studies and oral history interviews on atheist propaganda of the 1960s and 1970s in the Mari Autonomous Republic on the Volga revealed a fascinating mix of the familiar and the strange. Propagandists worried about how to explain to village audiences what proteins are and how life could have originated from them, while cultural professionals sought to design secular rituals in such a way that they would provide substitutes for the beauty of religious liturgies, but without overwhelming audiences emotionally in the way that religious practice supposedly did (Luehrmann 2011).

The ethical assumptions expressed by atheist propagandists—that the spread of atheism would eliminate barriers of ethnicity, age, and gender sustained by religious traditions, and would focus people's energies on their this-worldly responsibilities to a society of fellow human beings—seemed quaintly utopian in the context of my concurrent fieldwork among post-Soviet religious organizations. Here, I encountered returnees to ancestral religions who regretted the inter-religious and inter-ethnic marriages that they or their children had entered into during more secular times; evangelical converts who claimed that the only way to improve Russia's economy is to bring more people to Jesus; and the increasing confidence and cultural power of the Russian Orthodox Church. In the aftermath of decades of struggle between atheism and religiosity, it was not clear which side had hegemony over which. This allowed for a study that treated both sides as equally in need of explanation and focused on their mutually constitutive relationship.

Part of this evolving relationship between religion and non-religion in the Soviet Union was fueled by the development of empirical sociology during the second half of the twentieth century. Like their Western counterparts, atheist scholars focused on religious practitioners as repugnant others with puzzling practices and ideas. The political framework within which they worked forbade any hint at empathetic engagement. But upon reading their published works and archival transcripts of their debates, atheist scholars of the Khrushchev and Brezhnev era turn out to be quite reflexive about their work and ready to question its methodological and theoretical assumptions. While critical of their research subjects, they took considerable risks by pointing out that religious practices remained part of the lives of many Soviet citizens and by advocating for theoretical models of historical development that would account for this. They thus present an interesting case study of an antagonistic stance toward research subjects.

Religion through an Atheist Lens

With the exception of a few legally recognized and carefully controlled centers of theological education, all scholarly inquiry on religion in the Soviet Union took place under the heading of 'scientific atheism' (Shakhnovich 2006). Some scholars who were formerly part of this discipline now claim that they were always interested in studying religion but had no other way to gain access to knowledge about it (Viktor Shnirelman, pers. communication, 2011). While it is impossible to evaluate such retrospective claims, the fact remains that all scholarly descriptions of religious life during the Soviet period had to situate themselves within a framework of expectation that religion would eventually disappear. Operating within these non-negotiable ideological constraints, university departments and research institutes dedicated to scientific atheism started to produce increasingly sophisticated empirical research on religious practices in the Soviet Union in the 1960s. One reason for this was the growing realization that, despite decades of socialist development, religion was not going away by itself and that previously promoted assumptions about religious believers could no longer hold true. Steady or even rising numbers of infant baptisms throughout the 1950s and 1960s, for instance, could hardly be explained by the notion that only class enemies and old people would continue to cling to religion under socialism (Lane 1978).

Especially when a new wave of anti-religious attacks during the early Khrushchev years failed to yield the desired effects, rising numbers of scholars called for more careful inquiry into what became known as 'the causes of the vitality of religious survivals in socialist society'. In spite of resistance from philosophers who held that empirical research could add no new insights to the truths expounded by Marxism-Leninism, this was a time when empirical sociology and ethnography were re-emerging as legitimate academic disciplines after having been virtually stamped out in the 1930s (First 2008; Luehrmann 2005; Slezkine 1991).

Scholars who advocated for a resumption of empirical studies argued that only living examples could show the processes by which new social relations and new people come into being. Some of the first studies began shortly before Stalin's death in 1953 and were conducted in villages with collectivized agriculture. As they began to publish results during the Khrushchev Thaw, scholars underscored the immense changes in social life and family structures that collectivization had brought about. An early outcome was the 1958 study *The Village of Viriatino in Past and Present*, published by a group of scholars from Moscow's Institute of Ethnography after two years of intermittent ethnographic research between 1952 and 1954 (Kushner 1958; see also Benet 1970). Themes of modernization and improvement loom large, but even in a study that was designed to ask primarily about material culture, workdays, and family structure, the findings point to the theme of religious change and persistence.

Making inquiries about kinship and marriage practices, the ethnographers recorded memories of two early Communist Party activists from the 1920s. During this period, Communist Youth League members found brides who agreed to forego a church wedding, but their parents forced them into a compromise. Instead of holding the Russian Orthodox ceremony inside the church, the couples had to circle the church three times—a number denoting the Christian notion of the Trinity that was also familiar from Orthodox Christian ritual (Kushner 1958: 206). Starting in the late 1950s, studies of the lives of recent migrants to the expanding Soviet cities also showed the persistence of religiously inspired life-cycle rituals among populations whose rapidly changing material circumstances should, by Marxist standards, have transformed their consciousness toward atheism (Urazmanova 2000).

Contrary to what is sometimes claimed (Shlapentokh 1987), these early experiments with empirical ethnography and sociology were conducted by scholars loyal to the government and the Communist Party who explicitly sought ways to make their studies seem relevant to the cause of communism. But the trend toward empirical studies and the erosion of historical-materialist certainties that ensued were not without critics. At a 1963 conference organized to discuss the first draft of a collectively authored book on the 'spiritual world' of Soviet citizens during the transition from socialism to full-fledged communism (Stepanian 1966), the economic philosopher Petr Nikolaevich Fedoseev warned in his opening statement that "facts from particular conversations with workers" could at best "enliven" an account of contemporary Soviet reality. However, it was the scholars' job to place those facts within the right philosophical and temporal framework: "[W]hat is needed is a philosophical sociological analysis from the angle of vision of what is happening, from the angle of vision of what is to come, what are the tendencies of development, and how we can practically assist in the education and formation of the new human being, in the development of the spiritual life of socialist society."[5]

Not surprisingly, given its politically sensitive nature, religion as an explicit topic of study emerged relatively late, and the scholars who examined it took special care to heed the call to place empirical data in the right "tendencies of development" to serve the "formation of the new human being." In 1964, the Moscow Academy of the Social Sciences, which was directly subordinate to the Central Committee of the Communist Party, established an Institute of Scientific Atheism. Its researchers soon began to conduct large-scale studies based on standardized questionnaires that covered themes such as everyday life, national traditions, culture, and religious beliefs. The first studies were carried out in the Penza Region in 1968–1970 and in the Chechen-Ingush Autonomous Republic in 1970–1971. In the Mari Republic, more than 600 rural teachers and employees of cultural institutions interviewed respondents in towns and villages in 1972–1973. Variations followed in other Russian regions and Soviet republics over the course of the next four years, always with the assistance of local Communist Party members, who were largely responsible for administering the surveys (Pivovarov 1971, 1976; Smolkin-Rothrock 2009).

By linking questions about religious belief or its absence to questions about age, educational level, occupation, housing conditions, access to social and cultural services, and knowledge about and evaluation of ethnic traditions, these studies sought to find out why certain people participated in religious practices while others abandoned them. The reason for combining such a wide variety of topics in one questionnaire was twofold. First, the sociologists designing the surveys were well aware that people would try to please the interviewers and present themselves as more atheist than they really were, even if they were promised anonymity. Placing questions about religion at the end of a lengthy survey of more than 300 questions was meant to give the interviewer time to gain the trust of the respondent and receive more reliable answers (Solov'ev 1977: 13; 1987: 15).

The second purpose of the wide range of questions was to generate statistics that would serve as evidence of the superiority of atheist convictions. To achieve this goal, the sociologists correlated statements about the presence or absence of religious belief with other kinds of information contained in the survey. Through a method of regression analysis that was new in the Soviet Union at the time and included early forms of computer technology, atheists, when compared to believers, were shown to be more likely to participate in voluntary social service or trade union activities and to put the interests of society before their own (Solov'ev 1977: 100; 1987: 144–145). In the Mari Republic, the repeat survey in 1985 differentiated between atheists who had previously believed but then abandoned their religion and those who had never held any religious beliefs. Responses to such questions were correlated with information about age and place of birth (Solov'ev 1987: 30). The resulting data were meant to show the generational dynamics of the decline of religious belief and the growth of atheism, producing the view of 'dynamic tendencies' that was required of socialist statistics.

Despite the attempts to produce data that would be useful to the building of communism, the published results of this and other surveys openly challenged the idea that only ignorant or disloyal people would hold on to religious convictions. Instead, they presented conclusions that criticized party and government agencies for not providing enough cultural services for rural residents and failing to create more child care options for young parents, which left them with no choice but to give in to the demands of grandparents to baptize or circumcise their children (Sofronov 1973). Sociologists also raised difficult questions about the role of religious practice for members of ethnic minorities, hinting that for some people religion was connected to complicated communal loyalties, rather than being merely a false explanatory framework for the uneducated (Solov'ev 1977: 73–74; see also Luehrmann 2012).

Critical Attention

The project of talking to religious believers, asking them about their experiences and practices, and then publishing the results remained risky in the Soviet Union. But by the middle of the Brezhnev era, it had also acquired a measure of respectability, with the understanding that the ultimate purpose was the building of a secular communist society. At the discussion of the survey results at the Mari Republic's Communist Party plenum in 1975, the first secretary of the party fully acknowledged the unpleasant nature of some of the findings, only to turn them into a call to action for his subordinates. If 4.7 percent of teachers and 15.6 percent of medical professionals called themselves religious believers or people wavering between belief and unbelief, and if 15 percent of white-collar workers had not read a single book during the month that the study was carried out and 26 percent of party members had icons in their home, the remedy was both further study and improved political education:

> A person who has linked his life to the party of Lenin, to please his mother-in-law or whomever else, lives year in and year out under the god corner with the

image of the mother of god or Nicholas the miracle worker, and we consider him an ideological fighter for the policies of the party ... We need a serious reorganization of the work on forming a scientific worldview, of atheist education, of the organization of the study of problems of atheism and religion by members of the Komsomol and Communist Party, by diverse groups of the intelligentsia, by all categories of toilers.[6]

Note that the party secretary calls for Komsomol and Communist Party members to study "problems of atheism and religion," giving political approval to scholarly attempts to generate and disseminate knowledge about religion. The speech still presents religious paraphernalia and rituals as aspects of past social relations that should be targeted for elimination. Yet the underlying force of that past no longer lies in the evil intentions of former elites and those bent on wrecking the economy; instead, it can be found in more intimate structures of familial authority and affection. The male party member is assumed to tolerate icons in the home to please his mother-in-law and perhaps, by extension, his wife.[7]

On the part of the sociologists, one conclusion emerging from the empirical studies was to explain the tenacity of religion within certain families and social groups by reference to isolation from the wider Soviet public sphere. Even after controlling for differences in age and urban or rural residence, the follow-up study still indicated that religious believers read fewer books per month and watched fewer films (Solov'ev 1987). Elderly rural residents interviewed in an earlier, small-scale study complained that there was no place for them to meet other than the church, because all activities in the village's clubhouse were geared toward young people (Sofronov 1973).

In a stark reversal of Emile Durkheim's ([1914] 1998) identification of society as the true referent of religious ideas and practices, Soviet atheists came to see religion as a fragmentizing, isolating force that thrived on boundaries and severed connections. They saw walls of authority that prevented the transfer of progressive ideas from younger to older generations; geographic and cultural distances that separated the countryside from the city; traditions of distrust and economic specialization that separated members of different ethnic groups. At a time when functionalist analyses of religion in the English-speaking world emphasized its role in providing social values (Parsons 1960), Soviet atheist scholars were at pains to show that morality did not originate from religion but was merely appropriated by religious thought. "[M]orality is secular in origin," insisted the elderly philosopher Nikolai Ivanovich Gubanov during a meeting of the executive board of the Knowledge Society. "We work on separating morality from religion in order to define and highlight secular morality."[8]

But was any of this atheism 'real'? Or were scholarly and popular professions of atheism just a pretense to protect the study and practice of religion from state sanctions? Between 1985 and 2004, many respondents to sociological surveys in the Mari Republic changed their professed views. The number of declared religious believers rose from 13.5 percent in 1985 to 43 percent in 1995 and 68.2 percent in 2004. The number of atheists fell from 32.2 percent in 1985 (70 percent if one adds those who indicated "indifference to matters of religion") to 16.6

percent in 2004 (Shabykov et al. 2005: 10, 346; Solov'ev 1987: 118). In Russia as a whole, however, the number of unbelievers remained around 20 percent in 2011, 20 years after the end of atheist propaganda (Levada Center 2012: 170). This suggests that, for some people at least, more was going on than just ideological show.

In 2005, I interviewed Viktor Solov'ev, the sociologist who carried out the surveys in the Mari Republic. He remained one of the few avowed atheists whom I was able to meet during my research. Born in 1934 in a remote Mari village, he had built his career by combining Communist Party work with scholarly inquiry and public lecturing. After retiring from sociological research, he served as an associate dean in the faculty of law at Mari State University, where he taught courses on church-state relations that encouraged students to question the role of the Russian Orthodox Church in contemporary Russia. Quick to acknowledge that his loyalty to atheism was unusual among his academic peers, he made fun of colleagues who had promoted atheism for most of their lives and now presented at the theological conferences that the local diocese of the Russian Orthodox Church organized in collaboration with various state agencies. For Solov'ev and many other observers, the motivations behind post-Soviet professions and performances of religiosity are no less dubious than Soviet-era professions and performances of atheism.

Without getting too deeply into the issues of sincerity and knowledge of other people's beliefs, which constitute another difficult chapter in the history of anthropology (Robbins and Rumsey 2008; Wilson 1970), for the purposes of this chapter it is enough to note that even while declaring allegiance to atheism, empirical scholars of religion undertook politically and intellectually risky work. They documented and interpreted the views and, in some cases, the voices of religious believers, who in previous decades would at best have been ignored and at worst persecuted by representatives of the Soviet state. They insisted that there were ways of combining the minutiae of empirical data collection with an interest in dynamic tendencies and long-term change, and that the tendencies and changes in religious life spoke not merely of restriction and decline, but of adaptation and reactions to current social problems. Some "survivals," as a speaker of the 1963 conference on the spiritual life of socialist society put it, were not caused simply by "inertia." Instead, there were "phenomena even in the present that nourish this survival and reproduce it."[9] The ideological mystery of the causes of unexpected survivals thus motivated a closer look at the dynamics of socialist society. One speaker cited the spread of alcohol use into formerly tea-drinking Central Asia as a problem that was caused, rather than solved, by Soviet secularizing policies.[10]

Late Soviet observers of religion retained significant blind spots. Their own orientation toward persuading and mobilizing audiences led them to interpret religious practices and objects as analogous to propaganda tools: the beauty of ritual served above all to attract the attention of followers, while icons in homes helped to spellbind people. This interpretation ignored and distorted the practices of contemplation and material mediation of non-human presence that were part of Russia's religious heritage. For example, atheist scholars described Russian Orthodox religious imagery as the propaganda posters of the church.

This interpretation ignored the visually inconspicuous nature of many icons, as well as the many non-visual means by which people interacted with them, such as touching, kissing, and gathering objects that had been in contact with them (Luehrmann 2010).

After decades of anthropological soul-searching, such creative misunderstandings, where scholars interpreted social phenomena in light of their own motivations, present no surprise. It is more remarkable that, remaining within an atheist framework, late Soviet scholars carved out a niche for the empirical study of religion under socialism. They challenged simplistic views of religion as an expression of ignorance or deceit, not out of an inherent sympathy toward religious believers, but in order to devise more effective secularizing policies while also creating legitimacy for themselves as empirical researchers.

Conclusion: Uses of Antagonism

Through their insistence on the tensions between religious practice and full participation in a society of human contemporaries, Soviet scholars raised several points that are noteworthy for anthropologists of religion today. First, their empirical approaches challenged not only Marxist orthodoxy but also Durkheimian views of religion as a source of social cohesion that are still current among Western social scientists and are making a comeback in post-Soviet Russia. Accounts of secularization tend to be based on a historical narrative where aspects of modern society, such as morality, law, and medicine, progressively detach and differentiate from the religious foundations in which they were once embedded. By seeing religion as a parasitic latecomer exploiting human propensities for altruism and collaboration, Soviet atheist thought provides a useful corrective to automatic assumptions that religious phenomena always belong to a deeper past than their seeming secular counterparts.

Second, the more Soviet sociology moved away from explaining religion as merely a survival of feudal or capitalist social relations, the more sharply it defined religion as anti-social. Whereas a common worry in contemporary religious studies is that many of its approaches presuppose highly text-based and rationalistic religions such as Protestant Christianity, the Soviet insistence on regarding religion as the opposite of society seems to fit ascetic and world-renouncing religions much better (Asad 1993; Riesebrodt 2007). Soviet atheists confronted religious traditions that involved progressive withdrawal from the world in old age and premiums placed on ritual expenditure (Bernstein 2013; Luehrmann 2012; Rogers 2009). Taking up their intuition that religion pulls people away from human social bonds and everyday economic rationalities might be a step toward diversifying the forms of religiosity that inform theoretical models of religion.

Soviet atheists were certainly not alone in acknowledging the destructive edge that religious demands can add to political and social cleavages (Kapferer 1988; Orsi 2005). What distinguished them was that they combined the ethnographic virtue of close attention with a political commitment to changing what they saw—a strategy that many readers today would consider unprofessional. But today, as then, keeping one's gaze fixed on 'repugnant cultural others' seems to require affective resources of negative or positive charge. In times and places where the power imbalances between secular and religious actors are far less one-sided than they were in the Soviet Union, it seems important to retain the possibility of a critical stance and place it alongside more empathetic approaches to understanding.

Sonja Luehrmann is an Associate Professor of Anthropology at Simon Fraser University. She is the author of *Secularism Soviet Style: Teaching Atheism and Religion in a Volga Republic* (2011) and *Religion in Secular Archives: Soviet Atheism and Historical Knowledge* (2015).

Notes

1. For the sense of perfunctory emptiness emanating from atheist institutions toward the end of the perestroika period, see Bruce Grant's (2011) account of the virtually abandoned House of Scientific Atheism in Moscow in the spring of 1989.
2. Some of the most compelling critiques once again come from post-colonial studies, where secular conventions of politics and historiography are challenged for what they obscure about the histories and political motivations of colonized populations (Chakrabarty 2000; Nandy 1998). For anthropology, the most influential work has been that of Talal Asad, as discussed below.
3. Across a distance of more than 20 years, there are similarities in narrative structure between Renato Rosaldo's (1989) classic account of how he came to understand Ilongot headhunters' talk of rage in a new way after the death of his wife and Tanya Luhrmann's (2012: 325) account of how sharing the visceral as well as the cognitive experiences of learning to be an evangelical Christian helped her experience "what I believe the Gospels mean by joy."
4. There are signs that non-religious people are being discovered as ethnographic subjects. In addition to the chapters in this volume, see Engelke (2015) and forthcoming work by Lorna Mumford.
5. State Archive of the Russian Federation (GARF), f. R-9547, op. 1, d. 1314, l. 17, 9–11 May 1963.
6. State Archive of the Republic of Marii El (GARME), f. P-1, op. 41, d. 27, l. 32, 25 July 1975.
7. See Northrop (2004: 176) for a discussion of the strategic advantages of such a feminization of religious beliefs for couples and atheist bureaucrats alike.
8. GARF, f. A-561, op. 1, d. 184, l. 19, 29 April 1958. See also GARF, f. R-9547, op. 1, d. 1311, l. 341–347, 20–23 February 1963. For more on Gubanov's work in the Knowledge Society, see Smolkin-Rothrock (2014).
9. GARF, f. R-9547, op. 1, d. 1314, l. 457, May 1963.
10. Ibid., l. 286.

References

Asad, Talal, ed. 1973. *Anthropology and the Colonial Encounter.* Atlantic Highlands, NJ: Humanities Press.

Asad, Talal. 1993. *Genealogies of Religion: Discipline and Reasons of Power in Christianity and Islam.* Baltimore: Johns Hopkins University Press.

Asad, Talal. 2003. *Formations of the Secular: Christianity, Islam, Modernity.* Stanford, CA: Stanford University Press.

Asad, Talal. 2006. "Trying to Understand French Secularism." Pp. 494–526 in *Political Theologies: Public Religions in a Post-Secular World,* ed. Hent de Vries and Lawrence E. Sullivan. New York: Fordham University Press.

Bantjes, Adrian A. 1997. "Idolatry and Iconoclasm in Revolutionary Mexico: The De-Christianization Campaigns, 1929–1940." *Mexican Studies/Estudios Mexicanos* 13, no. 1: 87–120.

Benet, Sula, ed. and trans. 1970. *The Village of Viriatino: An Ethnographic Study of a Russian Village from Before the Revolution to the Present.* Garden City, NY: Doubleday.

Bernstein, Anya. 2013. *Religious Bodies Politic: Rituals of Sovereignty in Buryat Buddhism.* Chicago: University of Chicago Press.

Bhargava, Rajeev, ed. 1998a. *Secularism and Its Critics.* Delhi: Oxford University Press.

Bhargava, Rajeev. 1998b. "What Is Secularism For?" Pp. 486–542 in Bhargava 1998a.

Bilgrami, Akeel. 1992. "What Is a Muslim? Fundamental Commitment and Cultural Identity." *Critical Inquiry* 18, no. 4: 821–842.

Blanes, Ruy L. 2006. "The Atheist Anthropologist: Believers and Non-believers in Anthropological Fieldwork." *Social Anthropology* 14, no. 2: 223–234.

Chakrabarty, Dipesh. 2000. *Provincializing Europe: Postcolonial Thought and Historical Difference.* Princeton, NJ: Princeton University Press.

Chumachenko, Tatiana. 2002. *Church and State in Soviet Russia: Russian Orthodoxy from World War II to the Khrushchev Years.* Ed. and trans. Edward Roslof. Armonk, NY: Sharpe.

Clifford, James. 2005. "Rearticulating Anthropology." Pp. 24–48 in *Unwrapping the Sacred Bundle: Reflections on the Disciplining of Anthropology,* ed. Daniel Segal and Sylvia Yanagisako. Durham, NC: Duke University Press.

Clifford, James, and George E. Marcus, eds. 1986. *Writing Culture: The Poetics and Politics of Ethnography.* Berkeley: University of California Press.

Crapanzano, Vincent. 1980. *Tuhami: Portrait of a Moroccan.* Chicago: University of Chicago Press.

Davies, James, and Dimitrina Spencer, eds. 2010. *Emotions in the Field: The Psychology and Anthropology of Fieldwork Experience.* Stanford, CA: Stanford University Press.

Dragadze, Tamara. 1993. "The Domestication of Religion under Soviet Communism." Pp. 148–156 in *Socialism: Ideals, Ideologies, and Local Practice,* ed. C. M. Hann. London: Routledge.

Durkheim, Emile. [1914] 1998. *Les formes élémentaires de la vie religieuse.* Paris: Quadrige/Presses universitaires de France.

Engelke, Matthew. 2015. "The Coffin Question: Death and Materiality in Humanist Funerals." *Material Religion* 11, no. 1: 26–48.

Farman, Abou. 2013. "Speculative Matter: Secular Bodies, Minds, and Persons." *Cultural Anthropology* 28, no. 4: 737–759.

Faubion, James D. 2001. *The Shadows and Lights of Waco: Millennialism Today.* Princeton, NJ: Princeton University Press.

Favret-Saada, Jeanne. 1977. *Les mots, la mort, les sorts.* Paris: Gallimard.

First, Joshua. 2008. "From Spectator to 'Differentiated' Consumer: Film Audience Research in the Era of Developed Socialism (1965–80)." *Kritika* 9, no. 2: 317–344.

Froese, Paul. 2008. *The Plot to Kill God: Findings from the Soviet Experiment in Secularization.* Berkeley: University of California Press.

Gärtner, Christel, Detlef Pollack, and Monika Wohlrab-Sahr, eds. 2003. *Atheismus und religiöse Indifferenz.* Opladen: Leske und Budrich.

Gellner, Ernest. 1970. "Concepts and Society." Pp. 18–49 in Wilson 1970.

Goossaert, Vincent, and David Palmer. 2011. *The Religious Question in Modern China.* Chicago: University of Chicago Press.

Grant, Bruce. 2011. "Epilogue: Recognizing Soviet Culture." Pp. 263–276 in *Reconstructing the House of Culture: Community, Self, and the Makings of Culture in Russia and Beyond*, ed. Brian Donahoe and Joachim O. Habeck. New York: Berghahn Books.

Greene, Robert H. 2009. *Bodies Like Bright Stars: Saints and Relics in Orthodox Russia.* DeKalb: Northern Illinois University Press.

Guha, Ranajit. 1988. "The Prose of Counter-Insurgency." Pp. 45–86 in *Selected Subaltern Studies,* ed. Ranajit Guha and Gayatri Spivak. New York: Oxford University Press.

Harding, Susan. 1991. "Representing Fundamentalism: The Problem of the Repugnant Cultural Other." *Social Research* 58, no. 2: 373–393.

Hirschkind, Charles. 2011. "Is There a Secular Body?" *Cultural Anthropology* 26, no. 4: 633–647.

Husband, William. 2000. *Godless Communists: Atheism and Society in Soviet Russia, 1917–1932.* DeKalb: Northern Illinois University Press.

Kapferer, Bruce. 1988. *Legends of People, Myths of State: Violence, Intolerance, and Political Culture in Sri Lanka and Australia.* Washington, DC: Smithsonian Institution Press.

Keane, Webb. 2003. "Self-Interpretation, Agency, and the Objects of Anthropology: Reflections on a Genealogy." *Comparative Studies in Society and History* 45, no. 2: 222–248.

Khalid, Adeeb. 2006. "Backwardness and the Quest for Civilization: Early Soviet Central Asia in Comparative Perspective." *Slavic Review* 65, no. 2: 231–251.

Kleinman, Sherryl, and Martha A. Copp. 1993. *Emotions and Fieldwork.* London: Sage.

Kohl, Karl-Heinz. 1979. *Exotik als Beruf: Zum Begriff der ethnographischen Erfahrung bei B. Malinowski, E. E. Evans-Pritchard und C. Lévi-Strauss.* Wiesbaden: Heymann.

Kushner, P. I., ed. 1958. *Selo Viriatino v proshlom i nastoiashchem: Opyt etnograficheskogo izucheniia russkoi kolkhoznoi derevni.* Moscow: Akademiia nauk SSSR.

Lane, Christel. 1978. *Christian Religion in the Soviet Union: A Sociological Study.* London: George Allen and Unwin.

Levada Center. 2012. *Obshchestvennoe mnenie—2011: Ezhegodnik.* Moscow: Levada tsentr.

Luehrmann, Sonja. 2005. "Russian Colonialism and the Asiatic Mode of Production: (Post-)Soviet Ethnography Goes to Alaska." *Slavic Review* 64, no. 4: 851–871.

Luehrmann, Sonja. 2010. "A Dual Struggle of Images on Russia's Middle Volga: Icon Veneration in the Face of Protestant and Pagan Critique." Pp. 56–78 in *Eastern Christians in Anthropological Perspective*, ed. C. M. Hann and Hermann Goltz. Berkeley: University of California Press.

Luehrmann, Sonja. 2011. *Secularism Soviet Style: Teaching Atheism and Religion in a Volga Republic.* Bloomington: Indiana University Press.

Luehrmann, Sonja. 2012. "A Multi-Religious Region in an Atheist State: Union-Wide Policies Meet Communal Distinctions in the Postwar Mari Republic." Pp. 272–301 in *State Secularism and Lived Religion in Soviet Russia and Ukraine*, ed. Catherine Wanner. New York: Oxford University Press.

Luhrmann, Tanya M. 2012. *When God Talks Back: Understanding the American Evangelical Relationship with God*. New York: Vintage.

Mahmood, Saba. 2001. "Feminist Theory, Embodiment, and the Docile Agent: Some Reflections on the Egyptian Islamic Revival." *Cultural Anthropology* 16, no. 2: 202–236.

Mahmood, Saba. 2005. *Politics of Piety: The Islamic Revival and the Feminist Subject*. Princeton, NJ: Princeton University Press.

Mahmood, Saba. 2008. "Is Critique Secular? A Symposium at UC Berkeley." *Public Culture* 20, no. 3: 447–452.

Mitrofanov, Georgii. 2002. *Istoriia Russkoi Pravoslavnoi Tserkvi, 1900–1927*. Saint Petersburg: Satis.

Nandy, Ashis. 1998. "The Politics of Secularism and the Recovery of Religious Tolerance." Pp. 321–344 in Bhargava 1998a.

Navaro-Yashin, Yael. 2002. *Faces of the State: Secularism and Public Life in Turkey*. Princeton, NJ: Princeton University Press.

Northrop, Douglas. 2004. *Veiled Empire: Gender and Power in Stalinist Central Asia*. Ithaca, NY: Cornell University Press.

Orsi, Robert. 2005. *Between Heaven and Earth: The Religious Worlds People Make and the Scholars Who Study Them*. Princeton, NJ: Princeton University Press.

Ortner, Sherry. 1995. "Resistance and the Problem of Ethnographic Refusal." *Comparative Studies in Society and History* 37, no. 1: 173–193.

Parsons, Talcott. 1960. *Structure and Process in Modern Societies*. Glencoe, IL: Free Press.

Pivovarov, Viktor G. 1971. *Byt, kul'tura, natsional'nye traditsii i verovaniia naseleniia Checheno-ingushskoi ASSR (Osnovnye zadachi, instrumentarii, protsedury i nauchno-organizatsionnyi plan konkretno-sotsiologicheskogo issledovaniia)*. Groznyi: Checheno-ingushskoe knizhnoe izdatel'stvo.

Pivovarov, Viktor G. 1976. *Religioznost': Opyt i problemy izucheniia*. Ioshkar-Ola: Mariiskoe knizhnoe izdatel'stvo.

Riesebrodt, Martin. 2007. *Cultus und Heilsversprechen: Eine Theorie der Religionen*. Munich: Beck.

Robbins, Joel, and Alan Rumsey. 2008. "Introduction: Cultural and Linguistic Anthropology and the Opacity of Other Minds." *Anthropological Quarterly* 81, no. 2: 407–420.

Rogers, Douglas. 2009. *The Old Faith and the Russian Land: A Historical Ethnography of Ethics in the Urals*. Ithaca, NY: Cornell University Press.

Rolf, Malte. 2006. *Das sowjetische Massenfest*. Hamburg: Hamburger Edition.

Rosaldo, Renato. 1989. *Culture and Truth: The Remaking of Social Analysis*. Boston: Beacon.

Shabykov, Vitalii I., S. N. Isanbaev, and E. A. Ozhiganova, eds. 2005. *Religioznoe soznanie naseleniia Respubliki Marii El (Materialy sotsiologicheskikh issledovanii 1994 i 2004 godov)*. Joshkar-Ola: MarNII.

Shakhnovich, Marianna. 2006. *Ocherki po istorii religiovedeniia*. Saint Petersburg: Izdatel'stvo Sankt-Peterburgskogo universiteta.

Shlapentokh, Vladimir. 1987. *The Politics of Sociology in the Soviet Union*. Boulder: Westview.

Şincan, Anca. 2010. " From Bottom to the Top and Back: On How to Build a Church in Communist Romania." Pp. 191–216 in *Christianity and Modernity in Eastern Europe*, ed. Bruce Berglund and Brian Porter-Szűcs. Budapest: Central European University Press.

Slezkine, Yuri. 1991. "The Fall of Soviet Ethnography, 1928–38." *Current Anthropology* 32, no. 4: 476–484.

Smolkin-Rothrock, Victoria. 2009. "Sviato mesto pusto ne byvaet: Ateisticheskoe vospitanie v Sovetskom Soiuze, 1964–1968." *Neprikosnovennyi zapas* 65: 36–52.

Smolkin-Rothrock, Victoria. 2014. "The Ticket to the Soviet Soul: Science, Religion, and the Spiritual Crisis of Late Soviet Atheism." *Russian Review* 73, no. 2: 171–197.

Sofronov, Nikolai S. 1973. *Ateisticheskoe vospitanie kolkhoznogo krest'ianstva*. Ioshkar-Ola: Mariiskoe knizhnoe izdatel'stvo.

Solov'ev, Viktor S. 1977. *Sotsiologicheskie issledovania—v praktiku ideologicheskoi raboty: Nekotorye itogi izucheniia problem byta, kul'tury, traditsii i verovanii naseleniia Mariiskoi ASSR*. Ioshkar-Ola: Mariiskoe knizhnoe izdatel'stvo.

Solov'ev, Viktor S. 1987. *Po puti dukhovnogo progressa: Nekotorye itogi povtornogo sotsiologicheskogo issledovaniia problem byta, kul'tury, natsional'nykh traditsii, ateizma i verovanii naseleniia Mariiskoi ASSR*. Ioshkar-Ola: Mariiskoe knizhnoe izdatel'stvo.

Stepanian, Tsolak A., ed. 1966. *Stroitel'stvo kommunizma i dukhovnyi mir cheloveka*. Moscow: Nauka.

Urazmanova, Raufa K. 2000. *Byt neftiannikov-tatar iugo-vostoka Tatarstana (1950–1960e gody): Etnosotsiologicheskie issledovaniia*. Al'met'evsk: Al'met'evskaia entsiklopediia.

Wilson, Bryan, ed. 1970. *Rationality*. Evanston, IL: Harper & Row.

Chapter 6

CONFESSIONAL ANTHROPOLOGY

Galina Oustinova-Stjepanovic

"If one has no faith, is there any reason why one should be interested?" (Berger 2004: 1). This question springs from two common assumptions—that theology is interesting only for believers, while anthropology is inevitably a non-theistic discipline that consists of secular endeavors of non-believers to "explain [religion] away" (Binsbergen 1991: 336). However, within theology, conceptualized as an established academic field, there are uncertainties as to whether theology is indeed a confessional discipline that attracts only religious people (Bowie 1998). Scholars have been asking if, as an exercise in philosophical thinking, theologies can be understood across the faith–non-faith divide. For example, can an atheist study theology (Cush 2009)? Is a theologian ill-equipped to undertake a non-confessional study of religion (Yong 2012: 18)? These concerns about subjective religiosity or the non-religion of a researcher are analogous to the questions raised in anthropology about its methodological and epistemological foundations as a secular social science (Bielo 2014: 7). So, is anthropology of religion a confessional discipline of a kind? Does an anthropologist have to 'believe' to carry out research among seriously religious people? This chapter

Notes for this chapter begin on page 130.

revisits the debates about how the atheism of anthropology and of anthropologists enables or impedes ethnographic research and the production of anthropological knowledge.

Methodological Atheism

When E. E. Evans-Pritchard (1962: 29) delivered the Aquinas Lecture in 1959, he described the historical attitude of the early French, American, and British social anthropologists to religions as "hostile." In his view, the reason for hostility toward 'religion' was the assumed incompatibility of religious views and "the scientific logic of society" (ibid.) that the founding anthropologists hoped to uncover. According to Evans-Pritchard, his contemporaries perpetuated the belittling tradition of seeing religions as superstitions. Not only anthropologists, but a believing theologian might find stories of dart-throwing witches to be nonsensical gobbledygook (Harris 2010). Although hostility might still be a plausible attitude among anthropologists when selecting a research topic, the deliberate disregard of witches and theologians and the lampooning of religious matters as irrational are rare today, at least among those anthropologists who do not think that any science is inevitably incommensurable with religious convictions and practices and who question the notion of science per se (Proctor 2005).

However, having curtailed the maligning of religions with reference to Enlightenment reason and positivism, anthropologists often conceptualize religious traditions as a case of socially efficacious acts of imagination (Eipper 2001: 31), as an epiphenomenon or a means to a larger 'social' end. This recalcitrant anthropological tendency to explain 'religion' away in instrumental and non-theistic terms is the reason why many anthropologists have focused on the sociological, psychological, moral, and political uses of religious ideas and practices rather than on religious traditions in their own right. Such an instrumental stance ignores multiple aspects of people's own perceptions and practical orientations in life by treating important religious relations as a hindrance to obtaining material of social, political, or scientific relevance. This suspicious professional position, described as "methodological atheism" by Peter Berger (1969: 180), would tolerate religious traditions as illusionary but useful meaning-making products, symbols, or representations of historical humanity.

Yet the instrumental approach is problematic in a number of ways. For example, such explanations run the risk of overlooking words, events, things, and religious encounters where meanings are deferred or fail and their 'instrumental' efficacy is limited (Engelke and Tomlinson 2006). Furthermore, strictly semiotic and operational approaches to religious traditions might neglect the ethnographically substantiated observation that religious rituals, languages, experiences, ideas, and so on emerge as creative forces of realities (Handelman 2005).

To tackle methodological atheism, anthropologists might refuse to analytically represent knowledge obtained in the field for fear of committing an "intellectual vivisection" of psychologizing or anthropologizing indigenous religiosity

(Binsbergen 1991: 336–337). On the one hand, this raises a question of what can be learned from this refusal. On the other, one must not forget that instrumentalism can be an indigenous position of religiously motivated people. As anthropologists are calling for non-instrumental approaches to religious traditions (Boddy 1994), theological schools are coming up with functional and medical findings that prayers and kneeling in supplication stimulate the circulation of oxygen in blood vessels and extend longevity (Starrett 1998).

In light of the above controversies and anxieties, what is the predicament of an atheist anthropologist? Anthropologically sensitized to the dangers of mocking and instrumentalizing religious traditions, an atheist anthropologist might yearn to produce an ethnography that avoids biased and reductionist understanding of religious traditions. Yet, begging a practical recommendation for the accomplishment of 'participant observation', what should an anthropologist do about his or her subjective atheism to propel anthropological interpretations? Should atheist anthropologists renounce their subjective atheism and convert to belief to do their job as an anthropologist right? What are the limits of such tactical religiosity?

Anthropological Atheism

My question partly harks back to the MacIntyre-Winch debate on the possibilities concerning the intelligibility of (MacIntyre 1974: 62–77) and learning from (Winch 1974: 106) unfamiliar traditions, including religious ones. Alasdair MacIntyre explicitly asks if a skeptic and a believer can agree with their interlocutors on difficult religious issues such as salvation without sharing people's belief in God. MacIntyre (1974: 76) has answered his own inquiry in the negative: "[I]f I am right, understanding Christianity is incompatible with believing in it." A similar argument has been made by Meyer Fortes (1987: 288): "[A]nthropologists, I would argue, who are primarily observers, cannot but be agnostic if they want to achieve objectivity." He is critical of Evans-Pritchard's indictment of skeptical anthropologists because many non-religious anthropologists have contributed to the study of religions regardless of their personal religious convictions. The task of anthropology, Fortes continues, is not to adjudicate the metaphysical existence of gods but to illuminate the material, symbolic, and pragmatic efficacy of religion, including self-realization or the management of interpersonal relations (ibid.: 292). Winning Durkheimian plaudits, Fortes wraps up his argument saying that religion for anthropologists (and again in contrast to theologians) offers an insight into an 'objectification' of social forces (ibid.: 293) that constitute specifically anthropological areas of interest.

With regard to theology and art aesthetics, Alfred Gell (1999) also speaks in favor of dissociation from any fascination that religion and art might hold for anthropologists. Religion, magic, or art objects create enchantment by indexing magical powers and occluding the actual technologies of their production, which are the prime targets of anthropological analysis. Gell's arguments imply that religious enchantment might interfere with anthropological research into the conditions of production and techniques of human creativity behind religious artifacts, rituals, or relations. However, one might turn the tables on Gell by arguing that the all-pervasive celebration of human agency and mediation in constructing religious traditions "may undermine the conceptualisation of the Divine as that which transcends the human imagination" (Port 2011: 78). The result is that the non-human autonomous origins of visions, dreams, revelations, and other religious encounters that our interlocutors experience and narrate are rarely taken seriously (Mittermaier 2011).

For MacIntyre, Fortes, and Gell, 'belief' and anthropological practice should be kept apart. Does this approach signal a consequential refusal to participate in people's religious traditions? Katherine Ewing (1994) explores another subtle methodological dimension of the professional disregard of religious traditions, which she calls, after Berger's methodological atheism, 'anthropological atheism'. By contrast to Gell, Ewing suggests that the atheistic approach to people's religious experiences prevents anthropologists from getting deeply involved in situations leading to extraordinary events. Or, having encountered religious experiences, anthropologists edit them out in written ethnographies. For Ewing, anthropological atheism implies a taboo on going native, that is, on feeling and being like our religiously attuned interlocutors. Ewing claims that, by refusing to participate fully and religiously in people's life-worlds, an anthropologist commits a hegemonic act that denies equality to what anthropologists know as 'true' and what their interlocutors might hold in opposition to anthropological registers of being intellectual, historical, political, moral, and so on. A hegemonic act, to relate one of Ewing's examples, can be encapsulated in explaining a dream visitation by a Sufi saint exclusively in psychoanalytic terms of Freudian psychology.

However, Ewing's (1994) article is bedeviled with several problems. For a start, Ewing exaggerates the *a priori* atheist univocality among anthropologists and assembles a false dichotomy between believing interlocutors and non-believing anthropologists. Not all anthropologists "rule out the possibility of belief in another's reality" (ibid.: 572). 'Atheism' might also be a harsh overstatement of a more receptive position of anthropologists who do not militantly deny the existence of spirits but say, after Kant, that there can be no certainty that spirits and gods are empirically real. The *Encyclopedia of Unbelief* contrasts strong atheism (i.e., the denial of the facticity of gods) with weak atheism and agnosticism, or the impossibility of knowing for sure that any deity exists and, hence, not believing (Martin 2007: 89). It is an open-ended question whether anthropologists tend to gravitate to the strong or weak node of atheism. The most perplexing insinuation that Ewing makes is that a non-believing anthropologist is likely to privilege 'Western' theories, discourses, and secular explanations over local or combinatory (co-existing 'Western' and local) interpretations of anthropologists' interlocutors. To give an example, Ewing refers to the work of Tanya Luhrmann on witchcraft in Britain.

In her book, Luhrmann (1989: 18) makes a disclaimer about her own 'belief' in magic when she writes that she has never believed in magic and that she knows that any magical make-believe is not real. Although Luhrmann has participated in the magical practices and training of her interlocutors during her fieldwork, she frames her analysis in terms of the rationality and irrationality of magical 'beliefs' in order to demonstrate how magical practices can be persuasive despite their dubious efficacy. Ewing (1994: 573) suggests that Luhrmann's disclaimer indicates that Luhrmann failed to question her own assumptions about the irrationality of magic. According to Ewing, Luhrmann paid lip service to people's felt 'beliefs' and rituals in the field when she later explained magical practices in terms of a drift into irrationality. Ewing argues that Luhrmann was constrained in her description by the above-mentioned taboo on believing and going native.

Unfortunately, Ewing's argument that non-belief is a hegemonic act conflates the problem of the subjective belief of anthropologists with their professional conduct—their participation, degree of engagement, and interaction—in the field. By focusing on Luhrmann's disbelief, Ewing (1994: 578) herself introduces through the back door the troubled assumption that beliefs are reflected in practices: an atheist would not take people's beliefs seriously and would treat people as 'objects' of research. Believing or non-believing creates, to put it simply, a gulf between 'us' and 'them', and an anthropologist who refuses (or perhaps finds it impossible) to believe forecloses the possibility of full participation and perspicacious anthropological analysis. Furthermore, Ewing formulates her otherwise astute contestation of anthropological atheism in the inadvertently cognitive or mentalist language of 'belief', which makes it easy to miss the performative and dispositional dimensions of being an atheist in the field.

Suspension of Disbelief and Performance

It is interesting that cognitive belief rather than performative savvy tends to be seen as the most taxing and demanding religious accomplishment. For a start, I disagree with Ewing that shared believing is conducive to deep involvement in people's worlds. Our interlocutors are not 'stable' believers, and they typically find it difficult to penetrate each other's minds despite their shared religious inheritance. Ethnographies, mine included, attest to people's peregrinations through moments of conviction, skepticism, and believing; their roaming through different denominations (Kirsch 2004); their elated successes or discouraging failures and struggles to accomplish religiosity; their articulated frustration and ineffable lassitude; their renewal of commitments, engagement in healings, persistence despite inefficacy, and so on. Similar eccentricities and instabilities of cognitive and practical believing might apply to anthropologists, while specific theological forms of believing and performing rituals are a cultural work of the religious people with whom we temporarily live. To impugn anthropologists who are reluctant to become religious in the field is to forget that religious assimilation is often perceived as an achievement, a gift bestowed by ancestors or gods (Binsbergen 1991), a talent revealed through years of training (Luhrmann et al. 2010), and not just an intellectual and professional decision to believe.

Furthermore, is 'belief' such a secret and peculiar state of the human mind that it takes a mystic to understand a mystic? Cognitive anthropologists have been arguing for some time that intuitive religious belief is a natural proclivity of the human species. For example, Justin Barrett (2004) explains that human cognition has universally shared non-reflective intuitions about whose agency is behind different events and actions, ordinary and extraordinary. A glass does not drop to the floor of its own accord. It takes somebody or something to push it, and this agent might as well be a dead ancestor. Reflective religious beliefs—namely, theologically elaborated and culturally transmitted forms of religious concepts and rituals such as monotheism—are learned on top of our intuitive cognitive processes and, I aver, are empirically accessible to anthropologists. I am greatly simplifying Barrett's interesting book, but its key argument can be read like this. Our mind has a cognitive proclivity to believe in invisible agents; therefore, we are all natural theists and being religious is a cognitive default.

Barrett (2004: 107–118) goes on to maintain that atheism, by contrast, is a very peculiar cognitive position acquired in very specific settings, such as, among others, the academic corridors of Western universities. Barrett does not suggest that Western scholars are bound to be atheists—just that one can arrive at the non-theistic cognitive position of an atheist more easily in today's academic environment, which emphasizes the social construction of religions and denaturalizes many religious 'givens'. It is worth considering whether non-believing anthropologists might be the odd ones out who manage to bend their naturally religious minds in order to learn cognitively difficult non-theistic ways of being in this world. Nonetheless, Barrett's arguments about the cognitive naturalness of belief should not be taken at face value (Geertz and Markusson 2010). One could suggest that being an atheist is no bigger a cognitive challenge than adhering to one's beliefs, but in some contexts being a proclaimed atheist or a believer is to run the socio-political risk of persecution. Cognition theories are ultimately secular, but they serve the point of showing that belief and atheism might not be mutually exclusive cognitive positions.

Returning to the methodological question of being an atheist anthropologist in the field, should anthropologists "factor their own religious backgrounds, beliefs, and experiences into their research and writing" (Stewart 2001: 325)? I think they should. For me, the subjective religious beliefs of an anthropologist and their embarrassing absence are a problem of method (Engelke 2002) and "perspectival variation" (Stewart 2001: 327), not an argument for a privileged or implausibly 'objective' vantage into people's theological interpretations and ritual performances (Bielo 2014). It is also a comparative method aiming to illuminate rather than dissolve this variation. As a method in the field, disbelief can be suspended (Kapferer 2001; Luhrmann 1989) to forestall derision or clear biases and to enable involvement in religious practices. This position, described by Amos Yong (2012: 21) as "methodological agnosticism," entails at least an attempt to refrain from judgment about the perceptions of religiously motivated people and their experiential effects.

However, Joel Kahn (2011: 80) argues that strategies such as the suspension of disbelief might bespeak inequality and asymmetry as they depend on 'bracketing' religious and non-religious worlds as separate realms. When anthropologists suspend disbelief, they reify their own world as a culture that can be isolated from experience. Bracketing does not facilitate dialogue because, for Kahn, understanding springs out of the fusion of interpretive horizons into a novel perception (ibid.: 82). This is an intriguing critique, but it is not evident what kind of encounters could produce a fusion of horizons and what this fusion would look like in practice.

At the same time, doubt might be propitious for fieldwork endeavors (Kapferer 2001). Doubt is also a cognitive strategy of unsettling confidences and putting checks on the desire to take something as either a rational or spiritual 'fact' (ibid.: 343). A spiritual given might easily refer to conceptual biases of believing anthropologists' first acquired religiosity, usually Judaism and Christianity, and resilient religious expectations, a situation that spells a probability for distortions, misunderstandings, and blind spots (Saler 1993: 199–200) as consequential as those produced by atheism, secularism, or agnosticism. In this case, the problem for an anthropologist is how to research different or her/his own religious traditions without sliding into "methodological theism" (Yong 2012: 24), a 'believer's' view on religion.

While methodological atheism, agnosticism, and theism represent distinct epistemological takes on the problem of understanding religion, my contention is that believing does not exhaust people's religiosity. For example, getting the hang of liturgies and rituals of worship does not automatically ensue from believing in an all-powerful God. Consider a carefully laid-out setting for learning how to go into trance among Muslim Malays: offerings are made, incense is lit, and the best floor mats are spread. A competent teacher reads incantations, yet a female student is unable to achieve trance—and, according to her teacher, she never will (Laderman 1996). Because subjective talent, learning, and public encouragement correlate, it is not easy to emerge as a virtuoso of a ritual practice. Similarly, a Korean trainee in shamanism could not unseal her 'gates' of inspired speech and divinatory oracles (Kendall 1996), a skill that did not come to her effortlessly regardless of her experiences of a spiritual calling in her dreams and despite having received the necessary training from advanced shamans.

Thus, even if an anthropologist embraces a belief in the facticity of gods and spirits, there are practical challenges to being religious. After all, a devout Catholic might ask an anthropologist "do you pray?" (Fabian 1995: 45), rather than "are you a believer?" (DiCarlo 2012: 66). Similarly, becoming born-again for fundamentalist Baptists entails not just the suspension of disbelief but a performative speech act, a public disavowal (Harding 2000: 59). Ritualizing and ritual participation constitute a different challenge from believing (Bielo 2014). In a nutshell, cognitive assumptions about the facticity of spirits, somehow perceived by anthropologists to be the means to being religious, do not cover all the aspects of participation in people's pragmatic and liturgical activities and religious realities. The theologian William Schweiker (2005) suggests that atheism works on the level of cognition and on the level of practice. One can differentiate between 'theoretical theism', that is, belief in God, and 'practical atheism', ritual and prosaic non-adherence to practices that create a religious sociality. A professor of theological ethics at the University of Chicago, Schweiker points out that "practical atheism is, religiously speaking, a betrayal of faith" (ibid.: 273). Methodologically, apart from belief, numerous factors play into interactive situations between interlocutors and anthropologists. A sound anthropological practice, however, is not to speculate about a winning combination of personal histories and fieldwork circumstances, but to put forward and unmask the vulnerability of the ethnographer's own research processes—one's tactics, choices, lies, secrets, and experiences.

Kim Knibbe and André Droogers (2011) propose the notion of 'methodological ludism' as a constructivist alternative to methodological atheism, agnosticism, and theism (rejection, neutrality, or endorsement of religious truth claims, respectively).[1] Methodological ludism is primarily concerned with interpretation, but it goes beyond belief and disbelief by drawing attention to learning and unlearning a new bodily and emotional habitus and acquiring a different sense of self through ritual participation (ibid.). Methodological ludism involves 'serious play', which is a common aspect of religious practice for all participants. It has a subjunctive 'as if' dimension that allows people to imagine and enter a transcendental or alternative reality while remaining aware of this conventional world (Yong 2012: 25). Serious play relies on the capacity to deploy two interpretive frames simultaneously, for example, doubting religious truth claims yet accepting them as they are (Knibbe and Droogers 2011). The methodological implication of serious play is that it activates a researcher's ability to view and interpret the world along two sight lines: that of a fieldworker and that of a ritual participant. The simultaneity of these perspectives prevents radical relativism and the hierarchical (de)valuation of religious and non-religious experiences, regardless of whether a researcher is an atheist, agnostic, or 'believer' (Yong 2012: 27–28).[2]

It is not clear how methodological ludism differs from familial anthropological practices of perspectivism and of reflexivity (which involves self-alienation but does not require a loss of self). However, I find the notion of methodological ludism relevant to my analysis because Knibbe and Droogers (2011: 294) recognize the limits of play and embodied participation. Some anthropologists experience 'strange events'—visions or shamanic encounters with extraordinary forces (Jacobs 2002; Stoller and Olkes 1987; Young and Goulet 1994). Yet it is often forgotten that anthropologists not only seek immersion but also tactically define the performative boundaries of their subjective participation in the ritual lives of their interlocutors (Dubisch 1995: 180–192). For example, clapping one's hands might be experienced as less irksome than saying "amen" or speaking in tongues (Blanes 2006: 230). Another anthropologist might remain deliberately detached from more radical forms of participation because rituals are expensive or time-consuming (Glazier 2008). During her fieldwork in a missionizing Buddhist temple in Taiwan, Hillary Crane (2014: 21) resisted participating in rituals that would signal her conversion and full membership in that religious community; she crawled on her knees as a pilgrim but would not take her vows. In other words, anthropologists look not only for immersion but for ways to avoid and opt out of certain aspects of people's religious worlds. In the next section, I will describe my encounter with an exorcist and confess to my inability to play with two interpretive frameworks, as well as my desire to pare down my physical exposure to ritual.

An Atheist Meets a Mystic

There are numerous mystical Sufi orders in Macedonia that intersect with different ethnicities, including Albanians, Turks, Roma, and others. These orders are a legacy of the Ottoman Empire, which withdrew from the region in the early twentieth century. Since then, some of the orders have weathered the Balkan and two world wars, hostilities of the royal and then socialist Yugoslavia, and today's economically and socially uncertain production of an EU-style democracy in independent Macedonia. Other dervish orders are on the brink of disappearance, struggling to attract new members and financial contributions. Many dervish orders have been abandoned, while new ones, especially makeshift halls of prayer (*semana*), are being established by mainly Roma Muslims.

Concerned about my personal atheism and the atheism of anthropology, in 2008 I embarked on a project about Muslim mystical religiosity in urban Macedonia. I made a conscious decision to suspend disbelief, yet I did not wish to engage in a long-term religious commitment beyond my fieldwork.[3] When I participated in dervish rituals, even if I mimicked my interlocutors' performances, I still participated as a historical self. Born in the late Soviet Union, I was not baptized because of a vehemently atheistic parent, although many people of my generation were. I had little opportunity as a child to learn any religious practices. Inspired by French existential philosophy, I later developed an articulate intellectual position against religion. In Macedonia, I misrepresented myself as a non-practicing Russian Orthodox. Religion became a nominal identity, as among some non-believing Jews in Copenhagen (Buckser 2008) or some university students in Skopje who define themselves as categorical Orthodox Christians even when they simultaneously subscribe to staunch atheism (Thiessen 2007: 48). The decision to misrepresent myself as a 'believer by identity' was made on the spot and very early in the field, without a sophisticated plan to mislead my interlocutors. Yet I worried about the ethical implications of gaining access to the field by false pretenses. I felt that being strategically untruthful in the field carried the connotations of inequality between interlocutors and anthropologist (Katz 1996: 172; Metcalf 2002; Wolf 1996b: 11–12). At the same time, I feared being discovered and ostracized. I was worried that my atheism might compromise both my rapport with my interlocutors and my discernment of anthropological problems. Nevertheless, I felt that I could engage productively with people's religious traditions.

Crucially, during many interviews and discussions, it was not my atheism in its intellectual, 'rational' mode that created temporary rifts between people and myself; rather, it was my other convictions, especially political ones. In mundane conversations, some of my political registers were at loggerheads with people's occasional anti-Semitic, anti-Christian, or misogynistic rhetoric, which was often validated by popular interpretations of the Qur'an. My interlocutors' endorsement of historical pogroms against Jews, articulated in the light of the Gaza conflict, upset more than metaphysical conversations about many-headed angels and demons (cf. Harding 2000: 165, 185). In other words, my fieldwork was not informed by the opposition between rational science and religious truth claims but by my ethical discomfort and disapproval of the religiously inflected political articulations of my interlocutors.

My research gravitated to lengthy theological discussions and the observation of male-only rituals as a female anthropologist sitting in the corner—until I met Bayrush. A dervish who could talk to snakes and had prophetic dreams and visions, Bayrush possessed an extraordinary sexual cum spiritual energy that made him irresistible to all women. He was also the most powerful of all the dervishes in Skopje because of his personal affinity, forged in his dreams, with the buried saint, Hamid Baba, the historical founder of the Blue Lodge in Skopje. This is how Bayrush described himself to me with a boastful smile a week into our acquaintance. He was gaunt and frail, with a trimmed black beard and deep dark eyes offset by the pale skin of an ill man with a weak heart. Sometimes he wore a robe of light brown nylon or, more conventionally, a pair of jeans matched by either a dark sweatshirt or a T-shirt with assorted golden letters that did not make up a word.

In addition to his duties as a deputy of the *shaykh* Baba Fariha, who was perennially absent from his own rituals and disinterested in all administrative and spiritual obligations, Bayrush had a spiritual routine. The dervish was emotionally attached to the tombs located in a separate crypt (*turbe*) of the lodge (*tekke*). It was a long rectangular room, slightly underground like a cellar and submerged in the twilight of dim electric bulbs. The windows of the crypt were now boarded up with large metal panels after somebody hurled a Molotov cocktail through a window, smashing the glass and setting the carpets on fire. Unidentified Wahhabis were blamed. The room sloped downward, giving the impression that the 12 cemented tombs were gliding down into the dark, like tragic green and gold ships. To the right of the entrance, there was the largest and the richest tomb of Hamid Baba, the founder, with a long string of prayer beads, a leather belt, and a red scarf thrown over it. Occasionally, a T-shirt or towel was placed on top of the coffin, to be charged with the saint's energy (fig. 1).

Every day, except Sundays, which Bayrush spent with his extensive family, the dervish arrived at the *tekke* at noon. He left his empty shoulder bag containing just a skinny wallet in the dilapidated library, cluttered with old bicycle wheels, a buzzing freezer, a broken wheelchair, and a metal cot. There was just one bookcase left in that library, with dusty memories of former theological literacy and past scholarly grandeur. Bayrush changed his shoes to rubber slippers and shuffled to a running water tap with a red plastic bucket and a piece of grimy cloth. Then he would enter the crypt to mop the tombs and an assorted collection of objects, including little boxes, candlesticks, paintings, and picture frames. Some of the objects, such as a carpet with a galloping Arab horseman, had some relevance to Islam.

FIGURE 1 The Tombs of the *Shaykhs* in the Blue Lodge

Photograph © 2009 Galina Oustinova-Stjepanovic

Having finished cleaning, Bayrush would kneel next to Hamid Baba's tomb, say a prayer, and get up and kiss the spot on the coffin where the right foot of the beloved saint was located. Bayrush circled the tomb and kissed different spots on the coffin. He kissed the leather belt bedecked with metal rings. He would then kiss the coffin of Fatima Badi, the wife of Hamid Baba, and the small coffin of Abdal, their baby, according to Bayrush, or of another nameless dervish, according to others. Finally, Bayrush would apply a drop of enchanted perfume from a tiny bottle that could be bought cheaply at the street market. It protected him from evil spirits, which he feared.

The dervish would sit in the corner on an old sheepskin and place in front of him his mobile phone, a bottle of Cokta (a local version of Coca-Cola), and a handwritten list of Allah's Ninety-Nine Beautiful Names, which he would recite in a rapid-fire manner a thousand times each, interspersing his monotonous ritual with a *fatiha* prayer. His spiritual power, Bayrush asserted, came directly from Hamid Baba and was consolidated in his daily exercises of reciting the beautiful names of Allah. At the time of my research, Bayrush never attempted to memorize the names, not a negligible trifle if one considers the theological hypothesis that the Divine presence comes into being to the extent that the names take possession of the mind that recites them (Burckhardt 2006: 15).

Dervish rituals and prayers demand the repetition of Allah's names so that the words colonize a person's mind. This is not a sign of inferior cognitive faculty, as the colonial administrations in Egypt and Yemen claimed, but a vehicle of enacting presences (Messick 1989). However, Bayrush did not seem to know this hypothesis, and he continued to rely on his handwritten memory aid with Allah's names, which, due to wear and tear, he occasionally replaced, either with a photocopy of the list of the names from a book or another rewritten bit of paper. His day of cleaning and praying would conclude with a modest meal of white bread and chicken pâté, which he would eat while watching the five o'clock news on the black-and-white portable television in a small utility room of the *tekke*.

Despite the regularity of his prayers, Bayrush did not mind interruptions, answered all phone calls, enjoyed my questioning, and rushed outside every time he thought he heard a client's voice or footsteps. Most clients (*mush-teriya*), men and women, came to the tombs to lodge a prayer of petition with the saints and Allah. Many were diagnosed by Bayrush with spirit possession. Bayrush insisted that he had the 'energy' to help people, while other dervishes influenced by reformed versions of Islam routinely dismissed people's suspicions of a djinn affliction as 'superstitions'.

Bayrush was eager to demonstrate his 'energy' to me, and one day, when I complained of a stubborn headache, he led me to the far end of the crypt and asked me to sit down between two tombs. Bayrush instructed me to dangle my feet inside a hole in the ground, its cracked mouth partly covered by an old carpet. The place was cool and comfortable in the intense heat of the Macedonian August. I was told to put my forehead on the coffin to my left and to think about God (*misli na gospod*). Later I looked at the architectural plan of the crypt hanging on the wall and realized that I was sitting between the female and male coffins. Bayrush speculated that the left tomb of Sejide Badi would help women's worries, while the right one of *shaykh* Ibrahim Baba would heal men's problems. But that exhausted our inferences about left-right symbolism. So I was sitting in the energy hole trying to think about God, which I found exasperating. I wanted to experiment with participation and performance, not only to keep up appearances but as a form of introverted self-transformation. I tried to repeat a name of Allah after Bayrush to imagine a relationship with God, but my mind would drift away. I recalled that many of my interlocutors complained about how difficult it was to concentrate on a God that has no humanly imaginable form, according to Islamic theological definitions of Allah. At that moment, my field notes remind me, I was anthropologizing my experience and badly so: it all boiled down to sitting between two tombs hoping for a headache to go away. Although an atheist, I was beginning to grasp experientially the human hardship of thinking and talking to a Being, theologically described as inconceivable, invisible, and silent.

I opened my eyes at some point to peep at an elderly woman who nearly fell into the crypt. Obese, she had difficulty walking around the tombs, and Bayrush helped her climb through three loops of a giant rosary hanging from the support posts of the *turbe*. Bayrush returned to pick me up from the hole and led me to the same rosary beads. I stepped through the loops swinging close to the floor, first with my right leg and then my left. Next, he took me to the tomb of the founder of the lodge. There, standing on the carpet between two coffins, I kissed the foot of the saint and hopped over a long string of smaller beads, as if I was jumping a rope. Then I had to kiss the saint's broad leather belt. Bayrush put the belt around my waist. It was short and would not meet behind my back, but it was wide enough to cover my abdomen. Bayrush started chanting under his breath. He fetched a locked padlock, a plain one available at any store, and told me to unlock it. The locking and unlocking were repeated three times. The lock opened with a friendly well-oiled click. The last thing to do was to swallow a mandatory chunk of sugar from a small tin box placed at the foot of the tomb. That sealed our transaction.

We spent the rest of the day busy with little chores. We sprinkled the concrete floor of the courtyard with water and, having locked up everything, let a large shabby dog out of its cage to bark in the yard at night. We finally left the lodge, planning to have a meal together. I imagined we would sit in a small street café, but Bayrush invited himself to my flat not far from the lodge. During our meal, Bayrush decided that he wanted to tell me more about djinn spirits. These were dangerous and secret "things." According to Bayrush, "djinn spirits catch people and live inside them, so people sometimes have to eat two times more, for themselves and their djinn spirit. Djinn spirits ruin people's memory and induce vomiting. People feel heaviness in their chest and headaches at the back of their head. Often djinn spirits sleep with women, and occasionally women do not even need a husband. They just live with spirits. These women go to the toilet often because their djinn spirit is sitting in the loo." Bayrush encountered a female djinn spirit, who opened her mouth broadly so that he could see all her teeth and tried to kiss him. She wanted to sleep with him and tried to seduce him. "This happens and people do not even know if this is a real person who is trying to seduce them. Only children are spared, until the age of 16, because God protects them," Bayrush warned me.

Listening to Bayrush was interesting, and I wanted to learn more about where and how exactly djinn spirits attack people. Bayrush asked me to stretch my right palm toward him. He pressed the tip of my middle finger with his fingernail several times and repeated the process with my left hand. He instructed me to get up and put his fingers on my ears, blocking the sound. His thumbs were on my forehead between my eyebrows. He was rubbing the spot on my head viciously and then asked me if I felt vertigo. I said no and continued to look into Bayrush's eyes, which were tired and traversed with little blood vessels. He repeated the process several times while mumbling a prayer under his breath. Suddenly he nudged me in my stomach with the fingers of his left hand, causing sharp pain. I recoiled and screamed in surprise. The dervish asked me to confirm if I was in pain. I said I was. Bayrush told me that I had been hit (*pogodjena*) by a djinn, but I was not possessed. I had a gram of bad energy, just a morsel; he picked up a bread crumb to demonstrate the amount. Ill at ease and confused, I wished for the procedure to be over. I hoped we could go back to storytelling, but Bayrush rubbed my forehead a bit longer and poked me a few times in the stomach, although more gently. I did not feel any pain, and Bayrush was satisfied with the results. He showed me his left hand, which was trembling because he had transferred the bad energy he had found in me into himself. To release this energy he would have to perform a special ritual to cleanse his own energy. Some dervishes, Bayrush explained, cooperated with djinn spirits and had secret rituals in the cemeteries.

Bayrush said that djinn spirits were dangerous because one might succumb to their powers in dreams or in reality. A person can be forced to copulate with a djinn spirit, male or female, and might be bitten. People's energy and health might be ruined and their fertility challenged. Djinn spirits enter people through their blood. If an afflicted person's finger is pierced sharply with a needle, then the possessed blood that appears in the wound is dark in color. The place where Bayrush was rubbing my forehead was the location of a djinn's eye, a third eye on a person's face through which a djinn was watching the world. Bayrush suddenly moved to the middle of the room and told me to "dance disco" for him. I was taken aback. What did he mean by 'disco'? Bayrush swayed his hips, showing me the movements of pop singers. I refused, pleading that I did not know how to dance. But Bayrush insisted: "Come on, dance disco for me." I refused again, but he continued to goad me.

The episode was disturbing. There is a difference between just listening to a story about a djinn and being subjected to manhandling and physical scrutiny during the search for a djinn or spots where evil forces could have hit me. The experience was disconcerting despite the fact that I did not believe Bayrush's stories about djinn spirits. To overcome methodological atheism, I publicly suspended disbelief and took what people told me for granted.[4] What people said, however, did not affect me as much as the ritual itself, which I found invasive, both physically and emotionally. After Bayrush's repeated forceful requests to dance disco for him, he continued telling me stories about sexual innuendos between people and djinn spirits and how his personal energy was craved by afflicted women. Those stories made me feel increasingly uncomfortable, and I started to suspect mild sexual harassment. The request to dance disco tipped me further in the direction of the analogy between a djinn attack and harassment. But within people's interpretive frameworks, stories of sexual relations between djinn spirits and humans, usually women, were commonplace. The event invited ambiguity between spiritual malevolence and sexual harassment.

Methodological ludism implies switching back and forth between perspectives while simultaneously juggling with two or more ways of classifying reality (Knibbe and Droogers 2011), but the above episode reveals my discomfort at moving between interpretive frameworks. Bayrush and I interacted within an explicitly religious frame of spirit possession that involved the sexual aggression of djinn spirits. Yet his words and actions also suggested sexual harassment. In this case, the 'religious' practice of possession overlapped with 'secular' harassment. However, I found it difficult to acknowledge 'secular' aspects within the ritual without compromising my commitment to the suspension of disbelief because the event was framed explicitly as exorcism. Sexual harassment was its latent content but of a metaphysical rather than mundane quality. To dismiss the metaphysical would be precisely to explain religion away as socio-political and gender power relations.

Also, the event pointed out the limits of participation that is characterized not so much by 'belief' but by the embodied and affective quality of ritual practices. Thinking that ethnographic participation could be willed, I was surprised to discover that participation in a religious ritual—being poked, touched, hurt, and befuddled—felt harmful. The exorcism contained an implicit corporeal threat. Rumors about the real or mythical Baba sunflower oil (*baba zeytin*) massaging women and about Bayrush writing the Qur'anic verses with his tongue on their bodies in the cemeteries of Skopje reached me later. And when I described my encounter to my female interlocutors, several alerted me to the danger of being forced to have non-consensual sex under the spiritual control of a healer.[5]

On some level I started to think that this ritual exorcism was not a way to solve problems, social, political, or psychological, but to generate problems and dangers in the first place. Robert Orsi (2005: 62) reminds us that devotion is a 'psychological playground' that "provokes uncertainty, dread, confusion, and panic." In fact, the moment "'when the transcendent breaks into time' ... is more confounding and unsettling" than meaningful (ibid.: 111). Since my exorcism began with a minor health complaint, I could not help but notice that if a slight headache could have been adequately cured with an aspirin, the situation with djinn spirits would turn a headache into a mysterious, threatening, and complicated affair that would need the resources of several people to manage it. A djinn-induced headache would become a time-, money-, and effort-consuming process of healing—an unappealing combination of 'ends and means'.

Indeed, over the next few days, Bayrush proceeded to cleanse me of "bad works." He would not explain if I was hexed or possessed, whether it was a human responsibility, and why it had happened to me. He lugged in a herbal solution in a plastic water bottle in which I had to bathe myself; then he brought me some herbal tea. All these ingredients were not cheap, but Bayrush charged me the going rate at the street market. He was not trying to rip me off; he was trying to liberate me from something that I did not sense and that did not play any significant role in my life. Bayrush feared rejection and was worried that I would flush the herbal solution in the toilet, but I reassured him that I would not. I kept my word, and that same evening I poured the brown liquid over myself in the tiled shower cabin of my modern flat in an apartment block, had a magical tea, and went to sleep wondering if I would dream of a visitation or wake up ill. But nothing happened. I reported my mundane experience to Bayrush who, nevertheless, declared that I had been freed of any spiritual worries. I started to avoid Bayrush as he continued to boast about his energy and rushed to diagnose petrified women with possession, fidgeting with a rusty pin that he would sometimes shove in their middle finger to extract a djinn and a dark bead of blood. Sometimes, as a prank, he was locked inside the crypt for an hour by a middle-aged female neighbor who, tongue-in-cheek, defied Bayrush's diagnosis that she was terminally possessed.

Dispositional Atheism

The suspension of disbelief constitutes a necessary methodological exercise—known as methodological atheism—that probes into the implicit biases of anthropologists and our discipline as such. However, disbelief is not the only impediment to participation. One thing I have learned from my encounter with Bayrush is that Bourdieu (1990: 68–69) had a point when he wrote that anthropologists who voluntarily and intellectually make a decision to believe still might fail to apprehend the subjective experience of being religious if they are not able to act through their bodies. This is especially the case if a practical side of belief is not only an intellectual or ethical connection but an emotional and physical commitment (Asad 1993). Ritual participation had caused me embodied discomfort and posed ontological menace to my sense of self by undermining my ability to comprehend the world around me.

In the course of my fieldwork, it has become clear that the 'pure intellectualism' of anthropology is frequently, if not always, complicated by the emotions, physicality, inhibitions, and idiosyncrasies of a researcher. We all have different proclivities toward being religious (Luhrmann 2010: 228). These "different proclivities, different psychological and bodily capacities" (ibid.: 233) are as crucial for fieldwork participation as are cognitive belief and knowing. In my understanding, these proclivities are not only psychological but historical. I trace my bodily and emotional unavailability to 'being godless' (see the introduction, this volume) and religiously untaught in the post-Soviet context (see Luehrmann, this volume). I think about this bodily and emotional unavailability in terms of a 'dispositional atheism', which plays an important role in undermining the strategy of methodological suspension of disbelief and in marking the limits of participation.

Charles Hirschkind's (2011) question as to whether there is a secular body is timely in this respect. We are familiar with secular philosophical thought and discourses, but what are the "embodied aptitudes of a secular subject" (ibid.: 633) in historical contexts where secularism is the very texture of everyday life (ibid.: 641)? Perhaps there is no such thing as an atheist body that one can easily recognize in the street. At the same time, one can understand how an atheist cringes away from religion and immunizes the self against the affective and physical encroachment of religion. Charles Taylor (2007: 38) suggests that in some contexts of modernity (perhaps of a particular European modernity) a disenchanted "buffered self" creates distance between oneself and religion, a demon, a witch, or divine retribution. My argument is that such a buffered self works to insulate oneself from these forces not only intellectually but physically and emotionally. Being poked by the religious finger of an exorcist ruptures the buffer.

Acknowledgments

I would like to express my gratitude to Charles Stewart, Ruth Mandel, Michael Lambek, Ger Duijzings, Jonathan Spencer, and the contributors to this volume for their insightful comments on earlier versions of this chapter. My PhD training and fieldwork were funded by a UCL Overseas Research Scholarship and the Marie Curie Social Anthropology Programme.

Galina Oustinova-Stjepanovic has been working as a Teaching Fellow in the Department of Anthropology at University College London since 2012. She is also a researcher in the Department of Anthropology at the University of Edinburgh. Her PhD project focused on religion, especially Sufi Islam, the sense of ritual and moral failure, and the marginality and historical subjectivities of Roma Muslims in Macedonia. Her research interests include anthropology of religion, especially Islam, political anthropology, anti-Zionism and notions of sovereignty in the Soviet Union and Russia, and the history of the secularization of Soviet Jews.

Notes

1. The idea of methodological ludism is compelling, but its defense is based on a mistaken representation of atheism and agnosticism. Knibbe and Droogers (2011) suggest that atheism, agnosticism, and theism rely exclusively on the positivist juxtaposition of religion with science, while methodological ludism is a more constructivist approach to religion. This argument, however, does not take into consideration the fact that, for example, some forms of atheism are shaped by non-religious notions of history, temporality, and personhood rather than by the strict separation of religion and science. In other words, articulations of atheism are not necessarily positivist and can be constructivist in their orientation.
2. Yong (2012) uses the term 'theologian' instead of 'believer'. In the opening paragraph of this chapter, I refer to an ongoing debate about the assumption that theologians are necessarily believers. I have refrained from adopting Yong's terminology because it is not clear to me to what extent a study of theology requires a confessional membership.
3. I was not openly pressured to convert by my interlocutors, who frequently cited a Qur'anic verse that there is no compulsion in religion. Having said that, some people thought that it was inevitable that sooner or later I would do so because it was 'common sense' to be a Muslim. Susan Harding (1987: 168) suggests that during conversion people become convinced that God exists: "[T]o continue to think otherwise would be irrational; it is disbelief that is false and unthinking." Technologies of conversion differ, of course. Harding describes a particular linguistic process when converts are invaded by the Word of God delivered through the language of Christian fundamental Baptists.
4. The suspension of disbelief occasionally backfired when I was deliberately told cock-and-bull stories to test me and to expose my gullibility and 'insincerity'. The

most productive form of interaction was an ordinary conversation with its misunderstandings, clarifications, questions, contestations, and so on.

5. Subsequently, I witnessed identical rituals when women were brought to Bayrush by their husbands who complained that their wives had refused them sex and were aloof and depressed. Unfailingly, Bayrush explained that those women had had spiritual lovers and performed his exorcism, after which the women, who usually looked scared and forlorn, were whisked away into the busy city streets. I did not have a chance to arrange an interview with them or exchange more than a few superficial words. Although I do not know what happened before and after Bayrush's rituals, those ritual scenes connoted spousal and spiritual aggression in their own right. Isabelle Nabokov (1997) gives an example of a violent exorcism in South India that forces women to confess their illicit sexual desires. The South Indian exorcism was used against women who attempted to run away from their husbands. Accusations that women were possessed by demons did not empower women or offer an outlet for protest. On the contrary, women were subjected to humiliating and painful procedures in order to impress on them the expectation of what it takes to be a good wife. This is a plausible account of Macedonian exorcism, but it is essential to find out how the husbands and exorcists experience these rituals. Bayrush, for example, claimed that he was scared and drained by encounters with djinn spirits.

References

Asad, Talal. 1993. *Genealogies of Religion: Discipline and Reasons of Power in Christianity and Islam*. Baltimore: Johns Hopkins University Press.

Barrett, Justin. 2004. *Why Would Anyone Believe in God?* Walnut Creek, CA: Altamira Press.

Berger, Peter. 1969. *Social Reality of Religion*. London: Faber.

Berger, Peter. 2004. *Questions of Faith: A Skeptical Affirmation of Christianity*. Malden, MA: Blackwell.

Bielo, James. 2014. "Introduction: Writing Religion." Pp. 1–10 in Crane and Weibel 2014.

Binsbergen, Wim van. 1991. "Becoming a *Sangoma*: Religious Anthropological Fieldwork in Francistown, Botswana." *Journal of Religion in Africa* 21, no. 4: 309–344.

Blanes, Ruy L. 2006. "The Atheist Anthropologist: Believers and Non-Believers in Anthropological Fieldwork." *Social Anthropology* 14, no. 2: 223–234.

Boddy, Janice. 1994. "Spirit Possession Revisited: Beyond Instrumentality." *Annual Review of Anthropology* 23: 407–434.

Bourdieu, Pierre. 1990. *The Logic of Practice*. Trans. Richard Nice. Cambridge: Polity Press.

Bowie, Fiona. 1998. "Trespassing on Sacred Domains: A Feminist Anthropological Approach to Theology and Religious Studies." *Journal in Feminist Studies of Religion* 14, no. 1: 40–62.

Buckser, Andrew. 2008. "Cultural Change and the Meanings of Belief in Jewish Copenhagen." *Social Analysis* 52, no. 1: 39–55.

Burckhardt, Titus. 2006. "Sufi Doctrine and Method." Pp. 1–20. In *Sufism: Love and Wisdom*, ed. Jean-Louis Michon and Roger Gaetani. Bloomington, IN: World Wisdom.

Crane, Hillary K. 2014. "Flirting with Conversion: Negotiating Researcher Non-Belief with Missionaries." Pp. 11–24 in Crane and Weibel 2014.

Crane, Hillary K., and Deana L. Weibel, eds. 2014. *Missionary Impositions: Conversion, Resistance, and Other Challenges to Objectivity in Religious Ethnography*. Lanham, MD: Lexington Books.

Cush, Denise. 2009. "Religious Studies versus Theology: Why I'm Still Glad That I Converted from Theology to Religious Studies." Pp. 15–31 in *Theology and Religious Studies in Higher Education: Global Perspectives*, ed. Darlene L. Bird and Simon Smith. London: Continuum.

DiCarlo, Lisa. 2012. "I'm Just a Soul Whose Intentions Are Good: Observations from the Back Pew." Pp. 83–90 in Crane and Weibel 2012.

Dubisch, Jill. 1995. *In a Different Place: Pilgrimage, Gender, and Politics at a Greek Island Shrine*. Princeton, NJ: Princeton University Press.

Eipper, Chris. 2001. "The Virgin, the Visionary and the Atheistic Ethnographer: Anthropological Inquiry in the Light of Irish Apparitions." *Anthropological Forum* 11, no. 1: 21–37.

Engelke, Matthew. 2002. "The Problem of Belief: Evans-Pritchard and Victor Turner on 'The Inner Life.'" *Anthropology Today* 18, no. 6: 3–8.

Engelke, Matthew, and Matt Tomlinson, eds. 2006. *The Limits of Meaning: Case Studies in the Anthropology of Christianity*. New York and Oxford: Berghahn.

Evans-Pritchard, E. E. 1962. *Essays in Social Anthropology*. London: Faber and Faber.

Ewing, Katherine. 1994. "Dreams from a Saint: Anthropological Atheism and the Temptation to Believe." *American Anthropologist* 96, no. 3: 571–583.

Fabian, Johannes. 1995. "Ethnographic Misunderstanding and the Perils of Context." *American Anthropologist* 97, no. 1: 41–50.

Fortes, Meyer. 1987. *Religion, Morality and the Person: Essays on Tallensi Religion*. Cambridge: Cambridge University Press.

Geertz, Armin, and Gudmundur I. Markusson. 2010. "Religion Is Natural, Atheism Is Not: On Why Everybody Is Both Right and Wrong." *Religion* 40, no. 3: 152–165.

Gell, Alfred. 1999. *The Art of Anthropology: Essays and Diagrams*. Ed. Eric Hirsch. London: Athlone Press.

Glazier, Stephen D. 2008. "Demanding Deities and Reluctant Devotees: Belief and Unbelief in the Trinidadian Orisa Movement." *Social Analysis* 52, no. 1: 19–38.

Handelman, Don. 2005. "Introduction: Why Ritual in Its Own Right? How So?" Pp. 1–32 in *Ritual in Its Own Right: Exploring the Dynamics of Transformation*, ed. Don Handelman and Galina Lindquist. New York: Berghahn Books.

Harding, Susan 1987. "Convicted by the Holy Spirit: The Rhetoric of Fundamental Baptist Conversion." *American Ethnologist* 14, no. 1: 167–181.

Harding, Susan. 2000. *The Book of Jerry Falwell: Fundamentalist Language and Politics*. Princeton, NJ: Princeton University Press.

Harris, Paul. 2010. "Do Children Think That Miracles Are Just Fairy Stories?" Paper presented at LSE Anthropology Seminar. http://www.cognitionandculture.net/Lectures (accessed 15 January 2011).

Hirschkind, Charles. 2011. "Is There a Secular Body?" *Cultural Anthropology* 26, no. 4: 633–647.

Jacobs, Janet. 2002. "Transitional Identities: Self, Other, and the Ethnographic Process." Pp. 88–99 in *Personal Knowledge and Beyond: Reshaping the Ethnography of Religion*, ed. James V. Spickard, J. Shawn Landres, and Meredith B. McGuire. New York: New York University Press.

Kahn, Joel. 2011. "Understanding: Between Belief and Unbelief." *Australian Journal of Anthropology* 22, no. 1: 76–88.

Kapferer, Bruce. 2001. "Anthropology: The Paradox of the Secular." *Social Anthropology* 9, no. 3: 341–344.

Katz, Cindi. 1996. "The Expeditions of Conjurers: Ethnography, Power, and Pretense."
    Pp. 170–184 in Wolf 1996a.
Kendall, Laurel. 1996. "Initiating Performance: The Story of Chini, a Korean Shaman."
    Pp. 17–58 in Laderman and Roseman 1996.
Kirsch, Thomas. 2004. "Restaging the Will to Believe: Religious Pluralism, Anti-syncre-
    tism, and the Problem of Belief." *American Anthropologist* 106, no. 4: 699–709.
Knibbe, Kim and André Droogers. 2011. "Methodological Ludism and the Academic
    Study of Religion." *Method & Theory in the Study of Religion* 23, no. 3–4: 283–303.
Laderman, Carol. 1996. "The Poetics of Healing in Malay Shamanistic Performances."
    Pp. 115–142 in Laderman and Roseman 1996.
Laderman, Carol, and Marina Roseman, eds. 1996. *The Performance of Healing.* New
    York: Routledge.
Luhrmann, Tanya. 1989. *Persuasions of the Witch's Craft: Ritual Magic in Contempo-
    rary England.* Oxford: Basil Blackwell.
Luhrmann, Tanya. 2010. "What Counts as Data?" Pp. 212–238 in *Emotions in the Field:
    The Psychology and Anthropology of Fieldwork Experience,* ed. James Davies and
    Dimitrina Spencer. Stanford, CA: Stanford University Press.
Luhrmann, Tanya, Howard Nusbaum, and Ronald Thisted. 2010. "The Absorption
    Hypothesis: Learning to Hear God in Evangelical Christianity." *American Anthro-
    pologist* 112, no. 1: 66–78.
MacIntyre, Alasdair. 1974. "Is Understanding Religion Compatible with Believing?" Pp.
    62–77 in Wilson 1974.
Martin, Michael. 2007. "Atheism." Pp. 87–96 in *The Encyclopedia of Unbelief,* ed. Tom
    Flynn. New York: Prometheus Books.
Messick, Brinkley. 1989. "Just Writing: Paradox and Political Economy in Yemeni Legal
    Documents." *Cultural Anthropology* 4, no. 1: 26–50.
Metcalf, Peter. 2002. *They Lie, We Lie: Getting on with Anthropology.* London: Routledge.
Mittermaier, Amira. 2011. *Dreams That Matter: Egyptian Landscapes of the Imagina-
    tion.* Berkeley: University of California Press.
Nabokov, Isabelle. 1997. "Expel the Lover, Recover the Wife: Symbolic Analysis of a
    South Indian Exorcism." *Journal of the Royal Anthropological Institute* 3, no. 2:
    297–316.
Orsi, Robert. 2005. *Between Heaven and Earth: The Religious Worlds People Make and
    the Scholars Who Study Them.* Princeton, NJ: Princeton University Press.
Port, Mattijs van de. 2011. "(Not) Made by the Human Hand: Media Consciousness and
    Immediacy in the Cultural Production of the Real." *Social Anthropology* 19, no. 1:
    74–89.
Proctor, James D., ed. 2005. *Science, Religion, and the Human Experience.* Oxford:
    Oxford University Press.
Saler, Benson. 1993. *Conceptualizing Religion: Immanent Anthropologists, Transcendent
    Natives, and Unbounded Categories.* Leiden: E.J. Brill.
Schweiker, William. 2005. "Thinkpiece: The Varieties and Revisions of Atheism."
    Zygon 40, no. 2: 267–276.
Starrett, Gregory. 1998. *Putting Islam to Work: Education, Politics, and Religious Trans-
    formation in Egypt.* Berkeley: University of California Press.
Stewart, Charles. 2001. "Secularism as an Impediment to Anthropological Research."
    Social Anthropology 9, no. 3: 325–328.
Stoller, Paul, and Cheryl Olkes. 1987. *In Sorcery's Shadow: A Memoir of Apprenticeship
    among the Songhay of Niger.* Chicago: Chicago University Press.
Taylor, Charles. 2007. *A Secular Age.* Cambridge, MA: Belknap Press of Harvard Uni-
    versity Press.

Thiessen, Ilká. 2007. *Waiting for Macedonia: Identity in a Changing World*. Toronto: University of Toronto Press.

Wilson, Bryan R., ed. 1974. *Rationality*. Oxford: Basil Blackwell.

Winch, Peter. 1974. "Understanding a Primitive Society." Pp. 78–111 in Wilson 1974.

Wolf, Diane L., ed. 1996a. *Feminist Dilemmas in Fieldwork*. Boulder, CO: Westview Press.

Wolf, Diane L. 1996b. "Situating Feminist Dilemmas in Fieldwork." Pp. 1–55 in Wolf 1996a.

Yong, Amos. 2012. "Observation-Participation-Subjunctivation: Methodological Play and Meaning-Making in the Study of Religion and Theology." *Religious Studies and Theology* 31, no. 1: 17–40.

Young, David E., and Jean-Guy Goulet, eds. 1994. *Being Changed: The Anthropology of Extraordinary Experience*. Orchard Park, NY: Broadview Press.

AFTERWORD
On Atheism and Non-Religion

Matthew Engelke

We all have our conceptual bugbears, terms which, as anthropologists, cause us trouble. Over the past couple of years, an increasing number of anthropologists working in the anthropology of religion have had to face some newly prominent ones: atheism, godlessness, and (worst of all) non-religion.

I do not wholly like these terms. They are troublesome words, especially if deployed in hopes of having much analytic purchase. For all they seem to do in such cases is pull us back to what they are trying to get away from: God, gods, and religion. Godlessness, atheism, and non-religion are always beholden to something else.

To say I do not like these terms is not to say I do not admire the chapters collected in this volume. Indeed, it is a welcome addition to the growing body of literature on atheist and humanist organizations, secularist ideologies, secular embodiments, and the everyday dispositions of the godless, which range from aggressive to ambivalent. In the process of their explorations, these chapters trace forms of atheism and non-religiosity and godlessness from East Anglia to Angola. They document the importance of these conceptual compasses to how people live, die, doubt, get angry, believe in something, know something, and even listen to the radio. Several of the contributions also have a reflexive element, using case studies to revisit classic debates in anthropology over method and ethnographic authority.

The more reflexive discussions in these papers prompt a further consideration, which I would like to raise here. This concerns how to relate an 'anthropology of non-religion' to the anthropology of religion.

I have complained about troublesome words. To make matters worse, the anthropology of religion had issues before the godless came into view. For at least two generations—certainly since Jack Goody's (1961) intervention—the anthropology of religion has grappled with whether and how to speak of 'religion' at all. 'Religion' is a troublesome word, as well. As with other sub-fields, the anthropology of religion has undergone a lot of auto- and self-critique. Much of this has been salutary and productive. But it only adds to the unease, frustration, and sometimes slight embarrassment that accompanies the study of 'non-religion'. It is as if the/non/allows/religion/a free pass: we focus on the negation and not the object being negated, although we do not accept the object in the first place.[1]

One thing that strikes me is how the trouble of negation seems to affect the study of (non-)religion in particular ways. Take a comparison with the anthropology of kinship. With David Schneider's (1984) *A Critique of the Study of Kinship* often cited as a turning point—coupled with feminist critiques from the 1970s—kinship became an increasingly troublesome word. But neither at the level of theoretical analysis nor that of ethnographic finding did we start to see the anthropology of 'non-kinship' as such. By 2000, a whole new rubric was coming into place, one based on 'cultures of relatedness' (Carsten 2000) and, in a wonderful play on words, 'relative values' (Franklin and McKinnon 2001). The new kinship studies continue to flourish, not least where they have included the study of people who (like atheists and the godless) reject the normative terms of self-identification and social connection.

What about an anthropology of non-economics? Again, this sub-field has moved well beyond the classic formula (the formalist vs. substantivist debates of yore), focusing increasingly on the emergence of alternative currencies and related rejections or reconfigurations of the dominant models of banking, exchange, and so forth.[2] Economic anthropology in this phase has also given rise to other conceptual formulations—such as the 'human economy' (Hart et al. 2010)—and has reinvigorated classic concerns—such as 'value' (Graeber 2001). Once again, in many instances, the synergy between the analytical rejection of the sufficiency or meaning of a key term, on the one hand, and what people and social groups are doing to express their dissatisfaction with (or rejection of) an orthodoxy, on the other hand, is strong. Occupy Wall Street is not a 'non-economic movement'.

And could we have an anthropology of non-politics? Not a chance. This is almost unthinkable, certainly at the analytical level, especially given how easily a conception of politics slides into a generic one of power—despite some unease with this fact (Spencer 1997; Vincent 2002). There are, of course, plenty of people and organizations who describe what they do as 'non-political' or 'apolitical', and there is a healthy literature on the concept of 'depoliticization'. But I have never read an anthropological analysis that take those claims and concepts at face value. Indeed, I would venture that, for most anthropologists, such claims only draw attention to the 'political' positioning of the people making them. In James Ferguson's (1994) seminal study of development in Africa, the 'anti-politics machine' cannot erase the politics. As Matei Candea (2011: 313) puts it: "Political reality is the ground from which everything (even the supposedly non-political) is made—politically."

It is here that some common ground can be found with the ways in which anthropologists treat religion and its non-religious others. As I have started to discuss elsewhere (Engelke 2014), it boils down to this. When it comes to intellectual history and social history alike, anthropologists and others in the human sciences often assume—or even argue outright—that some kind of non-religious formation, some kind of claim to godlessness, is a superficial feature betrayed by an underlying religious (or metaphysical or theological) continuity. This is not to say there is no recognition of a difference between the Soviet League of the Militant Godless, for example, and Opus Dei. But the extent of the difference is often downplayed. Regarding my own work on humanists in Britain, many colleagues (in anthropology and related fields) have said that the humanists just seem to be repackaging religion, rather than rejecting it. Similar kinds of observations are quite common. But consider this from the philosopher Richard Rorty (2005: 33), not on record in many other places for acknowledging the good points made by George W. Bush and not himself a Christian apologist: "President Bush made a good point when he said, in a speech designed to please Christian fundamentalists, that 'atheism is a faith' because it is 'subject to neither confirmation nor refutation by means of argument or evidence.'"

When it comes to the matter of intellectual history, the arguments and underlying understandings are often just as pronounced. In the human sciences most broadly, this is best represented by the frequency with which one particular sentence of Carl Schmitt's ([1934] 2005: 36) *Political Theology* is cited: "All significant concepts of the modern theory of the state are secularized theological concepts." As Paul Kahn (2011) has emphasized, however, what is equally notable is how this specific citation is not discussed in relation to the whole of *Political Theology*. That powerful sentence tends to get disembedded and circulated in relation to a whole host of projects, analyses, and agendas. And, as Bruce Robbins (2013) would want to point out, a lot more work needs to be done to understand the difference between theological concepts and *secularized* theological concepts.

So what is the relationship between religious and non-religious systems of thought, belief, and practice? Within Western traditions, at least, this often comes up in terms of Judeo-Christian (although largely Christian) heritage. And a key issue is the extent to which modernity and the ostensibly connected process of secularization have effected a fundamental transformation in the ways that people think, act, and organize themselves.

There is a set of tasks here for those of us interested in studying 'non-religion'. Theoretically and conceptually, one of the primary ones is to ask, so what? This is not a flippant question. But if we cannot escape theologizing, for instance—as some of those who invoke Schmitt are suggesting—what does that tells us? Does it suggest that we are deceiving ourselves as to the nature of society—or even the nature of reality—and that we ought to dispense with the naturalist axiomatic and return to or revive a supernaturalist one? Or does it suggest that we should become better students of intellectual history so as to understand more the form and content of the ideas we use in an effort to reveal the blind spots they produce in our analyses? A lot more work needs to be done on these questions.

Another reason to admire the chapters collected here is the extent to which they capture the need to document and understand the range of the world's atheists and other godless people and what they are up to. There is an urgency to these works. Whereas a century ago many anthropologists would have seen themselves as conducting 'salvage ethnography', here we have the inverse: not anxiety over disappearance, but excitement over emergence. This is not to say that the authors are neglectful of historical dynamics; indeed, in some cases, we are dealing with the legacies of Soviet and anti-colonial atheisms. And in India, as we are reminded, 'atheism' has several genealogies and trajectories. All the same, atheism is having a 'moment', indexed above all by the spectacular success of Richard Dawkins, the science writer. Dawkins has gone global and shapes the very ways in which anthropologists write about atheism and related concepts, even where his ideas seem totally irrelevant, such as Taiwan and the Philippines.

The urgency—and need—is also evident in the range of approaches taken. Some of the chapters in this collection are based on long-term qualitative research projects, the primary focus of which is godless people, and several of the authors have already established themselves in these areas (e.g., Copeman and Reddy 2012; Lee 2015; Luehrmann 2011; Quack 2012). In some of the chapters, however, the godless people are clearly a secondary focus of the author's research, or they are approached through archival or other textual materials. This latter type of focus is just as valuable as the former: we cannot assume that explicit, systematic, and sustained attention to an ethnographic object is always better than what we trace incidentally or opportunistically. Clearly, though, one of the underlying messages of this collection is that we need to get cracking on the research front. We need more ethnographies of atheism, of secular humanism, of ambivalent non-religiosity. And we need it from everywhere. Even when it comes to the West, we do not know enough about these social formations, dispositions, or even, as some of the contributors here want to suggest, 'cultures'.[3] And when it comes to the rest of the world—or, even more, the interconnections, negotiations, and revolts that take place within the context of post-colonial or post–Cold War framings—the need for such ethnographies is even more obvious. It is with this message in mind that I would like to offer the reflections to follow, using my own research on humanists in Britain to further draw out how we might consider 'godless people'.

In 2011, I conducted fieldwork on the British Humanist Association (BHA). I spent my days in the Association's offices on Gower Street, in central London, and participated in a local humanist group that is affiliated with it. I also focused on the Humanist Ceremonies network and, in particular, humanist funerals. I even trained to become a BHA-accredited humanist celebrant.

Formed in 1967, the BHA has its roots in the nineteenth century's ethical society movement. Today, its chief aim is to promote humanism "as an ethical and fulfilling non-religious lifestance involving a naturalistic view of the universe."[4] The Association has approximately 12,000 members (annual fees are £35), and 16,000 supporters (those who sign up for a weekly newsletter, or otherwise allow themselves to be contacted). According to a survey I conducted (N = 1166), 69 percent of the membership are male; 96 percent are "White British" or "White Other" (categories I borrowed from the UK's Office of National Statistics); 73 percent have university degrees; 80 percent donate monthly to charity. Much of what the BHA does is campaign work that targets education, constitutional reform, and human rights. Many people join the BHA, for example, because of their opposition to state-funded faith schools. Others join to support the Association's efforts to remove the right of 26 Church of England bishops to sit in the House of Lords. The BHA's most well-known campaign is the Atheist Bus Campaign, which ran in 2008. Started by the comedian Ariane Sherine and supported by Dawkins, this campaign raised over £150,000, received huge media exposure, and was emulated in a number of other countries. The point was to counter what Sherine, in particular, felt was a particularly nasty form of fire and brimstone Christianity that prophesied hell for some and heaven for others.

As mentioned above, the Association also coordinates ceremonies—naming ceremonies and weddings, in addition to funerals—via a network of nearly 300 celebrants in England and Wales. One of the reasons I was so interested in studying the BHA is because, unlike a lot of organizations in this area, it expresses a commitment to the ritual and experiential side of being non-religious. Indeed, one of the arguments I have been making to date is the need to explore the bodily and experiential side of humanism (see Engelke 2014, 2015; see also Hirschkind 2010). This is important, I think, because, mirroring certain late-modern understandings of religion, humanism is often projected or interpreted as in and of the mind. The embodiment of atheism and godlessness is, of course, also a prominent theme in this volume's chapters.

This ideational vision is reinforced by the Association's balance of esteemed humanists. During my research, the BHA's president was the well-known journalist Polly Toynbee; the current president is the physicist Jim Al-Khalili. The Association has a number of high-profile vice-presidents and distinguished supporters with academic and literary backgrounds, including Dawkins, A. C. Grayling, Salman Rushdie, Philip Pullman, Ian McEwan, and the late Terry Pratchett. The comedians Stephen Fry and Ricky Gervais are also BHA supporters, so the gravitas is sometimes complemented by levity. It is important to the Association to highlight all such well-known advocates because potential supporters and members may not have a good sense of what humanism is (a point I will come back to later). I repeatedly heard from members that they got interested in humanism and the BHA via their interest in these various public figures.

For many humanists, the troublesome nature of terms such as 'atheism' and 'non-religion' is not always seen as directly relevant to their commitments. While many humanists say they are atheists, the majority emphasize that they are first and foremost humanists and thus not beholden in the way I described at the outset of this piece. Elsewhere, I have considered the connections and disconnections between religion (especially Christianity) and humanism (see Engelke 2014). Although there is not space to do so here in real depth, with the points about 'godless people' in mind, I would like to make a few observations.

Many BHA members insist on thinking of humanism as a descriptive term, claiming that it is not necessary for self-understanding or in relation to an 'identity'. That is to say, humanists argue that there were humanists before there were 'humanists'. In presentations that I have seen Andrew Copson, the BHA's CEO, give and in many conversations that we have had, he has always emphasized that other people in other times quite clearly expressed what we would recognize today as humanist views. His examples include Cārvāka, the author of the Bārhaspatya-sutras in ancient India; Averroes, the twelfth-century philosopher of Cordoba; and others we might expect, such as some key Enlightenment thinkers. Central to the argument of the humanist movement is the belief that humanism is (to coin a phrase) 'always already', a constitutive element of the human condition. A major reason this argument is made is to challenge the notion that religion is the wellspring of morality and ethics—that religion has a monopoly over the good. Being 'good without God' has always been possible, according to humanists. They focus in particular on the Golden Rule: treat others as you would like to be treated yourself. They say that while this is sometimes assumed to be a Christian ideal, it is in fact both older than and not in any way dependent upon any Abrahamic ethic.

The idea that humanism exists as some kind of social substrate, and gets expressed or lived out in a variety of ways, is something I regularly heard from BHA members, supporters, and affiliates during our conversations and interviews. Consider the following six such examples. This is a lot, but it is an indication of just how often "coming to humanism," as I usually put it in my questions, is framed in this way.

I went up to Oxford, and there found the humanist group by chance, going to a meeting that looked interesting, and discovering what they were about and thinking, well, here's a label for what I've been all my life. – P ♂

I had humanist ideals, but didn't know there was such a thing as humanism, in terms of an organization. It was only in adulthood that I heard about the humanist organization. And I came to the humanist association via an interest in the celebrant side—of becoming a celebrant. And I guess my values are essentially humanist: I just didn't know that there was a name for it. – S ♀

I looked it up after [my mother's funeral], the BHA, online, and liked what I saw. I identified with it. So after looking at it a few times, I then clicked 'join'. I started getting the newsletter, and really liking it. I didn't particularly think "I am a humanist" at that stage, but I really identified with it, and responded to everything that I saw, in the newsletters and on the website. – T ♀

I was a teacher for 20-odd years, and I used to have interesting discussions with my colleagues, many of whom were Christians, including the head of RE, who used to say, "Oh, maybe you're a Buddhist," and give me something about

Buddhism. I'd say, "No, not quite right. You know, I like a drink!" "Well, maybe you're a Quaker," she'd say. I don't believe in God—but that doesn't matter, apparently. But eventually she decided that I was a humanist, so, you know, she put a label on my set of beliefs. – M ♀

I haven't got an interesting journey to report. I'd say that just about five years ago, I happened to be idly wondering what the 'humanism' definition was, and I looked it up on the Internet, as one does, and saw the BHA list of what the humanists believe, and I thought, "Well, that pretty much sums up what I feel about life." Then I looked at the local group and saw that it had interesting discussions about moral issues, and I think I was attracted by the idea of a group that was looking at a wider range of moral issues, without a religious angle. And I've been involved in politics and environmental issues, and I thought it would be interesting to broaden out and join with a group locally. So that's it, for me. – O ♀

I didn't have a religious upbringing at all, my parents were atheists, no religious upbringing, and it just wasn't anything that entered one's mind. It was of no importance whatsoever—irrelevant. Until one of my professional colleagues, after we'd been chatting about something, he said, "With your views, you should join the British Humanist Association!" Which is what I did. – M ♂

There are many ways in which the promise of realization gets supported and inculcated within the BHA. A lot of them revolve around a certain promotion of science and reason inspired by the Enlightenment. Dawkins and other scientists who belong to and support the BHA promote this kind of realization. Science is absolutely crucial to many humanists I got to know, providing them with a master narrative of discovery, of realization—an all-encompassing framework with which to understand the world. The success and influence of Dawkins within organized non-religious movements and campaigns would be hard to overestimate. And as he is a vice-president of the BHA, this has been particularly important to the Association. In my survey of the BHA's membership, 72 percent said that they had read Dawkins's *The God Delusion*, and I gathered a not insignificant number of anecdotal coming-to-realization stories that hinge on reading one or another of his books (usually *The God Delusion*, sometimes *The Blind Watchmaker* or *The Selfish Gene*).

To be sure, not all members support Dawkins's views or his style of expressing them. And in any case, it is important for the staff, especially the CEO, to get the message out that humanism is more than an appreciation of science. One of the ways in which Copson tries to project a more diverse image is through varying the events program—events being a crucial forum in the construction of humanist publicity. For example, in 2011 he helped start an annual Shelley Lecture. The timing was notable because it was the bicentennial of Percy Bisshe Shelley being sent down from Oxford for having published *The Necessity of Atheism*. This lecture series focuses on contributions to humanist thought from more classically poetic and artistic minds.

Another way in which some humanists express their poetic side (broadly conceived) is through singing. In 2009 the BHA started a choir, and when he became CEO in January 2010, one of the songs Copson asked the choir to include in its repertoire is one that captures perfectly a certain vision of the humanist mind-set. Called "Do You Realize," it is by The Flaming Lips, an American indie rock band. The first few lines go: "Do you realize that you have the most beautiful face/Do you realize we're floating in space/Do you realize that happiness makes you cry/Do you realize that everyone you know someday will die." The song captures it all, really: beauty, love, science, the cosmos, death. Coming to have these things, coming to understand these things, coming to accept these things—it is all possible through the process of realization. This is a humanist anthem par excellence.

Before concluding, I ought to address further the idea of non-religion in all this. As a conscientious anthropologist, perhaps the first thing I should make clear is that my informants in the BHA would, as some of what I have said illustrates, *never* accept that humanism comes after religion. In a sense, one of the conceptual demands they are making is to return to an inquiry about human nature—something not much in favor in anthropology these days. From their point of view, the point of departure is never religion: religious traditions of thought, belief, and practice are only ever one set of ways to work out the human condition.

I might as well also note that humanists are often particularly frustrated when what they do is called 'non-religion'. It is this nominal form that really bothers them; the adjectival, 'non-religious', is slightly more acceptable—at least in the middle term (i.e., until religion as a concept no longer defines the social space that non-religion occupies). Copson put it to me this way:

> I don't like the noun 'non-religion' because I don't like humanism and other secular approaches to life being constantly, unnecessarily, defined by what they're not. I think it'd be the same as if you were to describe Christianity and Hinduism and Judaism and so on as 'non-humanisms'; I don't see why you should do it. I think it's demeaning, and it automatically sets you off in the wrong direction. Because although obviously humanists aren't religious, I don't think it's necessarily the most important thing. It's what they are positively: that they care about human values being founded on reason and experience, that they care about the scientific method as a way of understanding the world, that they care about treating other people well in the here and now for the sake of the here and now.

This effort to accentuate the positive was a common sentiment. As I have already said—but it bears repeating in a collection on 'godless people'—a lot of the humanists I got to know liked to call themselves humanists above anything else because it is not defining oneself in terms of what one is not. Again, most of these people were atheists, too, but that label seemed a dead end to them—ceding too much ground.

Getting back to the troubles faced by the anthropology of religion—to say nothing of the anthropology of non-religion—it is worth noting that humanists are no more uneasy with the label of it being a 'non-religion' than the Christians I have studied are uneasy with the label of Christianity as a 'religion' (Engelke 2013). Start talking to an evangelical Christian these days about their 'religion', and you are likely to get uncomfortable looks. The evangelicals I studied during a three-year project on public religion in Britain did not want to see Christianity as a religion. And this is not a new phenomenon. For a host of social, political, and theological reasons, 'religion' is often abandoned by those whom we might least expect, even as it is simultaneously embraced.

When Copson first told me that he did not like framing humanism in terms of religion, however, I balked. Nearly every public presentation of the BHA—not least its home page on the web—frames its work in relation to religion. And religion—especially Christianity—is a regular point of reference in humanist interactions and activities. There is a modest market of commodities for the godless, much of which—if not all—trades on anti-theism. A small minority of humanists sport T-shirts that say things like "Too stupid to understand science? Try religion!" and "Atheism: A non-prophet organization." At humanist pub quizzes, there is often a round of questions on religion—sometimes straightforward ones, sometimes mocking. When humanists hold meetings or otherwise gather socially, there is often a high level of metapragmatic signaling: they police themselves and one another on the use of phrases and terms that can be taken to have religious meanings. They joke, for example, when they unconsciously refer to the 'spirit' (of something), or snigger when they consciously joke about, say, issuing a fatwa. The first thing a humanist celebrant asks a chapel attendant to do at the council-run crematoria, where most of the funeral services are held, is to take down the cross that is almost always hanging on the front wall. One leading humanist waged a campaign in the 1970s to get her local London council to unbolt the cross that had until that point hung above the front of the chapel at a public crematorium. And now, at the City of London Cemetery and Crematorium, there is a small area, off behind the organ (which is heard less and less these days), where the staff keep a panoply of sacred symbols (Hindu, Sikh, Christian), each to be conveniently brought out as necessary.[5] In this day and age in Britain, whatever else they are, humanists are people who talk and think about religion.

The present-day portability of religious symbols in such civic spaces as cemetery chapels cries out for a figurative reading. For how can we not read the swapping out of signifiers of faith as a sign of changes afoot in the framing of our world? What happens when in England the cross comes down in a cemetery chapel? On the evidence of what humanists do, we are clearly not in a time where these signs have become floating signifiers, unmoored from each other and the social formations they represent. And yet it would not, as I have argued (Engelke 2014), be helpful or apt to call humanism a 'religion'—or even a 'non-religion', in any strong sense.

In a recent essay, Jürgen Habermas (2010) also reflects on these issues by turning to death. In 1991, the funeral of his friend Max Frisch was held in St. Peter's Church in Zurich. Frisch, an agnostic and intellectual, as Habermas tells us, "had sensed the awkwardness of non-religious burial practices and, by his choice of place, publicly declared that the enlightened modern age has failed to find a suitable replacement for a religious way of coping with the final *rite de passage* which brings life to a close" (ibid.: 15). For Habermas, the funeral was a "paradoxical event which tells us something about secular reason, namely that it is unsettled by the opaqueness of its merely apparently clarified relation to religion" (ibid.: 15–16). The title of Habermas's essay is "An Awareness of What Is Missing."

But what—if anything—is missing? Part of what this volume moves to address is the answer to this question. Another part of what it does, though, is to question the question itself. Both are productive endeavors. 'Being godless' can help us think of ways for anthropology and the human sciences to make sense of this state of affairs as we work to refine and sharpen our analytical tools for the understanding of religion—and, I suppose, non-religion.

Matthew Engelke is a Professor of Anthropology at the London School of Economics. He is the author of *A Problem of Presence: Beyond Scripture in an African Church* (2007), which won the 2008 Geertz Prize for Anthropology of Religion and the 2009 Turner Prize for Ethnographic Writing, and *God's Agents: Biblical Publicity in Contemporary England* (2013). He is the co-editor, with Joel Robbins, of "Global Christianity, Global Critique" (*South Atlantic Quarterly*, 2010). He has run Prickly Paradigm Press with Marshall Sahlins since 2002 and was the editor of the *Journal of the Royal Anthropological Institute* from 2010 to 2013. His current research and writing, funded by the Economic and Social Research Council (RES-000-22-4175), is on the British Humanist Association.

Notes

1. I will not address the anthropology of secularism here; it would, quite obviously, require an afterword of its own, for some different volume. It has in any case received a lot of separate attention.
2. For a reflection on these themes, see Bill Maurer (2012).
3. I am not on anthropology's anti-culture bandwagon, but in fact I do not think that 'culture' is the best rubric for what these chapters describe.
4. See http://humanists4science.blogspot.com/2011/04/bha-strategy-vision-mission-values-and.html.
5. See Engelke (2015) for a more detailed discussion about the use of sacred symbols and humanist funerals.

References

Candea, Matei. 2011. "'Our Division of the Universe': Making a Space for the Non-Political in the Anthropology of Politics." *Current Anthropology* 52, no. 3: 309–334.

Carsten, Janet, ed. 2000. *Cultures of Relatedness: New Approaches to the Study of Kinship.* Cambridge: Cambridge University Press.

Copeman, Jacob, and Deepa S. Reddy. 2012. "The Didactic Death: Publicity, Instruction, and Body Donation." *HAU: Journal of Ethnographic Theory* 2, no. 2: 59–83.

Engelke, Matthew. 2013. *God's Agents: Biblical Publicity in Contemporary England.* Berkeley: University of California Press.

Engelke, Matthew. 2014. "Christianity and the Anthropology of Secular Humanism." *Current Anthropology* 55, no. S10: S292–S301.

Engelke, Matthew. 2015. "The Coffin Question: Death and Materiality in Humanist Funerals." *Material Religion* 11, no. 1: 26–48.

Ferguson, James. 1994. *The Anti-Politics Machine: "Development," Depoliticization, and Bureaucratic Power in Lesotho.* Minneapolis: University of Minnesota Press.

Franklin, Sarah, and Susan McKinnon, eds. 2001. *Relative Values: Reconfiguring Kinship Studies.* Durham, NC: Duke University Press.

Goody, Jack. 1961. "Religion and Ritual: The Definitional Problem." *British Journal of Sociology* 14, no. 2: 142–164.

Graeber, David. 2001. *Toward an Anthropological Theory of Value: The False Coin of Our Own Dreams.* New York: Palgrave Macmillan.

Habermas, Jürgen. 2010. "An Awareness of What Is Missing." Pp. 15–23 in Jürgen Habermas, Michael Reder, Josef Schmidt, Norbert Briskorn, and Friedo Ricken, *An Awareness of What Is Missing: Faith and Reason in a Post-Secular Age.* Trans. Ciaran Cronin. Cambridge: Polity Press.

Hart, Keith, Jean-Louis Laville, and Antonio Cattani, eds. 2010. *The Human Economy.* Cambridge: Polity Press.

Hirschkind, Charles. 2010. "Is There a Secular Body?" The Immanent Frame. http://blogs.ssrc.org/tif/2010/11/15/secular-body/(accessed 20 August 2013).

Kahn, Paul W. 2011. *Political Theology: Four New Chapters on the Concept of Sovereignty.* New York: Columbia University Press.

Lee, Lois. 2015. *Recognizing the Nonreligious: Reimagining the Secular.* Oxford: Oxford University Press.

Luehrmann, Sonja. 2011. *Secularism Soviet Style: Teaching Atheism and Religion in a Volga Republic.* Bloomington: Indiana University Press.

Maurer, Bill. 2012. "Occupy Economic Anthropology." *Journal of the Royal Anthropological Institute* 18, no. 2: 54–60.

Quack, Johannes. 2012. *Disenchanting India: Organized Rationalism and Criticism of Religion in India.* New York: Oxford University Press.

Robbins, Bruce. 2013. "Is the Postcolonial Also Postsecular?" *boundary 2* 40, no. 1: 245–262.

Rorty, Richard. 2005. "Anticlericalism and Atheism." Pp. 29–42 in Richard Rorty and Gianni Vattimo, *The Future of Religion,* ed. Santiago Zabala. New York: Columbia University Press.

Schmitt, Carl. [1934] 2005. *Political Theology: Four Chapters on the Concept of Sovereignty.* Ed. and trans. George Schwab. Chicago: University of Chicago Press.

Schneider, David. 1984. *A Critique of the Study of Kinship.* Ann Arbor: University of Michigan Press.

Spencer, Jonathan. 1997. "Post-Colonialism and the Political Imagination." *Journal of the Royal Anthropological Institute* 3, no. 1: 1–19.

Vincent, Joan, ed. 2002. *The Anthropology of Politics: A Reader in Ethnography, Theory and Critique.* Oxford: Blackwell.

INDEX